FORCED SEXUAL INTERCOURSE
IN INTIMATE RELATIONSHIPS

Dedication

For my daughter, Jazymine C. Latham, and parents, Dave B. Johnson and Willie L. Johnson. A special dedication is given to my husband, Cartrell Latham, for his love, support, and sense of humor through the writing of this book.

Ida M. Johnson

Forced Sexual Intercourse in Intimate Relationships

IDA M. JOHNSON AND ROBERT T. SIGLER
Department of Criminal Justice
University of Alabama

Ashgate
DARTMOUTH

Aldershot • Brookfield USA • Singapore • Sydney

Published by
Dartmouth Publishing Company Limited
Ashgate Publishing Limited
Gower House
Croft Road
Aldershot
Hants GU11 3HR
England

Ashgate Publishing Company
Old Post Road
Brookfield
Vermont 05036
USA

British Library Cataloguing in Publication Data
Johnson, Ida M.
    Forced sexual intercourse in intimate relationships
    1.Acquaintance rape
    I.Title II.Sigler, Robert T.
    364.1'532

Library of Congress Cataloging-in-Publication Data
Johnson, Ida M.
    Forced sexual intercourse in intimate relationships / Ida M.
Johnson and Robert T. Sigler.
        p. cm.
    Includes bibliographical references and index.
    ISBN 1-85521-917-4
    1. Rape in marriage. 2. Acquaintance rape. I. Sigler, Robert T.
II. Title.
    HV6558.J64   1997
    362.883--dc21   96-48559
                                                        CIP

ISBN 1 85521 917 4

Printed and bound by Athenaeum Press, Ltd.,
Gateshead, Tyne & Wear.

Contents

List of Tables

Acknowledgements

The authors gratefully acknowledge the efforts of Beverly S. Curry, wife of Robert T. Sigler, for the many hours of labor editing, proofing, and formatting the manuscript. Her insistence on quality and precision has substantially improved this work.

1 Introduction

Forced sexual intercourse has gained steadily in importance as the status of women in our society has increased. The confusion and lack of clarity in definition, including the inability to establish a clear set of types or clear boundaries around the phenomenon, is extensive and political. The rhetoric, intensity, and lack of specificity and accuracy in research and stated positions work to the disadvantage of the women who are the victims in most of the incidents in which forced sexual intercourse is alleged and in many of the incidents in which force is used to gain sexual intercourse but is not labeled as inappropriate or unacceptable.

Two political positions tend to exert considerable influence on the character and direction of research design and model development. The first is identified as the feminist movement, which is, to some extent, driven by a victim orientation and which is, at times, a label which is externally imposed rather than a matter of self-identification adopted by researchers. Victim-oriented research is often driven by a need to enhance the victim status of one or more of the participants in the social interactions which produce the victimizations. One result is the exaggeration of the victimization by emphasizing extreme cases, characterizing extreme cases as common, and extending the definition of the offense behavior to increase the apparent incidence and prevalence of the victimization. Goals include the social redefinition of the offense behavior as unacceptable in all of its forms, the development of extended services for victims, and criminalization of the behavior or an increase in the enforcement of the law, if the behavior is prohibited by law.

The second and more recent movement is identified as sexist, a label which also usually is imposed by others and not accepted by the researchers who question the interpretations of research that is identified as feminist. Much of the focus of this line of research and dialogue is reactive rather than proactive and focuses on the prevalence and incidence figures advanced.

1

There is an assertion or an implication that the rates of victimization are exaggerated, and attempts to increase the level of control of dating and courtship and courtship behavior are excessive, setting standards for the behavior of men and women which are not realistic.

It is unfortunate that the separation between political agendas and research agendas, which is central to the conduct of objective research, appears to be weak in this area and appears to have produced an adversarial environment. It is noteworthy that in this environment a wide range of well-designed and executed research projects have focused on the various dimensions of forced sexual intercourse.

One area of research, which is extensive, measures community attitudes and examines the relationships among various attitudinal constructs, particularly those attitudes which influence the labeling of forced sexual intercourse as rape, as justified, or as mitigated by a range of contextual factors. Factors which have been found to affect the labeling of forced sexual intercourse include degree of association, orientation toward women, gender role stereotyping, social context, victim characteristics, victim acceptance of responsibility, unclear expectations for dating and consensual sexual exchanges, acceptance of rape myths, and definitions of appropriate masculine behavior.

Very few data have been gathered which focus on the offender and factors which influence his behavior. Available research focuses on the more extreme offenders - stranger rapists, violent rapists, and mentally ill rapists - with samples drawn from institutional populations or justice system records. Research focusing on less extreme offenders is limited by at least two factors: (1) the population of less extreme offenders is invisible. Most are not publicly accused or identified by their victims, many of whom do not define themselves as victims. (2) There are also indications in the literature that many of these men do not label their behavior as rape or perceive their behavior in this context as inappropriate. That is, they define their use of force in intimate relationships as normal and acceptable, thus they do not define themselves as offenders when responding to research questions posed in the best articulated of research projects.

Similar problems are revealed in the literature which focuses on victims. Much of the research focusing on the victims of forced sexual intercourse is based on samples drawn from clinical populations. As such, the focus is on those women who have been severely traumatized by their victimizations. Since the degree of trauma does not appear to be determined or limited by the type of forced sexual intercourse, client groups include those who have been victims of date and acquaintance rape but exclude those women who have managed to cope with their victimization. As is the case with offenders, many women do not define their experience as rape or as criminal. They accept responsibility for their victimization or define the behavior as within acceptable parameters. Some of these women do not identify themselves as victims when completing questionnaires, and, when they acknowledge that they have experienced force in intimate relationships, they do not respond as victims to items measuring a range of variables related to the events and their aftermath.

As a result of inconsistency in the definition(s) of forced sexual intercourse and the tendency for offenders and victims to define their experiences within the boundaries of appropriate behavior, the population of users and receivers of the use of force to gain sexual access has not been accurately defined. Estimates of the prevalence of forced sexual intercourse range from less than 10 percent to more than 60 percent of the adult female population. The most influential factor in explaining this variation appears to be the manner of operationalization of the definition of forced sexual intercourse, with relatively little variance by geographical location or composition of the target population. One persistent finding is that most victimization occurs before the age of 19. High school girls appear to be much more vulnerable than adult women, possibly because adult women have learned how to cope effectively with men who aggressively pursue sexual access.

The development of theory has tended to follow the pattern observed in the study of victims and offenders. Much more is written about the pathological stranger rapists and the severely traumatized victim than about relatively normal men and women involved in normal behavior which produces or progresses to unwanted and offensive behavior. More recent work has focused on the development of typologies, some of which attempt to address the social distance factor but direct little attention to the patterns of labeling in use by the actors.

In the final chapter, a preliminary model is presented which can be used as a basis for further research. A simple three-category typology for forced sexual intercourse is offered, with the suggestion that each of the three types should be treated as different behaviors rather than as different degrees of a single behavior. The three types are: (1) stranger rape in which the victim has little or no prior contact with the offender and cooperates only to the extent required by the degree of force applied or through fear of the consequences of non-compliance; (2) predatory rape in which a man, who intends or plans to rape his victim using any degree of deception or force required, entraps his victim by pretending to engage in legitimate dating behavior; and (3) date rape in which the man enters into legitimate dating behavior which, for a range of reasons, evolves into an exchange in which force is used to gain sexual access from an unwilling woman.

The model advanced is limited to the third type - date rape. Factors which are considered are the perception of man's intent, the woman's anticipation of sexual activity, the clarity of expectations, the man's labeling of the exchange, and the woman's labeling of the exchange. The model assumes: (1) dating is a normal process, (2) men persistently pursue sexual access, (3) women are held responsible for determining the rate at which a relationship proceeds and have personal standards regarding the speed at which the relationship will develop, and (4) that the expectations which women hold are not made explicit in most relationships.

If accurate knowledge and effective models addressing forced sexual intercourse are to be developed, some agreement must be reached as to the definitions which are to be used. Until this area develops sufficiently to permit some degree of consensus as to the parameters and classification of the phenomena, care must be exercised to state clearly the operational definitions and assumptions when the results of research are reported. As preliminary models are developed and tested, accurate explanations of the factors that contribute to the use of force in intimate relationships will emerge; these will provide activists with the knowledge needed to develop effective strategies to address the needs which they have identified.

2 Historical, Social, Cultural, and Legal Organization of Rape

Introduction

Forced sexual intercourse is as old as history itself. However, it has not always been viewed as a personal crime against the victim. Early in history, rape was an acceptable method of securing a wife. The institution of marriage was clearly supported by patriarchal attitudes that defined the male as the authoritarian figure who had the responsibility for controlling and dominating the woman. Prior to marriage, the woman was perceived to be the property of her father or male guardian; this ownership was transferred to the husband when the woman married. The woman's role in society was defined in terms of her ability to function in a subservient position and to procreate. This perception of the woman facilitated the historical perception of rape as a property crime instead of as personal violence.

Historically, rape, other than stranger rape, has been a concept lacking clarity and has been evaluated independently more than by an objective standard. In early Europe, rape was a general category which included some non-forced illicit sex. Types of illicit sex were not distinguished clearly, as the interest to be protected was the interest of the husband or father. In the United States, while all forced intercourse was subsumed under the category of rape, only stranger rape was controlled legally until recently. The legal issue today is still what types of forced sexual intercourse are actionable. As forced sexual intercourse in intimate relationships has moved conceptually toward separation from stranger rape, the need to know more about the use of force in intimate relationships has increased. An examination of this evolutionary process will allow the reader to consider many of today's confusing positions in historical perspective.

Women's Roles in Society

The word rape is derived from the Latin word *rapere* which means to steal, seize, or carry away (Warner, 1980). In early history, forcible rape represented an acceptable way for a man to secure a wife. The consequence of rape was forced marriage whereby a man took possession of a woman, raped her, and then brought her into the tribe as his wife. In ancient German society, the practice of bride purchase was common Males took possession of women who later became their wives. In this particular society, a marriageable girl was put up for bid by her father or male guardian and she went to the highest bidder. This system supported the inferior status of women as property of their fathers or male guardians. Again, rape was not viewed as a crime against the woman but as an act of theft or seizure of property from the victim's father. In the Germanic society, one form of punishment for rape was the *wergeld* system. The guilty assailant had to pay compensation to the victim's father in the amount of the bride price of the stolen or violated woman. Thus, the institution of marriage, in some areas, appears to have been institutionalized by the abduction and forcible rape of women as well as the auction of marriageable women to the highest bidder (Brownmiller, 1975).

Stranger rape persistently has been a universally proscribed act. This proscription has not always been keyed to the rights or needs of female victims. Throughout history, women have been perceived to be inferior to men and have been assigned roles of lesser status than those of their male counterparts. As early as the fifth century B.C. in Athens, a freeborn woman of the upper class was free in name but not in status and role. Such a woman was forced to spend her entire life physically confined to a separate part of the house (Dover, 1984). In spite of her upper class status, she could not vote, make contracts, or transact any business-related activities. She was allowed only to perform and participate in feminine activities which, in many cases, included hard work (e.g., weaving, dyeing clothes, spinning, cooking, and raising children). The view of women and their position in society as subordinate in relation to their male counterparts has been perpetuated through the patriarchal system (Dobash & Dobash, 1979; Brownmiller, 1975). This societal view of women has influenced greatly the development of our rape laws.

Traditional attitudes toward the crime of rape and the status of women also were dominant in America during the colonial period. During the colonial period, rape was seen as an expression of male power and domination, which was regulated by the courts and the community to maintain power and domination over women rather than to protect women from being violated. The woman was regarded not as a person in her own right, but as a sexual type, an inferior being (Koehler, 1980). Her primary roles in society were to become wife and mother. For the woman, sexuality was important in marriage not for sexual gratification, but for the procreation of legitimate offspring (Donat & D'Emilo, 1992). Thus, the church, courts, and community closely monitored the sexual behavior of women to ensure female chastity, fidelity, and the legitimacy of the husband's children.

During the colonial period, the value of a woman in society depended on her ability to marry and to procreate legitimate heirs. The woman's purity increased her chances of marrying. Women who were violated by an act of rape could not marry into a respectable family and, consequently, became an economic burden to their fathers for the rest of their lives.

Social class and marital status were important determinants of whether or not a rape case came before the courts. Rape cases in which the assailant's social class was lower than that of his victim, or those in which the victim was married and physically resisted the attack, were the ones most likely to come before the court. It also was necessary to show that the victim did not consent to the act of rape, meaning that she did not voluntarily engage in a sexual act with a man other than her husband. If she could not prove her resistance, she might be punished for the rape (Donat & D'Emilo, 1992).

During the first decades of the nineteenth century, the meaning of "sexuality" evolved from the need to procreate through the addition of courtship. At the same time, community controls on the woman began to relax, and the woman was allowed to make some choices, which included her decision to work outside the home. The woman no longer was restricted to the roles of mother and wife; she was allowed to enter the paid work force and earn wages. However, risks and vulnerability also came with this profound freedom. Prior to the nineteenth century, a woman could bargain with sexual favors (premarital intercourse) in exchange for a man's commitment to marry. If the woman became pregnant prior to marriage, it was assumed that the pregnancy would lead to marriage since the man already had committed himself to marriage by engaging in premarital intercourse. In spite of the existence of premarital sex, women still were expected to be pure and disinterested in sexual relations. Women who were not pure and who engaged in sexual intercourse (even against their will) were perceived to weaken the moral fabric of society (Freeman, 1981). They were perceived to be women who had fallen from grace; thus all blame for the crime of rape was heaped upon them.

The perception of women as being the property of their husbands or fathers is reflected in the early definitions of the crime of rape, which viewed rape not as an offense against the woman but as a crime against her husband or father (Brownmiller, 1975). Since the female was perceived as property of her husband or father (depending upon her marital status), monetary compensation was paid to the husband or father for damage to his property. This form of punishment failed to distinguish the female victim's rights from those of the husband or father, creating confusion in the early definition of rape.

Additionally, during the twentieth century, the focus of sexuality turned to the factors and contexts which influenced the prevalence of sexual behavior. The emphasis on theoretical explanations of sexual aggression focused primarily on understanding the plight of the male while ignoring the plight of the female (Donat & D'Emilo, 1992). Accordingly, the female's victimization was seen as a by-product of the male's pathology. The label of "sexual pathology", used to describe the violent male sex offender who could not control his sexual impulses, led to the reconceptualization of rape as an act of violence instead of an act of sex. During this period, the focus was on stranger rape. Forced sex in an intimate relationship was not considered to be rape or of public interest. Thus, the models of rape and rapists were limited to explanations for incidents in which strangers raped helpless women.

The perception of the rapist as being a violent mentally ill person facilitated the development of "sexual psychopath laws" which permitted rapists to be committed to state mental hospitals instead of jail. Sexual psychopath laws, which were designed to protect women, eventually divided the penalty for rape along racial lines, with white male rapists being labeled as mentally ill and sent to state hospitals and Black male rapists being labeled as violent and sent to jail (Freeman, 1981).

Historical analyses of rape have not always taken into consideration the historical factors related to Black women's rape experiences. In the American colonies, rape of Black women by white males served as an economic advancement to the labor force (Getman, 1984). In fact, by 1660, there were laws that encouraged sex between Black women and white males in order to procreate slave children and increase the slave population (Getman, 1984; Wriggins, 1983). During slavery, children were considered to be the property of their mothers, thus both mother and child became the property of the slave owner. As previously mentioned, the penalty for rape has always been executed along racial lines. For example, free or enslaved Black men convicted (and in some cases merely accused) of raping a white woman were often castrated or sentenced to death (Jordon, 1968). Virtually no penalties were applied to white males who raped Black women, because of the perception that the Black woman was the property of the white man.

Historically, rape of Black women by white men was not treated as seriously as the rape of white women by Black men or white men. Stereotypical views of Black women and men create disparities in the manner in which interracial rape cases are processed through the system. The historical slave period in America facilitated the deep-rooted stereotypical views held by society concerning the sexuality of Black men and women (Williams, 1984).

Historical Definitions and Punishments of Rape

Brownmiller's (1975) analysis of rape from a historical perspective found that rape was perceived as a property crime in several early societies (Athens, England, Greece, and Babylon) and included forms of sexual interaction other than stranger rape addressed earlier in this chapter. In Athenian society, the rape of a married woman was perceived as a lesser offense than the seduction of a married woman. Seduction was considered a more serious offense than rape because it was viewed as a premeditated act involving a lasting sexual relationship whereby the seducer gained the trust and loyalty of the woman and, thereby, gained access to her husband's household. While the punishment for rape was a monetary fine, the penalty for seduction was much more severe.

In cases of seduction, the aggrieved husband had the right to kill the seducer if he so desired. If he chose not to exercise this right, he could seek revenge on the seducer which resulted in public humiliation. While the wife was considered guiltless in cases of both rape and seduction, the husband of a raped or seduced wife was required by law to divorce the wife. Once she became a divorcee, the seduced woman had no opportunity to prove her innocence, and she became an outcast from society. Because the emphasis was on the husband's property value, consent was not a relevant factor. Since the discarded wife lost her status because of her decreased value rather than because of her immoral behavior, resistance or force was not a defense for her. The effect of this perspective can still be seen today when intercourse occurs with someone other than the woman's current mate. The emphasis, at times, appears to be on the loss of the man's status when his mate engages in intercourse with another, regardless of the degree of consent involved.

The historical laws of rape began to undergo change during the thirteenth century (Brownmiller, 1975). This change first occurred in medieval Europe. During the thirteenth century, European monarchies extended some protection of the law to married women who were raped. Prior to this time, a married woman who was raped was perceived to be just as guilty as her rapist (who was sometimes referred to as her lover), and she was put to death along with the rapist. With the development of the Statute of Westminster in 1285, the law specified that any man convicted of raping a married woman or virgin would be found guilty of a felony and put to death. In this era, rape was limited to instances in which force was used in non-intimate relationships. Implied consent was not an issue, in that any willing participation of the woman in activities leading up to the assault provided an effective defense, a principle which survived until quite recently.

In most countries, the law was more restrictive for virgins, perhaps because of the added value of virginity. A virgin who had been raped was required by law to initiate the legal process which would bring the rapist to trial. This process was often long and extremely embarrassing to the victim. Carter (1983) identified six steps which a woman had to take in order to bring her rapist to trial. She must: (a) create a public outcry over the crime as soon as possible, (b) exhibit her torn garments and bleeding to men of good standing in the neighboring towns, (c) explain the crime to local law officers, (d) make a formal accusation at the first county court to be held, (e) repeat her accusation before the coroner so that it could be taken down verbatim for the public records, and (f) prosecute the offender in the royal circuit court at the earliest opportunity. Because of this long, drawn-out process, embarrassment, and the possibility of being arrested and imprisoned for false accusation, many women preferred to avoid bringing charges against their assailant. The reluctance of the rape victim to become involved in prosecuting the rapist still exists today for many of the same reasons.

The reluctance of rape victims to initiate charges against rapists led to a revision of legal procedure. The prosecution of the offender could be undertaken in the name of the King if no accusation by the victim was made within forty days of the alleged offense. This right of the King to prosecute the rapist served as a method to protect wealthy families from unwanted marriages (Post, 1978).

Historically, the punishment for rape varied according to several factors: (1) the social and marital status of the victim, (2) where the rape occurred, and (3) the amount of resistance displayed by the victim (Warner, 1980). As the law existed, the rape of a married woman carried the penalty of death. The rape of an unmarried woman, on the other hand, carried the penalty of forced marriage to the victim and payment of three times her market value to her father. With the forced marriage, the rapist also was required by law not to divorce his rape victim. These types of punishments for rape of an unmarried woman punished not only the offender, but also the victim in the sense that her choice to marry and divorce was taken away from her. Women had few rights and the property orientation prevailed. The offender had to accept damaged property, with the no divorce clause designed to protect the women from being discarded at a later date.

The issue of rape was also considered in other ancient societies, such as those of the Babylonians and Hebrews (Brownmiller, 1975). The patriarchal society supported the male's right to exercise complete control over his wife, children, and slaves. Since women were perceived to be the property of their husbands, the act of rape became not a crime against the victim but a crime against the husband (i.e., damage to his personal goods). Accordingly, the Code of Hammurabi did not provide any penalties for the rape of a married women. In fact, there was no such acknowledgement that a married woman could be raped. If a married woman was violated through an act of sexual assault, regardless of the circumstances she was guilty of adultery and could be punished by drowning unless her husband intervened by pulling her from the water. Similarly, in the Hebrew society, the married woman who was raped was found to be equally guilty as the assailant and was usually stoned to death right along with her attacker. The penalty for rape for the victim was less severe if the woman was single and a virgin. According to Mosaic law, the assailant who raped an unbetrothed virgin outside the city walls was punished by having to pay the victim's father fifty silver coins, the price she would have brought in the bride market. Consequently, the victim and the assailant were ordered to be married. Again, the crime of rape was reduced to a crime against the property of the husband if the victim was married and of the father if the victim was unbetrothed.

According to early English law, the location of the rape played an important role in determining whether the victim was credible and whether there would be a punishment for the act. A woman raped within the city limits would be hesitant to report the rape for fear of being put to death, since it was believed that a rape could not occur within a crowded place without being detected. Then, as today, it was believed that the woman who failed to fight back or scream wanted to be raped. Such a woman, if married, was stoned to death because she was found guilty of committing adultery, a crime against her husband. In contrast, a woman raped in an open field - outside of the city limits - would be found not guilty, based on the assumption that even if the woman screamed, no one could hear her to come to her rescue. English laws and customs, including orientation toward forced sexual intercourse, were adopted in the United States.

Brownmiller's assertion that politics and the oppression of women rather than sexual frustration were the primary explanations of rape can be supported by historical data. It is evident that public brothels operated in numerous towns in the southeast of France during the fifteenth century. In addition to the brothels, prostitution was widely practiced at the bathhouses in various towns of France (Rossiaud, 1978). In spite of the fact that males had various opportunities to gain sexual access, rapes occurred frequently in the towns of France. Based on available statistics, approximately 80 percent of all rapes that occurred in the towns of France were gang rapes (Rossiaud, 1978). These rapes were perpetrated by young single men who did not possess a criminal record. One would think that since the young men did not have a criminal record, they would have disguised themselves when they committed the crime of rape. Instead, without concealing their identity, they would go to the young woman's home and start a disturbance outside her home with the intention of making her come outside. If the young woman did not come outside her home by herself, the young men would knock the door down, seize the woman, and force her outside where she would be beaten and raped. Interestingly, as a way to compensate for their behavior, the young men would attempt to force her to take money. At times, the beatings that the woman received were severe and, in some instances, resulted in permanent losses. For example, in one rape incident, a young woman was beaten so brutally that she was unable to return to work for several days, and, when she did, she was relieved of her position as a domestic servant. There were incidents of pregnant women being raped and dragged through the snow (Rossiaud, 1978). These cases support Brownmiller's view that rape was an act of violence rather than an act of passion and that the act of violence was used as a weapon of oppression against women.

The violence that accompanied historical rapes was not limited to the French society; it appears that violent rapes were universal. Ruggerio (1980), in his study of Venetian society during the Renaissance, reveals that the violence that accompanied rape was so prevalent and so severe that sexual gratification was almost forgotten. In one particular sexual assault case discussed by Ruggerio, the wife of a boatman was attacked by an assailant who, in addition to raping her, slashed her left arm with a knife, causing blood to gush forth, and, when her mother attempted to intervene, she also was beaten and cut above the eye.

Contemporary Definitions and Punishments of Rape in the United States

The definition of rape varies from state to state. During the first half of this century, definitions of rape focused exclusively on penile-vaginal intercourse (Russell, 1984; Quinsey, Chaplin & Barney, 1981; Rada, 1978). As the century progressed, other forms of sexual assault were added, with contemporary statutes including anal and oral intercourse and penetration with an object other than the penis (Koss, Gidycz, & Wisniewski, 1987; Struckman-Johnson, 1988; Muehlenhard & Linton, 1987; Kanin, 1967). More recent statutes classify crimes of sexual violence as all acts of penile/vaginal intercourse and all acts of forced sexual aggression, which often had been proscribed under sodomy and sexual abuse statutes.

Some definitions of rape have been broadened to include all nonconsensual sexual activity (Veronen, Kilpatrick, & Resick, 1983). Usually, when sexual violence does not include penetration, terminology other than rape is used. For example, terms such as sexual assault, sexual contact, sex play, sexual abuse, sexual aggression, and sexual coercion have been used to describe sexual violence without penetration. Regardless of the type of sexual assault, the focus is on the type of label attached to an act of sexual violence, and there are many similarities. Acts of sexual violence are often traumatic violations of the victim's body committed against the victim's will. These acts can be so devastating that the victim is deprived of both dignity and personal choice, and, in many instances, the acts leave lasting emotional trauma.

Most state laws concerning the definition of rape and sexual assault include the following elements: (1) the sexual act must be against the victim's will and without the victim's consent, (2) some degree of force, threat, or incapacitation must be used in committing the act, and (3) penile/vaginal penetration must occur (Estrich, 1987). The definition of rape is further delineated by the distinction between "simple" and "aggravated" rape (Estrich, 1987). Aggravated rape is rape that occurs in conjunction with some other crime. "Simple" rape occurs without the commission of another crime. Usually, forced sexual intercourse in friendship or intimate relationships, when defined as date rape, occurs without the commission of another crime, thus making it an act of simple rape and a criminal act, which is difficult to prosecute.

Acts of sexual violence have a long history. In fact, these types of sexual behaviors occurred frequently in society, but accurate terminology which the victims could use to describe their experience was not available. Not only was appropriate terminology not available to describe various forms of sexual violence, many victims did not know who to inform about the experience nor where to report it. Thus, it is not surprising that academicians did not begin to examine and identify the dimensions of the act of date rape until the mid-twentieth century (Parrot & Bechhofer, 1991).

Courtship and Dating

Some of the data which will be presented in this work suggest that forced sexual intercourse is not always defined as rape. In general, the forced sexual intercourse which is not labeled as rape by the victims has occurred in a courtship or dating context. In order to facilitate an understanding of the implications of the data, some attention must be paid to the evolution of dating, courtship, and intimate violence. Forced sexual intercourse between intimates or friends usually occurs within a marital, courtship, or dating context and will resist explanations which do not incorporate a familiarity with the research and theory which addresses this context.

Courtship is an activity with a lengthy past. Courtship as a set of activities in which couples engage as they seek suitable life mates has taken many forms but has been pervasive through time and present in most societies. Dating, a set of activities in which couples engage for recreation, emerged during the late 1800s and initially evolved from courtship rituals. As freedom for women expanded in the 1900s, the emphasis on recreation increased, and the emphasis on finding a mate decreased in dating. Today, recreational dating is an activity in its own right, but dating can lead to courtship or to the development of a relatively permanent relationship.

Historical Perspectives on Courtship and Dating

It is difficult to examine historical perspectives on courtship and dating without recognizing that the definitions of appropriate behavior, particularly individual freedom, have changed drastically over the years. While men traditionally have had the freedom to participate in recreation away from the protection of the family, women have been restricted to the family home and to carefully chaperoned social events. It was not until the industrial revolution that women began to work outside of the home and not until the 1900s that women began to associate freely in mixed-sex unchaperoned groups for recreation. It should be noted, however, that even today the separation between dating as recreation and dating as courtship is tenuous, at best.

Historical analysis in this area is somewhat limited. Information written about dating and courtship usually takes the form of diaries and letters (Rothman, 1950). As a result, the focus is on the patterns of thought and behavior of middle and upper class young men and women. Universal education did not develop until the 1900s; thus, writers tended to be children of the rich or at least reasonably affluent. It was these young adults who had the education and the leisure to maintain diaries and to write lengthy letters. Children of the less affluent did not acquire writing skills and did not have the leisure time to devote to elaborate courtships.

At the turn of the nineteenth century, dating occurred only in the context of courtship. Young men and young women could meet through church and family activities or through organized social activities, such as dances. Men and women were free to associate with and meet each other at dances. If the association moved beyond casual conversation in groups or dancing at parties, the activity was characterized as courtship with the possibility of marriage. By the end of the eighteenth century, young people were becoming responsible for courtship. Men and women were given considerable latitude in choosing their potential future mates. At this time, the standard for mate selection shifted from good provider or homemaker to romantic love.

Once courtship was begun, the couple frequently had some degree of freedom. While many activities occurred in the home of the young woman, the family would provide opportunities for the couple to be alone. Family members would leave the couple alone in the sitting room, or the couple would be allowed to move about the home and grounds unsupervised. Once the relationship was established, the young man would escort the young woman to church, picnics, dances, the theater, and other social activities. It was during the last quarter of the eighteenth century that young couples appear to have become more sexually active. The practice of bundling (couples spent the night in the same bed in their clothes with a board between them) was in vogue, and the number of couples expecting a child at the time of their marriage was higher than in preceding decades or later decades. Sex was recognized as a part of an intimate relationship, but sexual intercourse usually occurred only after engagement (Rothman, 1984). Forced sexual intercourse was a private matter which was guarded against by preventing possible intimacy before a relationship developed. In this context, the distinction between forced and consensual intercourse was not critical. That is, the practices protected young women both from evil men and from their own inclination to misbehavior.

As the nineteenth century emerged, the sexual nature of women began to be redefined. While women were expected to be sexual and passionate in the latter 1700s, they were expected to be moral and passionless in most of the 1800s. By the mid-1800s falling in love was a necessary condition for marriage. Early courtship/dating was characterized as friendship, with the friendship maintained until it became clear that love did exist. If love did not develop, the couple characterized their relationship as enduring friendship. During this period, bundling virtually disappeared, and courtship provided greater "protection" for the women. Men were expected to have natural passions, and women were expected to maintain control of the relationship (Rothman, 1984).

The commitment to romantic love continued into the 1900s, but women began experiencing greater freedom. The number of occupations which women could pursue, while still limited to "women's work", increased. More women were living independently in boarding houses, many of them some distance from their homes. Women still were expected to be modest and virtuous, still were responsible for controlling the relationships which they chose to pursue, and dating continued to be defined in terms of courtship. The extent to which men and women associated in non-courtship settings increased as co-educational colleges and universities emerged and women moved into the work place and out of the home. While work and social activities continued to remain somewhat sexually segregated, women and men tended to associate more frequently than in the past. Associations which developed in these settings tended to be defined in terms of friendship. Then, as today, however, these associations could lead to courtship (Rothman, 1984).

By the beginning of the twentieth century, dating as recreation was beginning to emerge as an activity not necessarily related to courtship. Women, particularly in the cities, were working all day in offices and were inclined to get out and do things rather than entertain gentleman callers in their homes or in their apartments. This shift from entertainment in the home of the woman to entertainment provided by the man established the basis for recreational dating. While separate from courtship, this activity was not necessarily divorced from sex. Sex was still a dangerous activity for women in the early 1900s, thus was approached with caution by most women. Premarital sex, however, was no longer taken as a sign of betrothal as had been the case in earlier centuries (Rothman, 1984).

As the nineteenth century passed and the twentieth century emerged, courtship was controlled carefully both by standards for appropriate social etiquette and through informal supervision by the parents of the young women and the community (Bailey, 1988; Rothman, 1984). Rules of good conduct and loose supervision served to protect the young women from inappropriate behavior (Lloyd, 1991). This system of informal gatekeeping gradually faded during the first decades of the twentieth century and was replaced by a system of dating which was defined and controlled to a great extent by the young people involved in the process rather than by their parents (Lloyd, 1991; Waller, 1951).

Couples in the early 1900s still attended the chaperoned parties, dances, and church socials of the preceding centuries, but they also engaged in unsupervized activities, such as visiting clubs, exhibitions, and shows in neighboring towns. These new activities involved a shift in the financial character of courtship as well as a shift in supervision (Rothman, 1984). Given the opportunities to be alone provided in both the 1700s and 1800s, it is possible that the shift in the financial dynamics was more important than the shift to less supervision by the family and by the community. Prior to the 1900s, costs of courtship were borne by the family of the women or by society. Courtship occurred in the woman's home or at public activities provided by the church or groups of families. The new activities tended to be commercial, and the man was expected to pay for the entertainment. These costs included transportation to distant towns (5-20 miles) and the cost of the entertainment.

Technology and social change, in the form of the automobile, the telephone, co-educational campuses, and new forms of commercial entertainment, were once again changing the way in which courtship was conducted. Children were being separated from the protected environment of the home at an earlier age. A few short decades before, women remained in the home until they sought employment in other towns, now they, in the company of their male companions, were leaving the protection/supervision of home and town to recreate while still "boys" and "girls". There was some reaction from concerned parents and the chaperon became an important person. In preceding centuries, the chaperon function had been provided informally by the family and the community. In the two decades immediately preceding and following the turn of the century, the chaperon function was frequently entrusted to a single person and provided in a formal rather than informal manner. So, at the same time, young men and women had social exchanges which were unsupervised and social activities which were strictly supervised, with considerable variation from family to family (Rothman, 1984). While recreation was becoming a more important function of dating, courtship (finding a suitable marriage partner) remained the primary function of dating. For most couples, premarital sex remained a sign of firm commitment to marriage. To a great extent, sex in the first decades of the twentieth century remained the prerogative of married couples. While sex continued to be defined in terms of marital relations, freedom within the marriage expanded. Marriage manuals of the time began to define sexual intercourse as having a recreation role as well as a procreation role - a position made possible in part by the introduction of rudimentary contraceptive devices and the popularity of Sigmund Freud (Rothman, 1984).

During the early decades of the twentieth century, control passed to the men as dating became the basis for courtship. During this period, control of the courtship process moved from the women and their families to the men. Before the turn of the century, courtship did not involve a financial investment. Activities in which the couple engaged were generally cost free. There was a financial interest to the extent that gentlemen did not court until they were financially independent to the point that they could support a family. The women and their families controlled both access and process through an elaborate system of rituals, such as calling cards, introductions, and the ability of the family to reject at the earliest stages the interests of the men (Bailey, 1988; Rothman, 1984). Parents and the community were unable to control dating, and dating now involved spending money. The resulting shift of emphasis from being a good provider to being a good date, coupled with the constraints imposed by the definition of women as passive and non-assertive, gave control of the access process to males. That is, women waited for men to ask them out. While some women developed elaborate strategies to attract the attention of desirable males, men had control of the process.

Women were rated as desirable based on the status of their family, their physical appearance, and their personalities. Desirableness was closely related to sexual attractiveness. Make-up, perfumes, and clothing were important assets.

Men were rated as desirable based on their possession of financial resources and the prestige of the groups to which they could claim membership; the worth of women was based on the quality of the men they could attract as dates. In the patriarchal system a woman's worth had been determined by the worth of her husband. This value was transferred from marriage to courtship as dating became accepted as the right and appropriate mechanism for socializing among the young (Bailey, 1988; Rothman, 1984). The process through which courtship and dating led toward courtship and marriage had different meaning for men than for women. For men, the theme was one of remaining in control of the relationship. For women, the theme was dependence on her partner (Lloyd, 1991). At the same time, the woman was held responsible for maintaining limits on (control of) the sexual dimensions of the relationship. If forced sexual intercourse occurred in this context, the victim was held accountable since it was her responsibility to control the degree of intimacy of the relationship.

Historical Perspectives on Violence and Aggression in Courtship and Marriage

Violence among intimates has become subject to scrutiny in the past two decades after centuries of classification as a taboo subject. This attention has tended to be specific, focusing first on spouse abuse (early 1800s), then on child abuse, then on spouse abuse again, and, most recently, on forced sexual intercourse between people who know each other. The more general concern focusing on violence between people involved or becoming involved in a personal/sexual relationship is emerging only now and has been characterized as intimate violence (Blackman, 1985). Much of what has been recorded historically about intimate violence has focused on spouse abuse.

Courtship and marriage are different stages in the same process and are influenced by basic values concerning the relationship between men and women. Throughout written history women have been subordinate to men. Written records indicate that women were subordinate to men in virtually every culture. The role of women in relation to men is defined by the religions of the West (Christianity and Judaism) in terms of obedience and submission. It has been suggested that one of the effects of religion has been to reinforce the subjugation of women (Daly, 1978; Dobash & Dobash, 1979; Okun, 1986; Wilson, 1978). These values were perpetuated through the patriarchal system of male dominance of families and inheritance and transmission of wealth through the male line or through the husbands of the daughters (Brownmiller, 1975; Dobash & Dobash, 1979).

Fathers and husbands were held responsible for the behavior of their daughters and wives and were expected to control them. If the women committed crimes, the men were held accountable for the damage. Men, as the dominant sex, were expected to discipline their women. In the exercise of this discipline men were expected to use reasonable physical force. Reasonable physical force was defined as including black eyes and broken noses (Dobash & Dobash, 1979). Community approval of the practice of the use of force by husbands to discipline wives continued uninterrupted into the twentieth century (Okun, 1986).

Intimate violence became an issue as the woman's suffrage movement gained strength in the 1920s, but lost prominence in the public eye as that movement waned and did not become salient again until the 1970s when pressure began to develop to force the justice system to treat marital violence as a criminal offense. While the feminist movement was not concerned with domestic affairs in the early years of the most recent resurgence of the women's movement, as women's roles changed and women became more involved in women's issues, domestic violence became a topic of concern (Okun, 1986). Attention was focused on practices of the justice system which effectively made marital violence a non-enforced offense in all but the most extreme cases.

Changes in Rape Laws

Changes in orientation toward domestic violence was one aspect of the convergence of two broader movements. Both domestic violence and forced sexual intercourse are behaviors which were addressed by the movement to redefine the relative status of women in our society and the movement to control or reduce violence. This dual influence can be seen clearly in efforts to revise the laws which addressed sexual misconduct. Changes in laws defining rape and rules of evidence have redefined the scope of behaviors to be addressed to include violent acts other than rape and have reduced the ability of offenders to rely on "character" issues as a defense.

Today, the criminal justice system is actively involved in the prosecution of cases of forced sexual intercourse. Laws regulating forced sexual intercourse have undergone substantial revision over the years. Many changes are reflections of changes in societal attitudes toward the crime of rape, the offender, and the victim. In this process, the perception of rape as an offense against the male (ie., husband or father) and not against the woman has been replaced with the perception of rape as an offense against the victim, that is, an offense against a person and not against property (Brownmiller, 1975).

In order to evaluate the extent to which laws regulating offensive sexual behavior have changed, the basic definition of rape must be examined. In general, rape is defined as a man engaging in sexual intercourse with a woman not his wife by force or threat of force against her will and without her consent (Estrich, 1987). While the definition appears to be clear, some forms of forced sexual intercourse have been excluded. According to this definition of rape, it is legally impossible for a husband to rape his wife. At one point in history, all laws relating to rape included the "marital rape exemption" (Russell, 1984). It was assumed that a husband could not be found guilty of raping his wife because by the act of marriage she had given prior consent to intercourse, a position which reflects the pervasiveness of the historical property orientation as much as it reflects implied consent. Forced sexual intercourse among married couples is the only form of forced sexual intercourse which has been persistently defined as beyond the interest of the state.

The women's movement was instrumental in drawing public attention to the phenomenon of rape during the 1970s, placing pressure on the legislatures to reform rape laws. The changing definition of women's rights included the assertion that the use of force to obtain sexual access is never justified. While pressure from the women's movement produced a number of positive reforms in the rape laws, many states were hesitant to change laws condoning spousal rape. Most of the reluctance to abolish the marital rape exemption was due to the perception that a couple's bedroom is private and the state has no right to invade the sanctity and intimacy of a marital relationship.

Despite efforts to abolish the marital rape exemption, a husband could legally force his wife to have intercourse in at least seven states as of 1990. There is a number of rationales or explanations for not abolishing the marital rape exemption, the most pervasive of which is the assertion that what occurs in a marriage is personal, private, and devoid of state interest. It is also argued that if wives were to charge their husbands with rape, the accusation would minimize the potential for reconciliation for the couple.

It is extremely difficult to reconcile a marriage once marital rape has occurred. Marital rape is just one extension of domestic violence (Russell, 1990; Finkelhor & Yllo, 1985). Both marital rape and physical abuse in marital and cohabitating relationships reinforce the belief that a woman has a responsibility to submit to her partner. It is possible that a similar rationale exists in some cases of and responses to date rape. When a young man takes a young woman on a date (which may include dinner, movie, or some other monetary activity) with the expectation that sexual intercourse will be the outcome and then forces her to engage in sexual intercourse against her will, his behavior is not consistently identified as rape.

The traditional definition of rape also has limited the crime to gender-based sexual acts with the man as the perpetrator and the woman as the victim. This view fails to acknowledge the fact that both men and women can be raped and that women now can be charged with rape if they participate in these acts. Many states now have created gender neutral laws to make it legally possible for women to rape men, and some states now have provisions for sexual assault between people of the same sex.

Other significant changes in rape laws have occurred in the areas of consent and the victim's prior criminal history. The most important defense central to the charge of rape is consent. By law, lack of consent in the area of rape is defined as engaging in sex by force or threat of force, against the victim's will, and without her permission. It is assumed that if consent is not given or if the victim only "says no" to sexual activity, she is responding in the way that she has been socialized to respond in that type of situation. In the area of rape, verbal consent is not expected of a woman who demonstrates certain kinds of behaviors. In fact, her self-expressions are considered evidence of consent to a sexual encounter. This implied consent perspective frequently was applied in cases of date rape in which a woman's actions were interpreted as willingness to have sex and has included such general behaviors as: going on a date, going to the offender's apartment, engaging in foreplay for a period of time before asking the male to stop, and dressing provocatively. These behaviors are perceived to be indicators that the woman wants to have sex, but, because of social and cultural norms, she is expected to say no to the sexual encounter although she really means yes. Consequently, no is not taken as denial of consent by the offender and those who share his cultural attitudes.

If these types of cultural attitudes predominate in rape laws and in the courtroom, the jury can conclude that a rape did not occur. Unless the testimony of the victim is strong and convincing concerning the fact that she did not consent, it will be difficult for the prosecution to obtain a conviction. If the victim internalizes self-blame for the forced sex, she may not define the act as rape and thus will not view herself as a legitimate victim. This emphasis on consent and the need to substantiate consent with circumstantial or objective evidence continues to make it extremely difficult to obtain a conviction in date rape cases and introduces confusion in the minds of men and women. This confusion can set the stage for rape.

Issues surrounding consent have led some states to reform their rape laws by removing some of the focus from the victim's behavior (Parrot & Bechhofer, 1991). At one time, rape laws measured non-consent of the victim by the extent to which she resisted her assailants or fought back; however, many states have shifted the focus from the victim's behavior to the offender's behavior by replacing the standard that a woman must show nonconsent by resisting "to the utmost" with a standard based on an examination of the acts of the offender. Although this new reform was designed to focus on the acts of the defendant to determine whether force was used, force is still defined by the court in terms of the woman's resistance (Estrich, 1987) and in terms of male standards.

Another area of rape law reform that had a significant impact on the definition of rape is the introduction of testimony concerning the victim's prior sexual history. Traditional procedural law allowed evidence of the woman's prior sexual behavior to be introduced in court. These new laws, called "shield laws" (Parrot & Bechhofer, 1991), were designed to counter the assumption that a promiscuous woman was more likely to consent to the alleged rape than a virgin (Tong, 1984). A woman with a reputation of being promiscuous would not be concerned about one more act of intercourse with the defendant. Revisions hold that prior sexual behavior does not imply consent and can not be used to justify the use of force in obtaining sexual access.

Prior sexual history is not only irrelevant to consent but also to the victim's credibility. A woman who was perceived to be pure, innocent, and a virgin was perceived to be more credible than a promiscuous woman. Thus, the system punished the woman for her sexual behavior and not the offender for his. Today, there have been some changes in rules of evidence concerning admissibility of testimony of the victim's prior sexual history. By

1990, more than 40 states had passed statutes that limited the ability of the defense to introduce evidence about the victim's past sexual history (Field & Bienen, 1980). The flexibility of these statutes varies from state to state; however, the most restrictive statute concerning introducing evidence about the victim's prior sexual history totally excludes the victim's past sexual behavior with anyone except the defendant.

Rape reform also has occurred in the area of rules of evidence. Reform statutes have abolished a number of evidentiary rules that identified rape as a crime to be tried differently from other crimes. Rules that were abolished include the requirement for special corroboration in rape cases, proof of resistance, and special instructions to the jury about the need for caution in assessing the testimony of the victim (Berger, Searles, & Neuman, 1988).

Another legislative change is redefining the crime of rape. At present, some states do not have specific rape statutes but, rather, have a series of graded offenses with the severity of the penalty depending on the degree of infliction of injury, the amount of coercion, and the age of the victim (Field & Bienen, 1980). The rationale of this particular change is to increase the conviction rate of rapists based on the assumption that the focus on the victim's injuries may produce more convictions on a wider range of offenses.

In another approach to reform, rape laws become sexual assault laws and sexual intercourse is removed as a focus. One example of this change is the new sexual assault legislation developed in Canada in 1983. This change in legislation shifted the emphasis from sex to violence. Consequently, the element of penetration has been replaced by the violence of the entire act; nevertheless, changing rape laws to sexual assault laws is not without its problems. The new legislation carries with it many of the same problems which existed under the old rape laws. It appears that under this new sexual assault legislation, the same elements are applied to both assault and sexual assault. Thus, there are no clear-cut boundaries to distinguish the differences in the legal elements for these two offenses. As a result, there is great potential for different interpretations of the actions that constitute a sexual assault.

The phenomenon of date rape was recognized by academicians by 1957; however, its recognition did not facilitate a substantial amount of research during the next two decades. The lack of academic research in this area and the development of social and legal policies on date rape only facilitated the belief that forced sex is acceptable under certain circumstances (Goodchilds, Zellman, Johnson & Giarrusso, 1988).

By the early 1970s, the women's movement in the United States brought the issue of rape to the public's attention as a serious social and legal problem. Consequently, rape crisis centers were developed across the nation, and a number of federal and state rape prevention programs were developed. As awareness of the problem increased, research and service emerged which focused on the plight of victims and their needs.

Throughout Western history and culture, there has been an underlying assumption that there is some tolerance for sexual violence and that this type of tolerance is reinforced by cultural beliefs. There are several factors that contribute to the cultural tolerance of rape of females: (1) the historical tradition of the patriarchal principle over women, (2) the historical perception that the woman encouraged sexual violence against herself by her dress or/and mannerism, and (3) laws which have made it difficult for the woman to come forth and press charges against her assailant (Dobash & Dobash, 1978). Tolerance of sexual violence against women only facilitates the acceptance of violence against women and the justification of some forms of forced sexual intercourse.

Summary

Date rape and rape are frequently perceived as being the same. A number of differences in historical perspective and in contemporary orientation must be understood before proceeding with an examination of forced sexual intercourse in an intimate or friendship relationship. While the focus of the research reported in this work is on forced sexual intercourse in friendship and intimate relationships, there is much in common among the various forms of forced sexual intercourse. Historically, women had few rights including the right to control their own sexual behavior. In centuries past, women were legally treated more as property to be controlled by the dominant male than as individual people. Under these circumstances, rape was treated as a crime of theft and the victim's owner (father or husband) was compensated for his loss. It was not until the twentieth century that rape began to be defined as an act of violence committed against a woman who was the victim, and that punishment was directed toward the male offender and not to the female victim. In the process, laws condemning these behaviors were broadened and trial procedures were modified. The concept of sexual assault emerged, and procedures which put the victims on trial were restricted.

As orientation toward women has changed, orientation toward sexual offenses has changed. The definition of rape has been broadened to include all forms of forced sexual intercourse and other offensive sexual behaviors. In the process, a new class of behavior, sexual assault, has been created which to some extent has replaced rape. The definition of forced sexual intercourse as rape or sexual assault still is influenced by historical factors in orientation toward rape. The most pervasive of these is perceived consent, the right (property) of men to sexual access in intimate relationships, and holding women accountable for their victimization in cases of sexual assault.

Courtship violence is similar in many ways to other forms of violence. Violence often is linked with aggression; however, aggression can occur without violence, and violence can occur without aggression. While some intimate violence can be explained in terms of aggression, this violence also can be produced by environmental pressures, by the actor's "personality", or by mutually accepted rituals or accepted patterns of behavior for some groups. Violence appears to be an acceptable response to problems in the United States. Violence is an option which individuals and groups can exercise if the cause is just. These values can and are used to support the decision to resolve disputes in intimate relationships. Women and children traditionally have been at a disadvantage in that men as husbands or fathers were expected to discipline their wives and children. This responsibility justified the use of physical force. The first reforms were designed to limit this force to force which would not cause death or great bodily harm.

Intimate violence is still in the process of redefinition. During this century child abuse, spouse abuse, and, most recently, elder abuse have been targets of social concern. Extreme cases have been documented and special interest groups have lobbied successfully for changes in the law and in the orientation of the justice system to spouse, child, and elder abuse, as well as to rape and sexual aggression. Things which in the past were considered to be private matters are now public matters and are addressed by social institutions.

As a part of this process, forced sexual intercourse has undergone substantial redefinition. Laws regarding rape have been expanded to include a broad range of sexually offensive behavior, with sexual assault and changes in the application of the rules of evidence permitting the successful prosecution of types of forced sexual intercourse which were not prosecutable in the past. There are still areas in which the application of public interest is limited. These areas include forced sexual intercourse among spouses and forced sexual intercourse among intimates (date or acquaintance rape). That is, some still consider this behavior as wrong but not a public/criminal matter.

Much of the research in all types of intimate violence focuses on the factors which are related to the use of or justification for the use of physical force. Attitudes toward women, attitudes toward the use of force, perceived provocative behavior of the victim, implied consent, perceived character of the victim, organizational membership, environmental pressure, masculine stereotypes, dominance, and financial investment have all been considered factors relevant to the use of force in intimate relationships. It appears at this point that future research must step back from the examination of prevalence, incidence, and individual factors and broaden the research frame to include the context in which these acts of violence occur. Date rape and acquaintance rape must be examined in the context of dating and courtship. There might be a relationship between the use of force or aggression in intimate relationships and the use of force to obtain sexual intercourse or sexual access. It is also possible that the values which define the appropriate behaviors for negotiating a dating, intimate, and/or sexual relationship are unclear and/or include the use of "acceptable" force. Such a situation would produce instances in which conflicting definitions would produce incidents of rape. If young women are to be adequately prepared to protect themselves, then accurate information must be available to inform the potential victims and their potential offenders of appropriate and inappropriate behaviors in dating and of the potential for confusion in situations in which the values are unclear.

References

Bailey, B. L. (1988), *From Front Porch to Back Seat: The History of Courtship in America*, The Johns Hopkins University Press, Baltimore, MD.

Berger, R. J., Searles, P. and Neuman, W. L. (1988), 'The Dimensions of Rape Reform Legislation', *Law and Society Review*, vol. 22, pp. 329-57.

Blackman, J. (1985), 'The Language of Sexual Violence: More than a Matter of Semantics', in S.R. Sunday and E. Tobach (eds), *Violence Against Women* (pp. 115-128), Gordian Press, New York.

Brownmiller, S. (1975), *Against Our Will: Men, Women and Rape*, Simon and Schuster, New York.

Carter, J. M. (1984), 'The Status of Rape in Thirteenth Century England: 1218-1276', *International Journal of Women's Studies*, vol. 7, pp. 248-59.

Daly, M. (1978), *Gynecology: The Meta-ethics of Radical Feminism*, Beacon Press, Boston.

Dobash, R.E. and Dobash, R. (1979), *Violence Against Wives: A Case Against the Patriarchy*, Free Press, New York.

Donat, P. L. N. and D'Emilo, J. (1992), 'A Feminist Redefinition of Rape and Sexual Assault: Historical Foundations and Change', *Journal of Social Issues*, vol. 48, pp. 9-22.

Dover, K. J. (1984), 'Classical Greek Attitudes to Sexual Behavior', in J. Peradotto and J. Sullivan (eds), *Women in the Ancient World: The Atrthusa Papers*, State University of New York Press, Albany, NY.

Estrich, S. (1987), *Real Rape*, Harvard University Press, Cambridge, MA.

Field, H.S. and Bienen, L.B. (1980), *Jurors and Rape: A Study in Psychology and Law*, Lexington Press, Lexington, MA.

Finkelhor, D. and Yllo, K. (1985), *License to Rape*, Rinehart and Winston, New York.

Freeman, J. (ed) (1989), *Women: A Feminist Perspective*, Mayfield, Palo Alto, CA.

Getman, K. (1984), 'Sexual Control in the Slaveholding South: The Implementation and Maintenance of a Racial Caste System', *Harvard Women's Law Review*, vol. 7, pp. 115-53.

Goodchilds, J. D., Zellman, G., Johnson, P. B. and Giarrusso, R. (1988), 'Adolescents and Their Perceptions of Sexual Interaction Outcomes', in A. W. Burgess (ed), *Sexual Assault* (Vol. 2, pp. 245-270), Garland, New York.

Jordon, W. (1968), *White Over Black: American Attitudes Toward the Negro*, University of North Carolina Press, Williamsburg, WV.

Kanin, E. J. (1967), 'Reference Groups and Sex Conduct Norm Violations', *Sociological Quarterly*, vol. 8, pp. 495-504.

Koehler, I. (1980), *A Search for Power: The "Weaker Sex" in Seventeenth-century New England*, University of Illinois Press, Urbana, IL.

Koss, M. P., Gidycz, C. A. and Wisniewski, N. (1987), 'The Scope of Rape: Incidence and Prevalence of Sexual Aggression and Victimization in a National Sample of Higher Education Students', *Journal of Counseling and Clinical Psychology*, vol. 55, pp. 162-70.

Lloyd, S. (1982), 'Premarital Abuse: A Social Psychological Perspective', *Journal of Family Issues*, vol. 3, pp. 79-91.

Muehlenhard, C. L. and Linton, M A. (1987), 'Date Rape and Sexual Aggression in Dating Situations: Incidence and Risk Factors', *Journal of Consulting Psychology*, vol.34, pp. 186-96.

Okun, L. (1986), *Woman Abuse*, Suny Press, Albany, NY.

Parrot, A. and Bechhofer, L. (1991), *Acquaintance Rape: The Hidden Cime*, Wiley, New York.

Post, J. B. (1978), 'Sir Thomas West and the Statute of Rapes, 1382', *Bulletin of the Institute of Historical Research*, vol. 53, pp. 24-30.

Quinsey, V. L., Chaplin, T. C. and Varney, G. (1981), 'A Comparison of Rapists' and Non-sex Offenders Sexual Preferences for Mutually Consenting Sex, Rape, and Physical Abuse of Women', *Behavioral Assessment*, vol. 3, pp. 127-35.

Rada, R. T. (ed) (1978), *Clinical Aspects of the Rapist*, Grune and Stratton, New York.

Rossiaud, J. (1978), 'Prostitution, Youth, and Society in the Towns of Southeastern France in the Fifteenth Century', in R. Forster and O. Ranum (eds), *Deviants and the Abandoned in French Society* (pp. 1-46), Johns Hopkins University Press, Washington, DC.

Rothman, E. K. (1984), *Hands and Hearts: A History of Courtship in America*, Basic Books, New York.

Ruggerio, G. (1980), *Violence in Early Renaissance Venice,* Rutgers University Press, Camden, NJ.

Russell (1990), *Violence in Intimate Relationships*, Prentice Hall, Englewood Cliffs, NJ.

Russell, D. E. H. (1984), *Sexual Exploitation: Rape, Child Sexual Abuse, and Workplace Harassment, Sage,* Beverly Hills, CA.

Struckman-Johnson, C. (1988), 'Forced Sex on Dates: It Happens to Men Too', *Journal of Sex Research*, vol. 24, pp. 234-40.

Tong, R. (1984), *Woman, Sex, and the Law,* Rowman & Allanheld, Totowa, NJ.

Veronen, L. J., Kilpatrick, D. G. and Resick, P. A. (1983), 'Treatment of Fear and Anxiety in Rape Victims: Implications for the Criminal Justice System', in W. H. Parsonage (ed), *Perspectives on Victimology* (pp. 148-159), Sage, Beverly Hills, CA.

Waller, W. (1951), *The Family: A Dynamic Interpretation*, Dryden, New York.

Warner, C. G. (1980), *Rape and Sexual Assault: Management and Intervention*, Aspen, Germantown, MD.

Williams, J. E. (1984), 'Secondary victimization: Confronting Public Attitudes about Rape', *Victimology: An International Journal*, vol. 9, pp. 66-81.

Wilson, J. (1978), *Religion in American Society: The Effective Presence*, Prentice Hall, Englewood Cliffs, NJ.

Wriggins, J. (1983), 'Rape, Racism, and the Law', *Harvard Women's Law Journal*, vol. 6, pp. 103-141.

3 Prevalence and Incidence

Introduction

Forced sexual intercourse is increasingly becoming of interest to activists and researchers. Forced sexual intercourse is, at best, a concept lacking clear definition, conceptual boundaries, and identified dimensions. Rape, sexual assault, and courtship violence share much of the behavior which appears to be relevant. Regardless of the approach, there appears to be a tendency to perceive forced sexual intercourse as an interaction between two actors, one of whom is an offensive man who acts (intends) to force his will on his female companion. Estimations of the incidence and prevalence of this phenomena have varied greatly from research project to research project. The variance in the findings reported among studies might represent variance in the phenomena studied. It is more likely, however, that much of the variance can be attributed to differences in the definitions of the behaviors studied and other differences in methodological technique. The analysis presented in this chapter includes data from two recent studies conducted by the authors which is combined with findings from a number of historical and contemporary studies which have sought to estimate the prevalence and/or incidence of forced sexual intercourse.

Rape and Sexual Assault

The definition of acts of forced sexual intercourse has changed a great deal over time. As indicated in Chapter Two, rape was originally perceived as an act against the husband or father of the victim (Clark & Lewis, 1977). The failure to distinguish the victim's rights from those of the husband/father introduced confusion in the early definitions of rape that continues today (Brownmiller, 1975). By the late 1970s, public awareness of rape issues had

31

increased and people were beginning to accept rape as a serious problem (Bourque, 1989; Rose, 1977). As a result of changing public attitudes, statutory changes were enacted in many states which redefined rape and introduced the concept of sexual assault, thus creating different degrees of rape (Parrot & Bechhofer, 1991, pp. 16-17).

While violence among dating couples has been studied for some time (Kanin, 1957), the term date rape did not emerge until the early 1980s. Studies have indicated that the majority of rapes occur between acquaintances (Rabkin, 1979; Koss, Dinero, Seibel, & Cox, 1988; Russell, 1984). Kanin's (1967) study of male undergraduates indicated that 26 percent reported having been sexually aggressive on a date in a way that led to the woman's fighting, crying, or screaming, while Russell (1984) found that of the rape victims identified in her study of 930 San Francisco residents, 88 percent knew their offender. Furthermore, a national survey indicated that 60 percent of the acquaintance-rape victims on college campuses occurred with casual or steady dates (Koss, Dinero, Seibel, & Cox, 1988).

The definition of behavior which includes the specific use of force in sexual interaction as rape can be clouded by the introduction of collateral factors. It has been suggested (Burt, 1980; Field, 1978; Muehlenhard, Friedman, & Thomas, 1985; Murnen, Perot, & Byrne, 1989) that there is a relationship between traditional sex role stereotyping and the perception of the act as rape. Griffin (1971) directed attention to the cultural supports for rape, leading to assertions that rape results from normal socialization processes. Warshaw (1988) addressed heterosexual rituals, suggesting sexual assertiveness on the part of the man and gatekeeping behaviors on the part of the woman may play a role in date rape. Parrot (1986) asserted that women who demonstrate the traditional female role of being passive, gentle, and sacrificing are more likely to be victims of rape than those who are assertive. Bridges and McGrail (1989) asserted that the model of rape which has been proposed by researchers such as Burt (1980) and Cherry (1983), which suggests that rape is an extension of the traditional behaviors and motives that operate in heterosexual situations, is particularly applicable to date rape.

The definition, nature, and frequency of occurrence of sexually offensive behaviors have been affected by changing social definitions of courtship and dating. During this century, courtship moved from control by social institutions to control by the participants, with a movement from supervised activities to informal dating as the primary courtship activity

(Bailey, 1988; Rothman, 1984; Waller, 1951). Exploitation and disorder began to appear in the dating process relatively early (Waller, 1937) and have continued to contemporary times (Makepeace, 1989). Violence (aggressive or forceful behavior) in courtship has been found to be relatively common, ranging from 30 percent to 50 percent in studies of the dating behavior of college students (Cate, Henton, Koval, Christopher, & Lloyd, 1982) and to be more extreme in inner city low income neighborhoods (Clark, Beckett, Wells, & Dungee-Anderson, 1994). This behavior has been attributed to a desire to control the situation (Stets & Pirog-Good, 1987; Follingstad, Rutledge, Polek, & McNeill-Hawkins, 1988). This use of controlling techniques may be supported by male peer groups (DeKeseredy, 1988) and may be interpreted as an expression of love rather than as an expression of hate (Cate, Henton, Koval, Christopher, & Lloyd, 1982).

Sexual assault is defined loosely and includes behaviors that are less intrusive than intercourse. Particularly when applied to a dating or courtship situation, the terms for sexual assault and their definitions vary widely and include sexual aggression (Amick & Calhoun, 1987; Kanin, 1957; Muehlenhard & Linton, 1987), sexual coercion (Fenstermaker, 1988), sexual victimization and rape (Koss, Dinero, Seibel, & Cox, 1988), courtship violence (Makepeace, 1981), and unwanted sexual intercourse (Ward, Chapman, Cohen, White, & Williams, 1991). In addition to the confusion caused by the differences in terms and definitions, the use of differing time frames (life time vs. fixed time frame) can cause confusion.

Official Estimates

Official estimates are found in the Uniform Crime Reports (UCR) and the reports from the National Crime Survey. There is general agreement that these sources of data are inaccurate and that they consistently underestimate rates of victimization in cases of sexual assault (DiVasto, Kaufman, Rosner, Jackson, Christy, Pearson, & Burgett, 1984; Johnson, 1980; Koss, Dinero, Seibel, & Cox, 1988; Koss, Gidycz, & Wisniewski, 1987; Ward, Chapman, Cohen, White, & Williams, 1991).

The Uniform Crime Reports are summaries of crimes reported to the police. Almost all police departments record almost all crimes reported to the police in the system. While the degree of cooperation and consistency in reporting has improved greatly in the past decade, the findings produced through analysis of UCR must be approached cautiously. Changes in crime rates over time computed from the UCR may reflect changes in technology and compliance rather than changes in the crime rates themselves. A number of other technical issues in data recording and compliant processing reinforces the need to exercise caution in accepting the validity of the UCR. While the new National Incident-Based Reporting System (NIBRS) is designed to reduce the impact of weakness of the UCR, the changes will have little impact on the primary weakness of reported crime-based statistics in the area of sexual assault. Both the UCR and the NIBRS are based on crimes reported to the police. A general weakness of both is that many crimes are not reported to the police, and it appears that this weakness is particularly relevant in estimates of the incidence and prevalence of sexual assault. Estimates of this error range from non-reporting by 75 percent of the victims to a Federal Bureau of Investigation estimate of a 90 percent non-report rate for sexual assaults (Divasto, Kaufman, Rosner, Jackson, Christy, Pearson, & Burgett, 1984).

The National Crime Survey (NCS) is conducted by the Department of Justice's Bureau of Justice Statistics. The NCS evolved from early victimization studies in major cities and the subsequent development of the National Crime Survey Panels. The major city orientation was dropped and the NCS is presently based on the early National Crime Survey Panel model. Randomly selected cohorts (panels) of citizens are interviewed at six-month intervals for three years. After three years, the cohort is replaced with a new cohort which is measured for three years. The intent of the NCS is to gather accurate measures of criminal victimization in the United States. The manner in which the NCS operationalizes its definition of sexual assault produces underestimates of the incidence and prevalence of these offenses (Koss, Gidycz, & Wisniewski, 1987). After asking about offenses such as whether the respondent was a victim of attacks with instruments such as knifes, guns, or other weapons, the subjects are asked if someone has harmed them in some other way. If the respondent responds affirmatively, the interviewer probes for type of harm, such as sexual assault. The use of a screening question such as this consistently reduces the reporting rate as subjects may not recognize that sexual assault is an appropriate response category for the item (Koss, Gidycz, & Wisniewski, 1987). When Koss, Gidycz, and Wisniewski (1987) compared their data with UCR rates, they found that their rates per 1,000 women were more than 10 times greater than NCS estimates. Even if one were to assume that college women were at greater risk than non-college women, a difference of this magnitude would indicate that the NCS data underestimate victimization in the area of sexual assault.

Johnson (1980) conducted an analysis of National Crime Survey data drawn from data gathered from the major urban area victimization studies. While he acknowledged the weaknesses inherent in the analysis of NCS data, his intent was to establish a minimum risk rate or floor for estimates of sexual assault by adjusting NCS data for age specific rates to determine a lifetime minimum risk estimate. The lifetime minimum risk rates for rape were 3.2 percent for white women and 6.4 percent for non-white women. The rates for attempted rape were 16 percent for white women and 18 percent for non-white women. He suggested that the differences in reporting rates by race is greater for rape than for attempted rape because white women are more hesitant to report a completed rape but not an attempted rape than minority women.

Brackman's (1993) analysis of official reports indicating that date rape was as likely to be reported as stranger rape in official statistics was challenged by Pollard (1995). Brackman (1993) responded by noting that the rate of reporting of date rape has increased at a higher rate than reports of stranger rape, which is reducing the disparity in reporting.

Official statistics are not a reliable source of information for estimating the incidence or prevalence of forced sexual intercourse other than in efforts such as Johnson's development of a minimal lifetime risk estimate. A number of studies in the past decade have attempted to establish more effective estimates of the degree of risk to which women are exposed for sexual assault.

Contemporary Research

Reported incident rates have varied greatly, from 10 percent for forced sexual intercourse (dates in past 12 months), 15 percent for all forced sexual intercourse (during lifetime) (Sigler & Wenstrom, 1991) and 15 percent for rape (Koss, Gidycz, & Wisniewski, 1987) to 37 percent for sexual aggression (lifetime) (Poppen & Segal, 1988). Estimates of number of victims of forced sexual intercourse on the campus which provided the setting for the studies conducted by the authors had ranged from 40 percent to 60 percent of the women on campus.

A number of scholars sought to measure the incidence and/or prevalence of date rape in the early 1980s (Hall & Flannery, 1984; Russell, 1984; Story, 1982). Of these, Russell's study (1984) was reported most thoroughly and persistently has been influential in setting the standard for subsequent studies. Russell conducted her study in San Francisco and drew her probability sample of women over the age of 18 with the assistance of a professional public opinion polling organization. The study sought to determine the prevalence of all forms of sexual assault, including rape and the sexual abuse of children. The data were collected by female interviewers. A semi-structured interview was used to gather data from 930 women. The interviewers were carefully trained to deal with the sensitive area of sexual assault to avoid the persistent under-reporting of sexual victimization characteristic of other studies gathering crime data. The study used the statutory definition of rape which includes force, threat of force, and incapacitation (asleep, drugs, unconscious). Using this definition, 24 percent of the women interviewed reported that they had been raped at some point in their life. Of these, 5 percent reported that their only victimization was to have been raped by their husbands after they were married.

As most studies of date rape exclude marital rape, the figure which is most appropriate for comparisons with other studies is 19 percent for the percentage of women who reported at least one rape by someone other than their husband. When attempted rapes were included, 44 percent of the subjects reported victimization, a rate which is somewhat higher than reported by other studies which have included attempted forced sexual intercourse (Wyatt, 1992). When attempted rapes by husbands are excluded, the 31 percent victimization rate reported more closely approximates Wyatt's estimate. Only one item in Russell's study used the word rape. When subjects were asked if they had been victims of rape or attempted rape, 22 percent of the subjects responded that they had been victims of rape or attempted rape. Thus, almost one-half of the victims did not describe their victimization as rape. Russell reports that one-half of the women who reported that they had been raped reported that they had been raped on more than one occasion by different assailants. The victimized subjects reported an average of two incidents of rape by two different assailants.

Two studies conducted in the late 1980s established an effective model based on measures of rates for college students (Koss, Dinero, Seibel, & Cox, 1988; Stets & Pirog-Good, 1989). Of the two, the study conducted by Koss and her colleagues was the more comprehensive as it was based on a complex national sample (Koss, Dinero, Seibel, & Cox, 1988; Koss, Gidycz, & Wisniewski, 1987). Data were gathered through the use of a self-administered questionnaire from over 6,000 students enrolled for classes at 32 colleges and universities across the United States. A sample of classes was selected using a stratified random cluster sampling process. The strata were geographically based with size of institution constituting additional stratum. The largest institution in each state was selected in addition to a random sample of the smaller institutions. The forced sexual intercourse measure asked subjects to report the use of unwanted physical force or threat of physical force to obtain sex. Six percent of the women reported the successful use of physical force to obtain sex from them, 9 percent reported the successful use of threat of force to obtain sex from them, 8 percent reported the successful use of alcohol or drugs to obtain sex against their wishes, 2 percent reported the successful use of position or authority to force sexual intercourse, and 25 percent reported the successful use of persistent arguments and pressure.

To assess the state of knowledge in this area, a number of recent studies and older studies which have been cited frequently in the literature were selected for review. The criteria for selection included: (1) data were gathered measuring forced sexual intercourse; (2) the presentation of the methodology used included a clear description of the definition of forced sexual intercourse operationalized, the sampling process, and the data collection processes; and, (3) sufficient information was included in the presentation of the data to permit the identification of the extent to which forced sexual intercourse was separated from other forms of offensive sexual behavior in the analysis.

The decision to accept studies which used sampling procedures that reflect disciplinary differences in acceptable methodology was very liberal. Thus, studies which sampled Human Sexuality classes, English classes, or volunteers from Psychology classes were included to permit the inclusion of studies which are frequently cited in the literature. Twenty studies reported in refereed journals and in conference papers from professional meetings were selected. Table 3.1 presents these studies in terms of rates, time span over which the reported behavior occurred, operational definition of forced sexual intercourse, sampling procedure, and geographical location. Most studies reported incidents for the subject's life; thus, much of the analysis will focus on these measures.

Similar results have been obtained in studies using similar methods. In the studies conducted by the authors of this book, a semi-structured questionnaire was administered to a random sample of men and women attending classes at a southern university. Fifty classes were selected from the list of all classes offered at the university during the spring semester of 1992. Of these classes, three were cancelled and four instructors denied

Table 3.1　Methodological factors for selected studies

Study	Rate (Per-cent)	Time Span	Factors		
			Definition	Sample	Locations
Graw & Ingram (1990)	10.0	Life	Date rape	Random college students	Six colleges/ three states
DiVasto et al. (1984)	8.2	Life	Rape	Non-random selected women's groups	Albuquerque/ community
Doyle & Burfeind (1994)	4.2	Year	Unwanted sexual intercourse	Mail, college students	Montana
Eltzeroth et al. (1994)	28.1 15.7	Life[5] Date/ life	Forced sexual intercourse	Mail, college students	Illinois
George et al. (1992)	5.9 16.7	Life	Unwanted sexual intercourse	Mail, college students	Piedmont, NC Los Angeles
Hall & Flannery (1984)	12.0	Life[4]	Forced sexual intercourse	Random digit dialing	Milwaukee/ community
Johnson et al. (1992)	19.0	Life	Unwanted drugs/ force	Random cluster, college students	U. of South Alabama
Johnson & Sigler (1992)	3.6 13.3 1.1 7.5 18.5	Year Life Year Life	Date, forced sex-ual intercourse Non-date Total victims	Random cluster, college students	U. of Alabama
Koss et al. (1988)	13.0 1.6 15.4	Life	Unwanted drugs/ Stranger Total victims	Random stratified cluster, college students	National
Mills & Granoff (1992)	17.7	Life	Rape or sexual assault[1]	College English classes	Hawaii
Muehlenhard & Linton (1987)	20.6	Life	Unwanted sexual intercourse	College psychology classes (extra credit)	Southwest
Murnen et al. (1989)	29.7	Life	Unwanted sexual intercourse	College psychology classes (extra credit)	New York

Table 3.1 Continued

	Rate (Percent)	Time Span	Factors Definition	Sample	Locations
Study					
Mynatt & Allgeier (1990)	26.0	Life	Forced sexual intercourse[2]	College psychology classes (extra credit)	Kentucky
Poppen & Segal (1988)	37.0	Life	Coerced sexual intercourse[3]	Stratified cluster, college students	Northeast
Russell (1984)	19.0	Life	Forced sexual intercourse, threat/drugs, incapacitated	Random sample, public interviews	San Francisco
	24.0		Marital included		
Sorenson et al. (1987)		Life	Sexual assault[1]	Random cluster, community inter-	Los Angeles
	19.9		Hispanic	views	
	9.4		White		
Stets & Pirog-Good (1989)		Year	Dating, aggression, Sex	Random cluster, college students	Midwest
	1.0		Physical force		
	8.0		No physical force		
Story (1988)					
1974 study	26.0	Life	Rape	College human	U. of Iowa
1980 study	14.0			sexuality classes	
Ward et al.	10.0	Acad. Year	Unwanted sexual intercourse	Random cluster, college students	
Wyatt (1992)		After age 18	Attempted rape[2]	Stratified random sample, community	Los Angeles
	25.0		African American		
	20.0		White		
Yegidis (1986)	3.2	Year	Forced sexual	83 percent of classes	U. of South
	7.9	Life	intercourse	with 100+ students	Florida

[1]Sexual assault included behaviors other than forced sexual intercourse.
[2]Subjects were given examples of non-physical force.
[3]Coercion included pressure from continued arguments.
[4]Based on adolescents (ages 14 to 17 years, inclusive).
[5]Twelve percent of the subjects reported offensive sexual behavior without penetration as forced sexual intercourse.

access to their classes. Data were collected during regular class time from 35 of the remaining 43 classes in the classrooms assigned to the courses. In five classes, the instructors permitted the researchers to distribute the instruments and campus mail envelopes addressed to the researchers with the verbal protocol.

The researchers chose to collect data from students in three music classes by mail. These were individual instruction classes in which the students worked in studios at different times during the week. The instructors in these classes delivered the instruments along with campus mail envelopes. Similar methods were used by Johnson, Palileo, and Gray (1992), Koss, Dinero, Seibel, and Cox (1988), Stets and Pirog-Good (1987, 1989) (upper level classes), Ward, Chapman, Cohen, White, and Williams (1991), and Yegidis (1986) (classes with more than 100 students). These studies report similar rates of victimization, with about 15 percent to 18 percent of the women reporting forced sexual intercourse by a stranger or on a date in their lifetime and 3 percent to 8 percent reporting forced sexual intercourse on a date in the past year. Yegidis (1986), who gathered data from large classes, reported the lowest rates while a similar study which used clusters drawn from residence halls reported higher rates (Poppen & Segal, 1988); a study which gathered data from English classes reported rates comparable to the studies which were based on samples of all classes (Mills & Granoff, 1992), as did a mailed survey research project to a simple random sample of enrolled students (Doyle & Burfeind, 1994). It should be noted, however, that Poppen and Segal (1988) used a very broad definition of sexual assault, which would produce the higher rates reported. A study based on human sexuality classes reported mixed results for the two different years in which data were gathered (14 percent and 26 percent) (Story, 1982). It is possible that self-selection operated, in that in one period (1974) victims were more likely to take human sexuality courses than in other years (1980), that there was a change in willingness to recognize victimization by the subjects in later years, that victimization declined, or that some other factor affected subject responses.

A second group of studies based on students consistently reported higher rates (20 percent to 29.7 percent). These studies gathered data from students who were part of a pool of students from psychology classes who agreed to participate in research projects to meet class requirements or to improve their grades (Muehlenhard & Linton, 1987; Murnen, Perot, & Byrne, 1989; Mynatt & Allgeier, 1990). These samples are not random, and, as a survey methodology was used, random assignment to experimental groups normally used to approach equivalence through the distribution of characteristics equally across groups in experimental designs was not a factor. The students were self-selected, both in terms of their willingness to participate in research and in the selection of participation in the sexual offense research project over participation in other available research projects.

There is very little similarity among studies which have gathered data from non-student populations in terms of methodology or in terms of findings. Most of these studies have focused on random samples of women from specific geographical areas but have used varying approaches to determining population lists, selecting subjects from the lists, definitions of forced sexual intercourse, and method of obtaining data. The reported rates ranged from about 8 percent reported from a study which sampled women's organizations (DiVasto, Kaufman, Rosner, Jackson, Christy, Pearson, and Burgett, 1984) to a high of 25 percent reported for attempted rape after the 18th birthday for African American women in Los Angles (Wyatt, 1992).

A number of specific factors appear to explain some of the variance in rates. Most of the studies reported here are based on lifetime experiences with one limited to incidents occurring after age 18 (Wyatt, 1992), one based on an academic year (Ward, Chapman, Cohen, White, & Williams, 1991), two based on one year (Doyle & Burfeind, 1994; Stets & Pirog-Good, 1989), and one measuring both (Yegidis, 1986).

The lowest rates reported are based on incidents reported for a twelve-month or academic year time frame, and the highest rates are from studies which measure lifetime rates (see Table 3.1). Those studies based on lifetime victimization, using random selection of subjects, with broad definitions of forced sexual intercourse, report moderate rates. Slightly higher rates are found in studies which are community based and thus include older women (Russell, 1984; Sorenson, Stein, Siegel, and Burnam, 1987, Wyatt, 1992). There is a lack of consistency in operationalization of forced sexual intercourse in these studies, thus the higher rates may be attributed to either the broader definitions or to the difference in time frame. It is likely that each accounts for some of the variance. The influence of time span may be slight if the rate of new victimization declines as women become older and better prepared to protect themselves. None of the studies express their findings in terms of yearly rates other than Johnson's (1980) study of National Crime Study data and the studies which measure victimization in a single year.

There is some support for the contention that rates of sexual assault decline as women grow older. In the study conducted by the authors, about 60 percent of the victims reported that their last victimization occurred before their 19th birthday, with ages 16, 17, and 18 accounting for virtually all of the victimization reported before age 19. Johnson's (1980) analysis of age-specific rates drawn from National Crime Survey data indicates that the highest rates are reported for 12-15 year old subjects (.00179) and for 16-19 year old subjects (.00185), with rates declining steadily as the age ranges increased after age 19, with women age 65-85 reporting a rate of .00021. DiVasto, Kaufman, Rosner, Jackson, Christy, Pearson, and Burgett (1984) found that about 50 percent of the assaults reported in their study occurred before the victims reached their 19th birthdays. This trend also can be seen in data limited to college experiences. Doyle and Burfeind (1994) found that 27 percent of the victims in their study of offenses in 1993 were 18, 20.1 percent were 19, and 12.8 percent were 20, with smaller percentages reported for the remaining age groups. While the findings reported here are from studies in which age of victimization was a secondary variable and not fully operationalized, the consistent trend in the data indicates that as women become older, victimization rates rapidly decline.

Results from the studies conducted by the authors of this book can best illustrate the differences for lifetime and one year rates. Subjects were asked to report incidents of forced sexual intercourse which occurred on a date and incidents which did not occur on a date. The data reported were collected in two sessions two years apart (1989 and 1991). Of the women in this study, 18.5 percent reported that they had been forced to have sex at some point during their lifetime (see Table 3.2). The majority of these incidents had occurred in dating situations both for lifetime victimization (13.3 percent) and for 1991 (3.6 percent). Fewer women reported being forced to have sex in a non-date situation both for lifetime (7.5 percent) and for 1991 (1.1 percent).

Fewer men reported forcing women to have sex (8.8 percent total) with men reporting proportionally more forced sex in a non-date situation (5.1 percent for lifetime, 1.3 percent 1991) than a date situation (5.5 percent for lifetime, 1.6 percent 1991) when compared with women (see Table 3.2).

Table 3.2 Prevalence of forced sexual intercourse

| | | | | | Prevalence | |
Type of incident	Victims No.	Per-cent	Offenders No.	Per-cent	Victims No.	Offenders No.
Total* 82	18.5	33	8.8	275[4]		230[5]
Date, 1991	16	3.6	6	1.6	54[1]	32[2]
Non-date, 1991	5	1.1	5	1.3	24[2]	29[2]
Date, lifetime	59	13.3	22	5.9	128[2]	122[3]
Non-date, life-time	33	7.5	19	5.1	69[2]	47[2]
Spouse 1		0				
Gang rape	5	1.1	1	.3		

*p < .001 for Pearson test for chi square for prevalence.

[1] One subject reported 20 instances.
[2] One subject reported 22 instances.
[3] One subject reported 20, 22, or 30.
[4] One victim reported 20, 29, 37, 66, or 88 instances.
[5] One offender reported 22 for each category, thus reported 88 incidents.

Incidence rates are high, with relatively little difference between men and women for reported incidents (women 275, men 230) (see Table 3.2). Most victims report only one (61 percent) or two (22 percent) incidents in their lifetime with similar results for offenders (50 percent and 19.2 percent) (see Table 3.3). However, there are more severe offenders than severe victims. One victim accounts for 88 (32 percent) of the victimizations while three men report more than 20 incidents. Although all three severe offenders reported that their victims used physical force (hitting) to resist them, only one identified himself as a rapist, and all three reported that their victims did not believe that they were being raped. In this sample, there is at least one, and probably three, very active predators.

While most studies measure both prevalence and incidence, most report on prevalence (the number of victims), rather than incidence (the number of offenses). The findings of the study reported here for incidence

Table 3.3 Incidence of forced sexual intercourse by type of incident

Type of incident	Number of Incidents												Total
	1		2		3		5-10		20-22		30		
	No.	Per-cent	No.	Per-cent	No.	Per-cent	No.	Per-cent	No.	Per-cent	No.	Per-cent	
On a date, 1991													
Victims	8	50.0	4	25.0	2	12.5	1	6.3	1	6.3	0	0.0	16
Offenders	2	33.3	1	16.7	1	16.7	1	16.7	1	16.7	0	0.0	6
On a date, life													
Victims	38	64.4	10	16.9	6	10.2	4	6.8	1	1.7	0	0.0	59
Offenders	10	45.5	3	13.6	1	4.5	5	22.6	2	9.0	1	4.5	22
Not a date, 1991													
Victims	4	80.0	0	0.0	0	0.0	0	0.0	1	20.0	0	0.0	5
Offenders	2	40.0	1	20.0	1	20.0	0	0.0	1	20.0	0	0.0	5
Not a date, life													
Victims	19	57.5	11	33.3	2	6.1	0	0.0	1	3.0	0	0.0	33
Offenders	12	63.2	5	26.3	1	5.3	0	0.0	1	5.3	0	0.0	19
Total													
Victims*	69	61.1	25	22.1	10	8.8	5	4.4	4	3.5	0	0.0	113
Offenders	25	50.0	10	19.2	4	7.7	6	11.5	5	9.6	1	1.9	52

*One victim checked 22 for each category. Thus, one victim accounts for all of the incidents reported in the 20-22 category.

are similar to those reported by Russell (1984) (mean = 1.9, n=50 percent of victims) with much higher rates (75 percent of the victims reported multiple incidents) reported by Mills and Granoff (1992). Three studies reported the number of offenses and the number of victims without reporting the percentages of victims who were victimized more than once. Two of these reported averages of about 1.5 incidents per victim (Doyle & Burfeind, 1994; Koss, Gidycz, & Wisniewski, 1987) while the third reported an average of almost three victimizations per victim (Wyatt, 1992).

Studies with the broadest definition of forced sexual intercourse report higher rates than studies with less restricted definitions. The highest rates are reported for studies in which subjects were given specific examples of force, which included non-physical force and which included behaviors other than sexual intercourse, such as attempted rape. Poppen and Segal (1988) reported a 37 percent victimization rate, but their definition included behaviors in which intercourse was not completed, as did Wyatt (1992), who reported victimization rates of 25 percent for African American women and 20 percent for Caucasian women. Murnen, Perot, and Byrne (1989) reported a rate of 29.75 percent, using a definition which specified unwanted rather than forced sexual intercourse. The remaining study which reported relatively high rates (26 percent) specified forced sexual intercourse but provided examples in which the force was not physical.

Measurement of forced sexual intercourse also is confused by the fact that some victims do not define their victimization as rape, as a crime, or as being severe. As noted earlier, when Russell's (1984) subjects were asked if they had been victims of rape or attempted rape only about half of the victims responded affirmatively. The authors' research supports this finding. The question raised suggests that forced sexual intercourse is not always perceived as rape by victims. This contention is supported by the perception of the incidents reported by both the victims and the offenders (Table 3.4). Half of the victims stated that they were not raped, 88 percent reported that they did not believe that the offender (their date) believed that he was raping them, and 14 percent believed that their assailant planned to rape them when he made the date. Almost 80 percent of the offenders chose not to characterize their action as rape, about 9 percent reported that their dates believed that they had been raped, and only one reported that he had planned to rape his date at the time he made the date.

The victims were less likely to trust their assailants after the incident (92 percent before to 26 percent after), but about one-third of the victims continued to date their assailants. Offenders report less loss of trust (88 percent for victims, 44 percent for offenders) and relatively high rates of continued dating (55 percent). More victims believed that their assailants planned to rape them than offenders reported planning to rape (Table 3.4). Both men (84 percent) and women (86.5 percent) reported that a man could use force and believe that he was not committing rape. Victims were more likely to make positive statements (48.9 percent) when describing their assailants than negative statements (17.8 percent) or negative and mixed statements (26.7 percent). Men's statements describing their victims were

Table 3.4 Perceptions of the incident

| | Victims | | Offenders | |
Perceptions	No.	Percent	No.	Percent
Subject thinks rape*	35	48.3	2	8.7
Other thinks rape	8	11.1	5	20.8
Planned to rape*	6	14.0	1	10.0
Trust before	45	91.8	15	88.2
Trust after	14	25.9	8	44.4
Continue to date	17	32.1	10	55.6
Force, not always rape	64	86.5	21	84.0

*p < .05 for Pearson's test for chi square.

Table 3.5 Perceptions of the person

| | Positive statements | | Mixed statements | | Negative statements | | Neutral statements | | |
Status	No.	Percent	No.	Percent	No.	Percent	No.	Percent	Total
Victim	22	48.9	4	8.9	8	17.8	11	24.4	45
Offender	9	64.3	3	21.4	1	7.1	1	7.1	14

predominately positive (64.3 percent) (Table 3.5).

Similar results have been reported in other empirical summaries. Doyle and Burfeind (1994) reported that 59 percent of the victims in their study stated that they did not believe that a crime had occurred. Koss, Dinero, and Seibel (1988) reported that about 12 percent of the victims in their study didn't define their experience as victimization and about half characterized the incident as one of miscommunication. About 15 percent of the victims felt that a crime had occurred but the crime was not rape, and about 24 percent described their victimization as rape. Murnen, Perot, and Byrne (1989) reported that women tend to blame themselves more than their assailant and that 25 percent of their victims reported that they remained friends with their assailants, 13.9 percent continued to date their assailants, and 11.1 percent continued to maintain a sexual relationship with their assailants. It should be noted that if these findings are accurate, studies which operationalize forced sexual intercourse with the terms rape or date rape will underestimate the incidence and prevalence of forced sexual intercourse.

Relatively little attention has been directed toward minority group status and victimization. The community studies which have focused on minority group status have found dramatic differences. Sorenson, Stein, Siegel, and Burnam (1987) found that Hispanic subjects reported victimization rates of 19.9 percent as compared with a 9.4 percent reported rate by the Caucasian subjects in their study. Wyatt (1992) reported similar differences in her analysis of reported victimization for African American women who reported a 25 percent victimization rate as compared with 20 percent reported by Caucasian women. It should be noted that the relationship between race and sexual assault found in the broader community may not hold for the academic community. There were no significant differences by race for any of the measures of sexual assault in the authors' study of college students and no consistency in direction for the small differences noted occasionally in the analysis.

There are also differences by geographical region; however, these differences tend to lack clarity and consistency. The one study which provides comparisons for geographical locations reported lower rates for Piedmont, North Carolina, than for Los Angeles, California (George, Winfield, & Blazer, 1992); however, considerable variation is noted among the three studies which collected data in Los Angeles. George, Winfield, & Blazer (1992) reported 16.7 percent; Sorenson, Stein, Siegel, & Burnam (1987) reported 19.9 percent and 9.4 percent; and Wyatt (1992) reported 20 percent (white) and 25 percent (Black). No substantial differences were apparent among the studies. All three use broad definitions of forced sexual intercourse and all three used random sampling in the selection of subjects.

Summary

This chapter has sought to review the efforts of scholars who have attempted to estimate the prevalence and/or incidence of forced sexual intercourse in the broader perspective that has emerged in the past two decades. It has been noted that a great deal of variance exists among the findings reported by various scholars. While a number of specific factors appear to influence the variation observed, basic methodology and definition used tend to have the greatest impact.

Two groups of studies using similar methodologies focusing on college students are identified. Those studies which are based on random cluster sampling of college students consistently demonstrate rates of about 18 percent for total victimization for forced sexual intercourse. Similar results are found for other studies using random sampling selection procedures of enrolled students and for relatively neutral targeted courses, such as English courses.

A second set of studies gathering data from student populations used a non-random selection process based on voluntary participation by students enrolled in psychology courses who seek to meet course requirements or to improve academic performance. In most cases, these students participate in laboratory experiments and are randomly assigned to experimental conditions. The random assignment assumption is not applicable to survey research of the type reported by the authors. These studies consistently report higher rates of victimization, which may reflect the self-selection nature of the process. That is, victims may be more likely to select a project which focuses on sexual behavior than some other form of research.

Most of the community studies which use random sampling and which use forced sexual intercourse or unwanted sexual intercourse as an operational definition report rates similar to the randomly selected college students. There is some variation in these studies, particularly those which draw their samples from Los Angeles, variance which can not be easily explained.

A need for continued fundamental research in this area clearly exists. In spite of relatively intense investigation in the past 15 years, the data are not available to answer a number of basic questions. Is forced sexual intercourse which occurs between intimates, in marriage, among casual acquaintances, or among strangers different types of behavior or basically the same behavior simply identified with labels which reflect social distance? If these are different types of behavior, are the risk factors different for the different types of behavior, are there common risk factors, or, for that matter, what are the risk factors in victimization by forced sexual intercourse?

There is a need to establish the parameters of the set of phenomena presently labeled forced sexual intercourse. The variables which are associated with forced sexual intercourse and how they interact with and modify it must be identified and the relationships thoroughly delineated.

References

Amick, A. and Calhoun, K. (1987), 'Resistance to Sexual Aggression: Personality, Attitudinal, and Situational Factors', *Archives of Sexual Behavior*, vol. 16, pp. 153-62.

Bailey, B. L. (1988), *From Front Porch to Back Seat: The History of Courtship in America*, The Johns Hopkins University Press, Baltimore, MD.

Barnett, N. J. and Field, H. S. (1977), 'Sex Differences in University Students' Attitudes toward Rape', *Journal of College Student Personnel*, vol. 18, pp. 93-6.

Barnes, G. E., Greenwood, L. and Sommer, R. (1991), *Family Relations*, vol. 40, pp. 37-44.

Bourque, L. B. (1989), *Defining Rape*, Duke University Press, Durham, NC.

Brackman, R. (1993), 'Reporting of Rape Victimization: Have Rape Reforms Made a Difference', *Criminal Justice and Behavior*, vol. 20, pp. 254-270.

Brackman, R. (1995), 'Is the Glass Half Empty or Half Full? A Response to Pollard', *Criminal Justice and Behavior*, vol. 22 (1), pp. 81-5.

Bridges, J. S. and McGrail C. A. (1989), 'Attributions of Responsibility for Date and Stranger Rape', *Sex Roles*, vol. 21(3/4), pp. 273-87.

Brownmiller, S. (1975), *Against Our Will: Men, Women, and Rape*, Simon and Schuster, New York.

Burt, M. (1980), 'Cultural Myths and Supports for Rape', *Journal of Personality and Social Psychology*, vol. 38, pp. 217-34.

Cate, R. M., Henton, J. M., Koval, J. E., Christopher, F. S. and Lloyd, S. A. (1982), 'Premarital Abuse: A Social Psychological Perspective', *Journal of Family Issues*, vol. 3, pp. 79-90.

Cherry, F. (1983), 'Gender Roles and Sexual Violence', in E. R. Allgeier and N. B. McCormick (eds), *Changing Boundaries: Gender Roles and Sexual Behavior*, Mayfield, Palo Alto, CA.

Clark, M. L., Beckett, J., Wells, M. and Dungee-Anderson, D. (1994), 'Courtship Violence Among African American College Students', *Journal of Black Psychology*, vol. 20(3), pp. 264-80.

Clark, S. M. and Lewis, D. J. (1977), *Rape: The Price of Coercive Sexuality*, Women's Educational Press, Toronto.

Cornell, N. and Wilson, C. (1974), *Rape: The First Source Book for Women*, The New American Library, New York.

DeKeseredy, W. S. (1988), *Woman Abuse in Dating Relationships: The Role of Male Peer Support*, Canadian Scholar's Press, Toronto.

DiVasto, P. V., Kaufman, A., Rosner, L., Jackson, R., Christy, J., Pearson, S. and Burgett, T. (1974), 'The Relevance of Sexually Stressful Events Among Females in the General

Population, *Archives of Sexual Behavior*, vol. 13, pp. 59-67.

Doyle, D. P. and Burfeind, J. W. (1994), *The University of Montana Sexual Victimization Survey*, University of Montana, Missoula, MT.

Eltzeroth, R., Charles, M. T., Kethineni, S. and Haghighi, B. (1994), *The Issues of Rape and Date Rape as Reported by Female and Male Students at the University of Illinois*, Police Training Institute, Champaign, IL.

Fenstermaker, S. (1988), 'Acquaintance Rape on Campus: Attributions of Responsibility and Crime', in M. Pirog-Good and J. Stets (eds), *Violence in Dating Relationships* (pp. 257-71), Praeger, New York.

Field, H. S. (1978), 'Attitudes Toward Rape: A Comparative Analysis of Police, Rapists, Crisis Counselors, and Citizens', *Journal of Personality and Social Psychology*, vol. 36, pp. 156-79.

Fischer, G. (1986), 'College Student Attitudes Toward Forcible Rape. I. Cognitive Predictors', *Archives of Sexual Behavior*, vol. 15, pp. 457-66.

Follingstad, D. R., Rutledge, L. R., Polek, D. S. and McNeill-Hawkins, K. (1988), 'Factors Associated with Patterns of Dating Violence toward College Women', *Journal of Family Violence*, vol. 3, pp. 169-82.

George, L. K., Winfield, I. and Blazer, D. G. (1992), 'Sociocultural Factors in Sexual Assault: Comparison of Two Representative Samples of Women', *Journal of Social Issues*, vol. 48 (1), pp. 105-25.

Griffin, S. (1971), 'The All-American Crime', *Ramparts*, vol. 10, pp. 26-35.

Hall, E. R. and Flannery, P. J. (1984), 'Prevalence and Correlates of Sexual Assault Experiences in Adolescents', *Victimology: An International Journal*, vol. 9, pp. 398-406.

Johnson, A. G. (1980), 'On the Prevalence of Rape in the United States', *Signs: Journal of Women in Culture and Society*, vol. 6, pp. 136-46.

Johnson, G. D., Palileo, G. J. and Gray, N. B. (1992), '"Date Rape" on a Southern College Campus: Reports from 1991', *Sociology and Social Research*, vol. 76 (6), pp. 37-44.

Kanin, E. J. (1957), 'Male Aggression in Dating-courtship Relations', *American Journal of Sociology*, vol. 63, pp. 197-204.

Kanin, E. J. (1967), 'Reference Groups and Sex Conduct Norm Violations', *Sociological Quarterly*, vol. 8, pp. 495-504.

Koss, M., Dinero, T., Seibel, C. and Cox, S. (1988), 'Stranger and Acquaintance Rape: Are There Differences in the Victims' experience', *Psychology of Women Quarterly*, vol. 12, pp. 1-23.

Koss, M., Gidycz, C. and Wisniewski, N. (1987), 'The Scope of Rape: Incidence and Prevalence of Sexual Aggression and Victimization in a National Sample of Higher Education Students', *Journal of Consulting and Clinical Psychology*, vol. 55, pp. 162-70.

Lloyd, S. A. (1991), 'The Darkside of Courtship: Violence and Sexual Exploitation', *Family Relations*, vol. 40, pp. 14-20.

Makepeace, J. (1981), 'Courtship Violence Among College Students', *Family Relations*, vol. 30, pp. 97-102.

Makepeace, J. (1989), 'Dating, Living Together and Courtship Violence', in M. Pirog-Good and J. Stets (eds), *Violence in Dating Relationships: Emerging Issues* (pp. 94-107), Praeger, New York.

Mill, J. S. (1870), *The Subjection of Women*, D. Appleton and Co., New York.

Mills, C. S. and Granoff, B. J. (1992), 'Date and Acquaintance Rape Among a Sample of College Students', *Social Work*, vol. 37, pp. 504-09.

Muehlenhard, C. L., Friedman, D. E. and Thomas, C. M. (1985), 'Is Date Rape Justifiable? The Effects of Dating Activity, Who Initiated, Who Paid, and Men's Attitudes toward Women', *Psychology of Women Quarterly*, vol. 9(3), pp. 297-310.

Muehlenhard, C. and Linton, M. (1987), 'Date Rape and Sexual Aggression in Dating Situations: Incidence and Risk Factors', *Journal of Counseling Psychology*, vol. 93, pp. 186-96.

Murnen, S. K., Perot, A. and Byrne, D. (1989), 'Coping with Unwanted Sexual Activity: Normative Responses, Situational Determinants, and Individual Differences', *Journal of Sex Research*, vol. 26(1), pp. 85-106.

Mynatt, C. R. and Allgeier, E. R. (1990), 'Risk Factors, Self-Attributions, and Adjustment Problems among Victims of Sexual Coercion', *Journal of Applied Social Psychology*, vol. 20(2), pp. 130-53.

Parrot, A. (1986), *Acquaintance Rape and Sexual Assault Prevention Training Manual* (2nd ed), Cornell University Press, New York.

Parrot, A. and Bechhofer, L. (1991), *Acquaintance Rape*, John Wiley & Sons, Inc., New York.

Pollard, P. (1995), 'Rape Reporting as a Function of Victim-Offender Status: A Critique of the Lack of Effect Reported by Brackman', *Criminal Justice and Behavior*, vol. 22(1), pp. 74-80.

Poppen, P. J. and Segal, N. J. (1988), 'The Influence of Sex and Sex Role Orientation on Sexual Coercion', *Sex Roles*, vol. 19, pp. 689-701.

Rabkin, J. G. (1979), 'The Epidemiology of Forcible Rape', *American Journal of Orethopsychiatry*, vol. 49, pp. 634-47.

Rose, V. M. (1977), 'Rape as a social problem: A Byproduct of the Feminist Movement', *Social Problems*, vol. 25, pp. 247-59.

Rothman, E. K. (1984), *Hands and Hearts: A History of Courtship in America*, Basic Books, New York.

Rouse, L. P., Breen, R. and Howell, M. (1988), 'Abuse in Intimate Relationships: A Comparison of Married and Dating College Students', *Journal of Interpersonal Violence*, vol. 3, pp. 414-29.

Rowland, J. (1985), *The Ultimate Violation*, Doubleday, New York.

Russell, D. E. (1975), *The Politics of Rape: The Victim's Perspective*, Stein and Day, New York.

Russell, D. E. H. (1984), *Sexual Exploitation: Rape, Child Sexual Abuse, and Workplace Harassment*, Sage, Beverly Hills, CA.

Sigler, R. T. and Haygood, D. (1987), 'The Criminalization of Forced Marital Intercourse', *Marriage and Family Review*, vol. 12(1-2), pp. 71-86.

Sigler, R. T. and Wenstrom, M. (1993), 'Incidence of Date Rape on a College Campus', *International Journal of Comparative and Applied Criminal Justice*, vol. 17, pp. 229-42.

Sorenson, S. B., Stein, J. A., Siegel, J. M. and Burnam, M. A. (1987), 'The Prevalence of Sexual Assault: The Los Angeles Epidemiologic Catchment Area Project', *American Journal of Epidemiology*, vol. 126, pp. 1154-64.

Stein, P. (1976), *Single*, Prentice Hall, Englewood Cliffs, NJ.

Stets, J. E. and Pirog-Good, M. A. (1987), 'Violence in Dating Relationships', *Social Psychology Quarterly*, vol. 50, pp. 237-46.

Stets, J. E. and Pirog-Good, M. A. (1989), 'Sexual Aggression and Control in Dating Relationships', *Journal of Applied Social Psychology*, vol. 19, pp. 1392-412.

Stets, J. E. and Pirog-Good, M. A. (1989), 'The Marriage License as a Hitting License: A Comparison of Assaults in Dating, Cohabiting, and Married Couples', in M. A. Pirog-Good and Stets, J. E. (eds), *Violence in Dating Relationships: Emerging Issues* (pp. 33-52), Praeger, New York.

Story, M. D. (1982), 'A Comparison of University Students Experience with Various Sexual Outlets in 1974 & 1980', *Adolescence*, vol. 17, pp. 737-47.

Waller, W. (1937), 'The Rating and Dating Complex', *American Sociological Review*, vol. 2, pp. 727-34.

Waller, W. (1951), *The Family: A Dynamic Interpretation*, Dryden, New York.

Ward, S. K., Chapman, K., Cohn, E., White, S. and Williams, K. (1991), Acquaintance Rape and the College Social Scene', *Family Relations*, vol. 40, pp. 65-71.

Warshaw, R. (1988), *I Never Called it Rape*, Harper and Row, New York.

Wilson, W. and Durenberger, R. (1982), 'Comparison or Rape and Attempted Rape Victims', *Psychological Reports*, vol. 50, pp. 198-9.

Wyatt, E. G. (1992), 'The Sociocultural Context of African American and White American Woman's Rape', *Journal of Social Issues*, vol. 48(1), pp. 77-91.

Yegidis, B. L. (1986), 'Date Rape and other Forced Sexual Encounters among College Students', *Journal of Sex Education and Therapy*, vol. 12, pp. 51-4.

4 Characteristics of Victims, Offenders, and the Context of Date Rape

Introduction

Prior to the 1980s, the crime of rape was viewed as a rare and random act primarily perpetrated by a stranger who represented a small portion of the male population (Johnson, 1980; Scully, 1990). Today, this view of the rapist has been extended to include a man who is known to the victim. One controversial issue focusing on the rapist is whether he is abnormal, suffering from various forms of sexually psychopathic diseases. Perhaps all rapists from all backgrounds have serious psychological difficulties which handicap them in relating to people in general and women in specific, and which lead them to act out their stress through sexual aggression (Groth, 1979).

This perception of the rapist suggests that the crime of rape is an infrequent act. In reality, rape is not a rare occurrence. A vast amount of sexual violence is perpetrated by male aggressors against women and a substantial amount of these violent acts are not reported. A comprehensive study by Koss and her colleagues (Koss, Gidyez, & Wisniewski, 1987; Koss, Dinero, Seibel, & Cox, 1988; Koss & Harvey, 1987; Koss, Leonard, Beezley, & Oros, 1985) of a sample of 3,187 women revealed that 866 had suffered a rape or an attempted rape. However, out of this sample only 5 percent, or 45, reported the incident to the police. Such instances of nonreporting are quite common in other studies as well. Acts of sexual aggression range from acts of sexual harassment to violent acts and sexual assaults. In two comprehensive studies of the prevalence of date rape, Russell (1984) found that the prevalence rate for women 18 and older was 44 percent. Koss and her associates (1985, 1987, 1988) found a prevalence rate of 27.5 percent since the age of 14 in a small sample of college women. To say that rape is a rare act of sexual aggression committed by a small segment of the male population is to suggest that most rapes are stranger rapes.

Rape is not limited to acts of violence committed by strangers; in many cases the victim knows her assailant. Koss et al. (1987) and Warshaw (1988) found that 84 percent of the female victims identified in their research either knew or were acquainted with their assailants, and at least 57 percent of all the rapes were date rapes. Further, only 5 percent of rapes were reported to the police, and only 27 percent of the women recognized or interpreted these actions as rape.

The nature of date rape is complex. Consensual sexual encounters free of force involve mutual interaction between consenting adults, a request for sex by the man and consent from the woman, or a request for sex by the woman and consent from the man. Non-consensual sexual encounters lack this level of clarity, and, in fact, range from instances in which one party is sure that the activity is consensual to those in which both parties are certain that the woman has been raped by the man. In between these extremes there is a range of an unlimited set of types or categories which are composed of combinations of uncertainty as to the exact nature of the interaction held by the man and by the woman involved. In some cases, the man is more likely to see the exchange as inappropriate or to accept responsibility; in others, the woman is more likely to see the exchange as inappropriate or to accept responsibility.

In cases of date rape, the man usually aggressively seeks sexual access, assumes consent, and proceeds without an explicit verbal request or consent. The man may believe that the woman's resistance is token resistance rather than an accurate expression of the woman's wishes. Consequently, misunderstandings and miscommunications may result, producing unwanted sexual intercourse or date rape (Goodchilds & Zellman, 1984; Muehlenhard, Friedman, & Thomas, 1985; Muehlenhard & Linton, 1987). In this situation, the man may overestimate the victim's sexual interest. In some cases, women also may be ambiguous in expressing a firm and consistent "no" to unwanted sexual advances, may be ambivalent about how far they want to go in an intimate situation, or may be uncertain about whether to engage in sexual activity (Muehlenhard & Hollabaugh, 1989). Beliefs about ambivalent feelings on the part of women can lead men to believe that the use of sexual coercion to gain sexual access is acceptable. Since men might believe that in sexually compromising situations women are expected to say "no" when they actually mean "yes", they might not perceive their tactics as aggressive and might feel fairly comfortable in using coercion or other aggressive techniques.

It has been found that some women are, in some sexual encounters, unable to effectively communicate their disinterest in unwanted sex

(Murnen, Perot, & Byrne, 1989). Both men and women college students have a difficult time verbalizing their ideas concerning their policies and preferences as to when it is appropriate to engage in sex. In many cases, young people rely on nonverbal signals to communicate in a sexual encounter. Sometimes, these nonverbal signals have different connotations for men and women (Goodchilds & Zellman, 1984).

It is generally accepted that men are much more promiscuous than women and that they are much more likely than women to attempt to influence their partners to have sexual relationships (Sorenson, Stein, Siegel, & Burnam, 1987). Women tend to be more selective than men in terms of limiting their sexual activity to the man with whom they have a relationship (Thornhill & Thornhill, 1983; Ellis, 1989). Women are also more likely to engage in consensual sexual activity for romance than for recreation (Gagnon, 1977).

In the context just described, it is difficult to identify victim or offender characteristics with any degree of clarity or specificity. As a result, much of the literature addressing these factors is contradictory. In light of the misconceptions about the crime of rape and the underreporting of rape by the victim, it is important to exercise caution when evaluating the findings regarding the reported characteristics of the victim, the offender, and the situation.

Characteristics of Rape Victims

In spite of the vast number of studies conducted on rape victims, there is a lack of consistent reliable findings which distinguish women who have been raped from other women. Most research studies conducted which focus on the rape victim are based on data collected from the woman after the rape has taken place which, in essence, requires the victim to recall her experiences.

The studies which are available tend to focus on what happens to the women after they have been assaulted. Psychological and physical damage, the difficulty in adjusting to their experience, and the impact of the experience on future relationships are frequently examined in detail.

Studies which have focused on the characteristics of rape victims have tended to profile victims of stranger rape or victims who have been traumatized by their assaults. Rape is a very complex phenomenon which has many dimensions: type of abuse, event characteristics, assailant characteristics and relationship to the victim, victim characteristics, and victim response during the aftermath (Burgess, 1991). The act of rape can include more than forced sexual intercourse. Rape also can include other forms of physical force and psychological abuse (Burgess, 1991). Physical abuse during a rape can include: being punched, hit or beaten; being cut, stabbed, or bitten; being tied up, restrained, gagged, or blindfolded; being burned; and being forced to walk or crawl a long distance. Psychological abuse can be caused by any of these factors or by the presence of a weapon and specific threats (harm to loved one, repeat rape, loss of job or income, disfigurement or physical injury, and death) used to control the victim or to gain access to the victim. Many of the psychological and emotional responses of the victim represent a cluster of somatic, cognitive, psychological, and behavioral symptoms which is identified as the rape trauma syndrome (Burgess & Holmstrom, 1974, 1980, 1983). This syndrome can occur in all types of rape.

The symptoms which represent the rape trauma syndrome occur in two stages: the acute or disorganization phase and the reorganization phase (Rapaport & Burkhart, 1984). In the acute or disorganization phase, the victim experiences many symptoms including guilt and shame. In this phase, she may experience digestive system disorders, headaches, and vaginal discharges. In this phase, the victim also can experience "expressive" reactions in which anger, fear, anxiety, tension, and crying are common. Other victims may exhibit a type of "controlled" reaction during which they remain calm, controlled, and subdued. This phase usually lasts for weeks.

In the reorganization phase, the victim may become depressed, show anger toward men, avoid others in social situations, and experience impaired memory or concentration and/or rapid mood swings. This phase could last for months or years. Following a rape (and sometimes up to many years later), the victim may experience three typical behavior patterns:

(1) withdraw from social interactions,
(2) attempt to repress memory of the rape, or
(3) exhibit a nondiscriminating sexual behavior pattern.
(Rapaport & Burkhart, 1984)

Although victims of rape have been the focus of numerous studies, little is known about the characteristics of these women. Most studies focus on women who have been identified through their participation in counseling, thus are based on victims who have been traumatized by their experience. There is a reluctance on the part of victims to come forward to talk about their experiences. In cases of date rape, even victims who are known to resident fellows and friends choose to decline to participate in research when discretely approached.

Many women have such low self-esteem and self-worth that they don't expect to be treated as equal, worthy people (Groth, 1979). Of course, some women have been socialized to perceive violence as normal and learn at an early age to be submissive in sexual encounters. Children and women who have been victims of incest or some other type of sexual abuse come to define themselves as sex objects (Hirsch, 1981).

More recent research reveals that victimized women tend to have had a greater number of dating and sexual partners, to experience their first sexual intercourse at a younger age and to have had more liberal sexual values than non-victimized women (Amick & Calhoun, 1989; Koss, 1985; Koss & Dinero, 1989). Koss and Dinero (1989) found that victimized women had a greater number of sexual partners prior to being raped. Regardless of these findings concerning the differences between victimized and non-victimized women, any woman is a potential victim.

Women of all races, social classes, and ages are vulnerable to being rape victims; however, women from specific age, social class, and racial groups may be at greater risk for being victimized. The most frequent ages of victims vary from one study to the next. Katz and Mazur's (1979) comprehensive review of rape victimization revealed that the "high-risk" age group for rape victims is composed of adolescents (ages 13-17). While it is difficult to determine the high-risk age group because so few cases are reported, several researchers report that the peak age for rape is 14 years of age (Hursch & Selkin, 1974; Katz & Mazur, 1979). Furthermore, research reveals that the majority of rape victims (87 percent) were between the ages of 14 and 30 years (Russell, 1984); however, when the victim's age was examined on a yearly basis, the most vulnerable ages were between 13 to 26 years of age.

One victim characteristic that most researchers agree on is lower socioeconomic status. Most of the data revealing that rape victims come from lower socioeconomic neighborhoods are gathered from police reports and FBI statistics. Thus, the data on the social class of rape victims may reflect the class status of those willing to rely on public assistance in their victimization and their willingness to contact the police. In contrast, rape victims from middle to upper classes might be more likely to seek medical care from a private physician (Katz & Mazur, 1979).

Koss, Dinero, Seibel, and Cox (1988) developed a research design to measure the responses of unreported and unacknowledged rape victims to produce data with greater generalizability. They administered a self-report questionnaire to a sample of 6,159 students, including 3,187 women, at 32 U.S. institutions of higher education. The study indicated that "stranger rape victims, compared with acquaintance rape victims, rated the offender as more aggressive; victims were more scared and felt that the man was more responsible for what happened. The groups of women did not differ in their ratings of the clarity with which they communicated nonconsent to the offender, ratings of the degree of resistance they offered, in their feelings of anger and depression during the assault, or in the extent to which they felt responsible for what happened" (p. 10). Close to one-half of the victims in both groups were drinking before their assault. The study also indicated that stranger rapes were more likely to involve threats of bodily harm, hitting and slapping, and a weapon. The two groups did not differ significantly in such behaviors as arm twisting, holding down, choking, and beating. The acquaintance and stranger rape victims were not found to differ significantly in avoidance strategies (turning cold, reasoning or pleading, crying or sobbing, running away, and physically struggling), which were reportedly used by one-half or more of both groups, but women assaulted by strangers were more likely to report that they screamed for help (Koss, Dinero, Seibel, & Cox, 1988).

For the most part, victims are not completely passive (Burgess, 1988). Victims resist by reasoning (84 percent) and physically struggling (70 percent). In spite of attempts to resist the sexual advances of offenders, many victims felt scared, angry, and depressed. While many of the victims felt responsible for what had happened, they believed that the offender was much more responsible for the rape. Interestingly, 42 percent of the women indicated that they would continue to date and to have sex with the offender on a later occasion. Many of the victims (41 percent) stated that they expected to be victimized again in the future, and only 27 percent of the women whose experience met the legal definition of rape labeled themselves as rape victims (Burgess, 1988, pp. 15-16).

Victims of date rape often don't regard themselves as having been raped (Jenkins & Dambrot, 1987). In this view of the assault, the victims do not define the experience as rape to themselves or to others. A study of respondents to the *Ms. Magazine* Campus Project on Sexual Assault found that almost three-quarters of the women who stated that they had been raped did not identify their experience as rape (Sweet, 1985). The victims felt at least somewhat responsible for the act and were, therefore, less likely to report the incident to the police. Of the women surveyed, more than one-third did not discuss their experience with anyone, and more than 90 percent did not tell the police. A victim's perception of date rape is influenced by a lack of self-esteem and the victim's difficulty with asserting herself. In one case, a victim being raped by her date at a fraternity party didn't scream for help because she did not want to embarrass the rapist (Leo, 1987, p. 77). Women in society today are more assertive than women 100 years ago, but women are still taught to be submissive to males, to be feminine and nice, and not to fight or make a scene.

Several studies have found self-attributions of responsibility by date rape victims. For example, McCahill, Meyer, and Fischman (1979) found that many rape victims think about their victimizations in terms of things that they could have done to avoid the incident, such as engaging in safer activities or by offering greater resistance when assaulted. Women are more likely to blame themselves for the rape when they are acquainted with the rapist and they did not respond well (fighting back through resistance or communicating a very clear "no") to the situation. On the other hand, women tend to blame the rapist for the victimization under the following conditions:

(1) if they did not know the man well,
(2) when a more obvious form of coercion was used such as physical force, and
(3) when the woman's response to the sexual advances was clear.
                              (Murnen, Perot, & Byrne, 1989)

In their study of 130 college women, Murnen et al. (1989) found that women generally responded passively to sexual advances and they tended to blame themselves for the rape. They also found that many of the women continued to date and to have a relationship with their assailant, which concurs with the finding of Burgess (1988) discussed above. This suggests that they blamed themselves for the sexual encounter and did not define their victimization as true rape.

Williams (1984) also presented data indicating that women may be reluctant to perceive some acts of sexual aggression by an acquaintance as coercive. Williams reported that women who were victims of rape by an acquaintance were less likely to view themselves as rape victims than women who were victims of rape by a stranger. In the former situation, where two persons are mutually attractive to each other, the victim may feel that she used poor judgment and is somehow responsible for the victimization.

Consistently, there seems to be an issue of miscommunication concerning the victim's verbal and nonverbal language as it related to her not giving consent to proceed as a participant in a sexual act. Usually, while the victim will say that her nonconsent to the sexual act was clear and straightforward, the offender will misinterpret her language (e.g., taking a no to mean yes) and conclude that the victim's nonconsent to have sexual intercourse was "not clear at all". It should be noted, however, that this may be a characteristic of the offender and not a characteristic of the victim (Burgess, 1988).

It has been found that some women are, in some sexual encounters, unable to effectively communicate their disinterest in unwanted sex (Murnen, Perot, & Byrne, 1989). Both men and women college students have a difficult time verbalizing their ideas about their policies and preferences as to when it is appropriate to engage in sex. Young people often rely on nonverbal signals to communicate in a sexual encounter and, at times, these nonverbal signals have different connotations for men and women (Goodchilds & Zellman, 1983). Compliant sexual activity and the absence of uncertain sexual intentions can produce rape (Shotland & Hunter, 1995).

It has been noted that victims of date rape tend to come from unhappy families (Makepeace, 1987) and from aggressive families (MacEwen, 1994). Barnes, Greenwood, and Sommer (1991) found that victims also have experienced violence and harsh parenting in their own family. They also found correlations between precipitating factors such as stress and the use of alcohol and sexual and physical violence in date rape.

Several risk factors are associated with the likelihood of being a victim of date rape. Research shows that age (women in their teens and early 20s) (Ageton, 1983, Katz, & Mazur, 1979; Russell, 1984), alienation from family and friends, identification with delinquent peers, participation in delinquent activities (Ageton, 1983), age at the onset of intercourse, number of consensual intercourse partners (Koss, 1985), adherence to liberal political views, and infrequent attendance of religious services (Mynatt & Allgeier, 1990) are associated with increased risk of date rape. In her study of a nationally representative sample of adolescent women, Ageton (1983) found that some of the adolescent factors (e.g., identification with delinquent peers and engaging in delinquent activities) predicted the likelihood of becoming a victim of sexual assault later in life.

While a broad range of factors have been identified with victims and victimization, there are relatively few persistent differences between women who are raped and other women. The identification of different types of victimization and the association of victim characteristics with types of victimization may add some clarity to many of the conflicting and inconsistent findings.

Characteristics of Rapists

In order to understand the crime of rape, it is important to understand the characteristics of the rapist. The mere fact that the use of force is a part of the rapist's repertoire indicates that all rapists have something in common; however, rapists are different in many respects. As a society, we tend to label and to define persons based on certain physical and psychological characteristics. Typically, stereotypical views of the rapist reveal him to be an obsessed, psychopathic madman (Allison & Wrightsman, 1993). However, this profile does not fit most rapists; there are a number of rapists who are not sick, diseased, or abnormal. Some studies have shown that less than 5 percent of rapists have been diagnosed as clinically psychotic at the time of the rape (Scully, 1990; Walby, 1990; Lottes, 1988). Bearing this in mind, other studies have found that the rapist is a normal male whose sexual aggressive act is an extension of normative sexual behavior in the male population (Scully & Marolla, 1985; Herman, 1989; Scher, 1988; Bart & O'Brien, 1985) or that men who use violence in courtship and dating have battering personalities (Ryan, 1995).

At one time, rape was defined as a gender-specific crime in which only males could be held legally responsible for the crime of rape. Later, states redefined the crime of rape, making it a gender-neutral crime. In spite of reconceptualization of the crime of rape, most rapists are men. Women's involvement in the crime of rape usually is limited to the role of victim except in rare cases in which the woman acts as an accessory. In most crimes, gender differences are discussed more often than gender similarities. For the most part, research has shown that men are more physically and sexually aggressive than women (Tarvis & Wade, 1985).

The stereotypical view of the rapist as sick and abnormal perpetuates the belief that rape is an infrequently occurring crime that is committed by a complete stranger. While some scholars would argue that the act of rape involves psychopathology, either moderate or severe (Cohen & Roth, 1987), social factors related to the act of rape can not be ignored (Allison & Wrightsman, 1993).

Numerous characteristics of the rapist have been identified; these characteristics vary according to the methodology used. The samples of rapists used to identify the characteristics of rapists range from incarcerated felons to descriptions of rapists in police reports (Amir, 1971; Groth, 1979). It is important to note that rape is one of the most underreported crimes and that the samples researchers use to measure the characteristics of rapists may be biased, since undetected rapists may be different in characteristics from detected rapes. Also, certain types of rapes (stranger rape) are more likely to be reported than others (date rape).

Several psychological typologies of the rapists have been developed. Types have ranged in width from two (Kopp, 1962) to seventeen (Gebhard, Gagon, Pomeroy, & Christenson, 1965). Kopp's (1962) types include rapists for whom rape is not common behavior and who feel guilty about their behavior and rapists who are anti-social and psychotic. The latter have no feelings of guilt. Their rapes are acts of aggression rather than acts of sex. Gebhard, Gagon, Pomeroy, & Christenson's, (1965) seventeen types include situational, relationship, and motivation factors. Rada's (1977) five types include psychotic rapists, situational stress rapists, masculine identity rapists, sadistic rapists, and sociopathic rapists. It is argued that regardless of the typology of rapists, both aggression and sex are involved in all types of rape.

There is general agreement that men are much more promiscuous than women, and that they are much more likely than women to attempt to influence their partners to have sexual relationships (Sorenson, Stein, Siegel, & Burnam, 1987). On the other hand, women tend to be more selective than males in terms of limiting their sexual activity to the man with whom they have a relationship (Shields & Shields, 1983: Thornhill & Thornhill, 1983; Ellis, 1989). Women are also more likely to become sexually active for romance rather than for recreation (Gagnon, 1977).

In any sexual coercive incident, it appears that sexual deprivation is an important issue. Kanin (1967; 1985) found that college men who were dissatisfied with the frequency of their sexual activity were more likely to engage in coercive sexual behavior. Furthermore, college men who used sexual coercion were likely to engage in sexual activity more frequently than college males who did not use sexual coercion, perhaps because they sought out sexual partners more frequently. According to Kanin (1985), men make a concerted effort to find women who will engage in sexual relations. Once these women are identified, men may use a variety of techniques (falsely professing love or attempting to get the woman intoxicated) to get the woman to comply. This suggests that while coercive and non-coercive behaviors are often used in the same exchange, coercive behavior is used as a last resort after other techniques have failed, especially when the victim and assailant are acquainted.

Several studies of college students have identified characteristics of men who admit to the use of force with their dates. These men were found to be more aggressive, more likely to view pornographic materials, more likely to use alcohol, more hostile toward women, and more likely to have peer groups that reinforced stereotypical views of women (Koss, Gidyez, & Wisniewski, 1987). Other studies have found that these men are more likely to condone rape and violence (Kanin, 1967; Koss, Leonard, Beezley, & Oros, 1985; Rapaport & Burkhart, 1984), and are more likely to hold traditional roles and are more likely to be sexually experienced (Koss, Leonard, Beezley, & Oros, 1985).

One of the most common predictors of date rape is the presence of violence in the perpetrator's family. While some researchers have found a relationship between violence in the offender's family and date rape (Bernard & Bernard, 1983; Roscoe & Benaske, 1985), other researchers have not observed such a relationship (Knudsen, 1988). Family aggression (MacEwen, 1994) and harsh parenting (which does not necessarily have to include physical abuse) (Gwartney-Gibbs, Stockard, & Brohmer, 1987), also have been cited as correlated with sexual violence in dating. This does not suggest that every person who is exposed to physical or sexual violence during childhood will engage in sexual or physical violence later in life.

Still another interesting factor relative to the characteristics of the rapist is lack of social skills and social development. Some studies have revealed that convicted rapists as compared to men serving time in prison for nonviolent, nonsexual crimes have a deficit in social skills and social grace which leads the rapist to misunderstand both the language and behavior of women (Abel, Bianchard, & Becker, 1978; Becker, Abel, Blanchard, Murphy, & Coleman, 1978).

Perhaps one common characteristic of the rapist is his adherence to traditional and cultural views. Usually, the rapist's traditional and cultural views mirror societal values and beliefs. Perhaps American culture plays a role in producing the rapist through a socialization process that emphasizes the teaching of power, control, dominance, competitiveness, anger, and aggression to men while at the same time discourages the teaching of open expressions of emotions, passivity, sharing, vulnerability, and cooperation (Herman, 1989). Thus, rape and other acts of sexual violence may be reproduced, perpetuated, and legitimatized through culturally induced myths that serve to excuse, justify, rationalize, and, in some cases, glorify male acts of violence against women (Matoesian, 1993).

Several studies have identified the characteristics of self-reported sexually aggressive men as follows: (1) They are more likely than other men to condone rape and violence against women (Kanin, 1967, Malamuth, 1987; Rapaport & Burkhart, 1984); (2) they are more likely to hold traditional gender role attitudes; (3) they are more sexually experienced than other men (Malamuth, 1987); and (4) they are more likely than other men to be hostile toward women, to have dominance as a motive for engaging in sex, to be sexually aroused by depictions of rape, to be irresponsible and lack a social conscience, and to have peer groups, such as fraternities, that pressure them to be sexual (Kanin, 1967, Rapaport & Burkhart, 1984; Malamuth, 1987).

Generally, characteristics of antisocial behavior have been used to predict sexual coercion. Men with histories of sexually coercive behavior have been found to more impulsive, to be less socialized, and to be more prone to violent behavior (Malamuth, 1987; Calhoun, Kelley, Amick, & Gardner, 1986; Rapaport & Burkhart, 1984) and are generally more aggressive and hostile individuals.

Furthermore, research has revealed a relationship between a man's willingness to use force and sexual violence. According to Allison, Adams, Bunce, Gilkerson, and Nelson (1992), men who report that they would force a woman to have sex if there was no risk of detection internalize masculine values and adhere to Machiavellian principles (Allison, Adams, Bunce, Gilkerson, & Nelson, 1992). Machiavellianism is a construct that refers to persons who characteristically manipulate others through guile, deceit, and opportunism, and includes a component centering on a zest for dominating and controlling others (Christie & Geis, 1970). This suggests that men who use sexual coercion are likely to experience emotion, especially hostility and anger, to a greater degree than men who do not use sexual coercion.

Recent studies focusing on the characteristics of rapists support the belief that rapists have a macho personality, which was found to be a good predictor of self-reported sexually coercive/assaultive behavior (Mosher & Anderson, 1984; Mahoney, Shively, & Traw, 1986). In addition, in a study of 392 college males, Tieger (1981) found that "normal" men who rated themselves as more likely to rape if they were certain they would not get caught held cultural beliefs that minimized their acts of violence and the negative impact that the rape would have on the victim while at the same time blaming the victim for the rape. Such a belief pattern only serves to assist men in disinhibiting sexual aggression (Bandura, Underwood, &

Fromson, 1975).

Malamuth, Briere, and Check (1986) found that rapists function in an atmosphere and environment that condones sexually aggressive behavior. Men who revealed that they would find being sexually forceful with women acceptable internalized rape supportive attitudes, approved of using aggression in nonsexual situations, and reported a high likelihood of themselves being sexually coercive. Kanin's (1984) study of date rape on a college campus revealed that date rapists were products of a highly sexually oriented peer-group socialization process, which may have started in the early years of high school. Such peer groups perceive the sexual conquering of a woman as enhancing their self-worth. Thus, these sexually aggressive men as compared to nonsexually aggressive men have had more sexual partners and are generally more sexually active (Kanin, 1984, p. 99).

A self-report study of a sample of college men comparing sexually aggressive males to nonsexually aggressive males conducted by Koss (1985) revealed that the former viewed sexual aggression as normal, had conservative attitudes toward female sexuality, reported greater rape-myth acceptance, regarded heterosexual relationships as game playing, held women more responsible for rape prevention, and reported traditional beliefs about women's roles.

In researching the characteristics of the rapist, it is important to recognize the fact that there is no single factor or set of factors which describes the rapist; characteristics of the rapist vary from one rapist to the next. For some rapists, many of the above characteristics will be found while for other rapists only a few characteristics will be present. To fully understand the complexity of the characteristics of rapists, research similar to that proposed for victims is required.

Interactional and Situational Factors

Forced sexual intercourse occurs in a context. Numerous factors, such as the relationship between the offender and the victim, socialization, gender patterns, and rape myths, affect the perceptions of and about the offenders and the victims. These factors, presented in detail in Chapter Five, will be reviewed briefly from the victim's and the offender's perspective here.

Degree of Relationship

Some studies have focused on the victim-offender relationship and the amount or degree of violence/force used (Amir 1971; Bart & O'Brien, 1981, 1985; Ellis, Atkeson, & Calhoun, 1981; Stuntz, 1975; Weis & Borges, 1973). Katz and Burt (1986) asserted that victims of rape between acquaintances feel more self blame than victims of stranger rape. Studies have shown that subjects interpret rape differently when rapists and victims are strangers than when they are acquaintances (L'Armand & Pepitone, 1982; Tetreault & Barnett, 1987). Koss, Dinero, Seibel, and Cox (1988) noted that most published studies of the victim-offender relationship have dichotomized the variable into stranger-versus-acquaintance categories, and that few rapes placed in the acquaintance category of these studies involved victims who were dating or who were married to their offender, while the acquaintance category tended to consist of offenders who had non-intimate and non-romantic relationships with the victim (pp. 3-4).

Koss, Dinero, Seibel, and Cox (1988) found that rapes by acquaintances, compared with strangers, were more likely to involve a single offender and multiple episodes, were less likely to be seen as rape or to be revealed to anyone, and were similar in terms of the victim's resistance (p. 1). In general, acquaintance rapes were rated as less violent than stranger rapes. The exception was rapes by husbands or other family members, which were rated as violent as stranger rapes but were much less likely to occur in a context of drinking or other drug use. In spite of these different crime characteristics, virtually no differences were found among the groups in levels of psychological symptoms (Koss et al., 1988).

The degree of the relationship between the victim and the offender plays an important role in all aspects of acquaintance rape. The range of the relationship varies from casual association (having just met in a bar or at a party) to the existence of a fairly stable relationship (couple being engaged or living together). This extreme range of relationships creates a difficult problem within the study of date rape. The fact that marital rape recently has become a criminal act in some states but not in others characterizes this problem. There is a question as to the point at which society has the right to intervene in the affairs of two people who have a somewhat established pattern of interaction. This hesitancy is complicated by the definition of the degree of association which constitutes a "relationship".

Socialization

A number of researchers have established a link between traditional views held by men and women and the perceptions which the victim and the rapist hold for themselves when rape occurs. Griffin (1971) directed attention to the cultural supports for rape, leading to assertions that rape results from normal socialization processes (Weis & Borges, 1973; Medea & Thompson, 1974; Russell, 1975, 1982; Weis & Weis, 1975; Jackson, 1978). Warshaw (1988) addressed heterosexual rituals, suggesting sexual assertiveness on the part of men and gatekeeping behaviors on the part of the women may play a role in date rape. Parrot (1986) asserted that women who demonstrate the traditional female role of being passive, gentle, and sacrificing are more likely to be victims of rape than those who are assertive. Bridges and McGrail (1989) suggested that rape is an extension of traditional behaviors and motives that operate in heterosexual situations.

It has been argued that popular conceptions of dating and courtship contribute to male sexual aggression and have shaped men and women's attitudes toward and perception of rape and the role that they play in acts of sexual aggression. For example, women have been socialized to believe that it is unladylike for them to initiate sexual advances to men, to acknowledge any enjoyment from a sexual act, to respond to a sexual act without making some type of resistance, or to have sexual relations unless they are involved in a love relationship. Women, for the most part, have not been socialized to effectively communicate their feelings of nonconsent in an assertive way (Russell, 1975). Men, on the other hand, are expected to be the initiators of sexual encounters, and they have been encouraged by society to enjoy their sexuality and to pursue their sexuality with numerous partners. Men have been socialized to be strong, forceful, dominant, superior, competitive, and tough, which encourages them to pursue sexual relationships that may be free of the emotional ties that many women seek in intimate relationships. Men's motives for sexual intercourse more often included pleasure, fun, and physical reasons; whereas women's motives emphasized love, commitment, and emotion. According to Russell (1975), this differential gender socialization of opposite qualities and opposite roles and goals in sexual and dating situations only perpetuates the crime of rape against women.

Myths About Rape

A number of widely held beliefs and attitudes exists about women and their traditional sex roles, many of which overlap with socialization issues. Traditional views concerning the sex roles of men and women help to shape the stereotypical views and myths about rape; this creates the settings which produce an act of violence (Burkhart & Fromuth, 1991). In fact, a number of men who hold traditional views of women and who support rape myths consistently have been involved in more sexual violence than men who do not believe in traditional sex roles (Lisak & Roth, 1988; Muehlenhard & Linton, 1987; Koss, Leonard, Beezley, & Oros, 1985). Of course, some of the traditional views held by rapists and potential rapists are reproduced and legitimized through societal held views which justify, rationalize, and support acts of rape.

There appears to be a close relationship between rape supportive myths, attitudes about the roles of men and women, attitudes which portray women as sex objects, and sexual aggression against women. According to Adler (1985), men who more strongly hold such attitudes are more likely to report sexually aggressive behavior. One factor which is sometimes overlooked in the discussion of adherence to traditional views about the roles of women and men is that these views are shared by both men and women and that women also internalize rape myths.

It is common for both men and women to believe that the woman asked to be raped by the way she was dressed; that a woman who goes to a man's house or apartment on their first date is expecting and willing to have sex; that a woman who is raped is really promiscuous or has a bad reputation; that saying yes to one man is saying yes to any man; or that a woman only says that she has been raped when she is angry with the man and wants to retaliate (Burt, 1980). Such negative attitudes only serve to justify and to deny the crime itself and the existence of the victimization. The adherence of the rapist to traditionally held beliefs about the roles of women places the blame for the rape on the woman by believing that some women deserve to be raped or ask to be raped by their dress or/and mannerism.

Such myths are perceived to be prejudicial, stereotypical, or false beliefs about rape, rape victims, and rapists (Burt, 1980). They allow men to both engage in the act of rape and to justify or rationalize their behavior after the act has occurred (Weis & Borges, 1973). Myths that women enjoy being raped and that they are responsible for the rape have been used as justification by convicted rapists to deny their role in the act and to avoid negative effects of their actions on their victims (Scully & Marolla, 1985a, 1985b). Interestingly, some convicted rapists never contemplated the possibility of prison because they did not define what they had done as wrong.

Summary

Forced sexual intercourse is more common than is reflected in official rape statistics. Forced sexual intercourse includes date rape, predatory date rape, and stranger rape. The nature of the range and types of victimizations is not clear; this prevents an effective assessment of victim characteristics, offender characteristics, and situational or context characteristics.

While there are no clear patterns, a number of characteristics have been found to be related to victimization. Those who had no intention of interacting sexually with their offenders often are traumatized severely regardless of, or perhaps because of, the degree of closeness of the relationship. In the rape trauma syndrome, victims go though specific stages of development as they seek to deal with their victimization.

General self-report studies have indicated that women who report that they have been forced to have sex when they didn't want to tended to be more socially and/or sexually active. That is, women who are more outgoing and socially active are more vulnerable to offenders. The most vulnerable women appear to be young girls from early adolescence to young adulthood who may not have learned to effectively protect themselves.

There is a tendency for women who have been forced to have sex by a date or an acquaintance to accept responsibility for their victimizations. They often do not describe their victimization as rape, will continue to associate with their offender, and do not report their victimization.

Most traditional profiles of rapists define the offender in terms of psychological pathology. It does seem, however, that many men who force women to have sex appear to be relatively normal. Various studies have associated dominance, aggression, holding traditional stereotypical views of women, alcohol, use of pornographic materials, violence and violent backgrounds, and hostility toward women with those who report that they have or are willing to use force to gain sexual access.

Most victims and subjects in studies of general student populations appear to have different perceptions of offenders and victims based on the degree of relationship between them. The closer the relationship, the less likely all types of subjects are to characterize forced sexual intercourse as rape, the women as victims, and the men as offenders. Socialization, gender roles, and rape myths also tend to produce a reduction in attribution of responsibility to men and victim status to women.

Future research must focus on the variations in the types of situations in which men use force to gain sexual access. If characteristics of victims, offenders, and context are examined in terms of type of victimization, the nature of victims, offenders, and contextual factors will be clarified.

References

Abel, G. G., Bianchard, E. B. and Becker, J. V. (1978), 'An Integrated Treatment Program for Rapists', in R. T. Rada (ed), *Clinical Aspects of the Rapist* (pp.161-214), Grune & Stratton, New York.

Adler, C. (1985), 'An Exploration of Self-Reported Sexually Aggressive Behavior', *Crime and Delinquency*, vol. 31(2), pp. 306-31.

Allison, J. A., Adams, D. L., Bunce, L. W., Gilkerson, T. and Nelson, K. (1992), 'The Rapist: Aggressive, Dangerous, Power Hungry, and Manipulative', paper presented at the Annual Meeting of Psychological and Educational Research, Emporia, KS.

Allison, J. A. and Wrightsman, L. S. (1993), *Rape: The Misunderstood Crime*, Sage, Newbury Park, CA.

Ageton, S. S. (1983), *Sexual Assault among Adolescents*, Lexington Press, Lexington, MA.

Amick, A. and Calhoun, K. (1987), 'Resistance to Sexual Aggression: Personality, Attitudinal, and Situational Factors', *Archives of Sexual Behavior*, vol. 16, pp. 153-62.

Amir, M. (1971), *Patterns of Forcible Rape*, University of Chicago Press, Chicago.

Bandura, A., Underwood, B. and Fromson, M. E. (1975), 'Disinhibition of Aggression through Diffusion of Responsibility and Dehumanization of Victims', *Journal of Research in Personality*, vol. 9, pp. 253-69.

Barnes, G. E., Greenwood, L. and Sommer, R. (1991), 'Courtship Violence in a Canadian Sample of Male College Students', *Family Relations*, vol. 40, pp. 37-44.

Bart, P. B. (1981), 'A Study of Women Who Were Both Raped and Avoided Rape', *Journal of Social Issues*, vol. 37(4), pp. 123-37.

Bart, P. B. and O'Brien, P. H. (1985), *Stopping Rape: Successful Survival Strategies*, Pergamon, Elmsford, NY.

Becker, J. V., Abel, G. G., Blanchard, E. B., Murphy, W. D. and Coleman, E. (1978), 'Evaluating Social Skills of Sexually Aggressives', *Criminal Justice and Behavior*, vol. 5, pp. 357-68.

Bernard, M. L. and Bernard, J. L. (1983), 'Violent Intimacy: The Family as a Model for Love Relationships', *Family Relations*, vol. 32, pp. 283-6.

Bridges, J. S. and McGrail, C. A. (1989), 'Attributions of Responsibility for Date and Stranger Rape', *Sex Roles*, vol. 21(3/4), pp. 273-86.

Burgess, A. W. (ed.) (1988), *Rape and Sexual Assault* (Vol. 2, pp. 193-220), Garland, New York.

Burgess, A. W. and Holmstrom, L. L. (1974), 'Rape Trauma Syndrome', *American Journal of Psychiatry*, vol. 131, pp. 981-6.

Burgess, A. W. and Holmstrom, L. L. (1980), 'Typology and the Coping Behavior of Rape Victims', in S. L. McCombie (ed), *The Rape Crisis Intervention Handbook*, Plenum, New York.

Burgess, A.W. and Holmstrom, L.L. (1983) 'The Rape Victim in the Emergency Ward', *American Journal of Nursing*, vol. 73(10), pp. 1740-5.

Burkhart, B. R. and Fromuth, M. E. (1991), 'Individual and Social Psychological Understanding of Sexual Coercion', in E. Gruerholz and M. A. Koralewski (eds), *Sexual Coercion: A Sourcebook on its Nature, Causes, and Prevention* (pp.75-89). Lexington Press, Lexington, MA.

Burt, M. (1980), 'Cultural Myths and Supports for Rape', *Journal of Personality and Social Psychology*, vol. 38, pp. 217-34.

Calhoun, K. S, Kelley, S. P., Amick, A. and Gardner, R. (1986), 'Research on Rape'. Paper presented at the Southeastern Psychological Association, Orlando, FL.

Christie, R. and Geis, F. L. (1970), *Studies in Machiavellianism*, Academic Press, New York.

Cohen, L. J. and Roth, S. (1987), 'The Psychological Aftermath of Rape: Long-term Effects and Individual Differences in Recovery', *Journal of Social and Clinical Psychology*, vol. 5, pp. 525-34.

Ellis, E. M., Atkeson, B. M. and Calhoun, K. S. (1981), 'An Assessment of Long-term Reaction to Rape', *Journal of Abnormal Psychology*, vol.90, 263-6.

Ellis, L. (1989), *Theories of rape: Inquiries into the Causes of Sexual Aggression*, Hemisphere Publishing, New York.

Gagnon, J. H. (1977), *Human Sexualities*, Scott Foresman, Glenview, IL.

Gebhard, P. H., Gagon, J. H., Pomeroy, W. B. and Christenson, C. V. (1965), *Sex Offenders: An Analysis of Types*, Harper and Row, New York.

Goodchilds, J. D. and Zellman, G. L. (1984), 'Sexual Signaling and Sexual Aggression in Adolescent Relationships', in N. M. Malamuth and E. Donnerstein (eds), *Pornography and Sexual Aggression* (pp. 233-243), Academic Press, Orlando , FL.

Griffin, S. (1971), 'The all-American Crime', *Ramparts*, vol. 10, pp. 26-35.

Groth, A. N. (1979), *Men who Rape: The Psychology of the Offender*, Plenum Press, New York.

Groth, A. N. and Birnbaum, H. J. (1985), *Men Who Rape: The Psychology of the Offender*, Plenum Press, New York.

Gwartney-Gibbs, P.A., Stockard, J. and Brohmer, S. (1987), 'Learning Courtship Aggression: The Influence of Parents, Peers, and Personal Experiences', *Family Relations*, vol. 36, pp. 276-82.

Herman, J. (1989), 'The Rape Culture', in J. Freeman (ed), *Women: A Feminist Perspective*, (pp. 20-44), Mayfield, Palo Alto, CA.

Hirsch, M. (1981), *Women and Violence*, Van Nostrand Reinhold, New York.

Hursch, C. and Selkin, J. (1984), *Rape Prevention Research Project*, Annual Report of the Violence Research Unit, Division of Psychiatric Service, Department of Health and Hospitals, Denver Anti-Crime Council, Denver, CO.

Jackson, S. (1978), 'The Social Context of Rape: Sexual Scripts and Motivation', *Women's Studies International Quarterly*, vol. 1, pp. 27-38.

Jenkins, M. and Dambrot, F. (1987), 'The Attribution of Date Rape: Observers' Attitudes and Sexual Experiences and the Dating Situation', *Journal of Applied Social Psychology*, vol. 17, pp. 875-95.

72   Forced sexual intercourse in intimate relationships

Johnson, A. G. (1980), 'On the Prevalence of Rape in the United States', *Signs: Journal of Women in Culture and Society*, vol. 6, pp. 136-46.

Kanin, E. J. (1967), 'Reference Groups and Sex Conduct Norm Violations', *Sociological Quarterly*, vol. 8, pp. 495-504.

Kanin, E. J. (1984), 'Date rape: Unofficial Criminals and Victims', *Victimology: An International Journal*, vol. 9(1), pp. 95-105.

Kanin, E. J. (1985), 'Date Rapists: Differential Sexual Socialization and Relative Deprivation', *Archives of Sexual Behavior*, vol. 14(3), pp. 219-31.

Katz, B. L. and Burt, M. R. (1986, August), 'Effects of Familiarity with the Rapist on Postrape Recovery', presented at the Annual Meeting of the American Psychological Association, Washington, DC.

Katz, S. and Mazur, M. A. (1979), *Understanding the Rape Victim: A Synthesis of Research Findings*, Wiley, New York.

Knudsen, D. D. (1988), *Child Protective Services: Discretion, Decisions, Dilemmas*, Charles C. Thomas, Springfield, IL.

Kopp, S. P. (1962), 'The Character Structure of Sex Offenders', *American Journal of Psychotherapy*, vol. 16, pp. 64-70.

Koss, M. P. (1985), 'The Hidden Rape Victim: Personality, Attitudinal, and Situational Characteristics', *Psychology of Women Quarterly*, vol. 9, pp. 193-212.

Koss, M. P. and Leonard, K. E. (1984), 'Sexually Aggressive Men: Empirical Findings and Theoretical Implications', in N. M. Malamuth and E. Donnerstein (eds), *Pornography and Sexual Aggression*, Academic Press, Orlando, FL.

Koss, M., Leonard, K. E., Beezley, D. A. and Oros, C. J. (1985), 'Non-stranger Sexual Aggression: A Discriminant Analysis of the Psychological Characteristics of Undetected Offenders', *Sex Roles*, vol. 12, pp. 981-92.

Koss, M. P., Gidycz, C. A. and Wisniewski, N. (1987), 'The Scope of Rape: Incidence and Prevalence of Sexual Aggression and Victimization in a National Sample of Higher Education Students', *Journal of Consulting and Clinical Psychology*, vol. 55, pp. 162-70.

Koss, M. and Harvey, M. (1987), *The Rape Victim*, The Greene Press, Lexington, MA.

Koss, M., Dinero, T., Seibel, C. and Cox, S. (1988), 'Stranger and Acquaintance Rape: Are There Differences in the Victim's Experience?', *Psychology of Women Quarterly*, vol. 12(1/2), pp. 1-24.

Koss, M. P. and Dinero, T. E. (1989), 'Discriminant Analysis of Risk Factors for Sexual Victimization Among a National Sample of College Women', *Journal of Consulting and Clinical Psychology*, vol. 57, pp. 242-50.

Koss, M. P., Woodruff, W. J. and Koss, P. G. (1990), 'Relation of Criminal Victimization to Health Perceptions among Women Medical Patients', *Journal of Consulting and Clinical Psychology*, vol. 58, pp. 147-52.

L'Armand, K. and Pepitone, A. (1982), 'Judgments of Rape: A Study of Victim-rapist Relationship and Victim Sexual History', *Personality and Social Psychology Bulletin*, vol. 8, pp. 134-9.

Leo, J. (1987, March, 23), 'When the Date Turns into Rape: Too Often the Attacker is the Clean-cut Acquaintance Next Door', *Time*, p. 77.

Lisak, D. and Roth, S. (1988), 'Motivational Factors in Nonincarcerated Sexually Aggressive Men', *Journal of Personality and Social Psychology*, vol. 55, pp. 795-8.

Lottes, I. L. (1988), 'Sexual Socialization and Attitudes Toward Rape', in A. W. Burgess (ed),

Rape and Sexual Assault (Vol. 2, pp. 193-220), Garland, New York.

MacEwen, K. E. (1994), 'Refining the Intergenerational Transmission Hypothesis', *Journal of Interpersonal Violence*, vol. 9(3), pp. 350-366.

Mahoney, E. R., Shively, M. D. and Traw, M. (1986), 'Sexual Coercion and Assault: Male Socialization and Female Risk', *Sexual Coercion and Assault*, vol. 1, pp. 2-8.

Makepeace, J. M. (1987), 'Social Factors and Victim-offender Differences in Courtship Violence', *Family Relations*, vol. 36, 987-91.

Malamuth, N. (1986), 'Predictors of Naturalistic Sexual Aggression', *Journal of Personality and Social Psychology*, vol. 22, pp. 474-95.

Malamuth, N., Briere, J. and Check, J. V. P. (1986), 'Sexual Arousal in Response to Aggression: Ideology, Aggressive, and Sexual Correlates', *Journal of Personality and Social Psychology*, vol. 50, pp. 330-40.

Matoesian, G. M. (1993), *Reproducing Rape: Domination Through Talk in the Courtroom*, University of Chicago Press, Chicago.

McCahill, T. W., Meyer, L. C. and Fischman, R. M. (1979), *The Aftermath of Rape*, Lexington Press, Lexington, MA.

Medea, A. and Thompson, K. (1974), *Against Rape*, Farrar, Straus & Giroux, New York.

Mosher, D. L. and Anderson, R. D. (1984), 'Macho Personality, Sexual Aggression, and Reactions to Guided Imagery of Realistic Rape', *Journal of Research in Personality*, vol. 20, pp. 77-94.

Muehlenhard, C. L., Friedman, D. E. and Thomas, C. M. (1985), 'Is Date Rape Justifiable? The Effects of Dating Activity, Who Initiated, Who Paid, and Men's Attitudes Toward Women', *Psychology of Women Quarterly*, vol. 9(3), pp. 297-310.

Muehlenhard, C. L. and Hollabaugh, L. C. (1988), 'Do Women Sometimes Say No When They Mean Yes? The Prevalence and Correlates of Women's Token Resistance to Sex', *Journal of Personality and Social Psychology*, vol. 54, pp. 872-8.

Muehlenhard, C. L. and Linton, M. (1987), 'Date Rape and Sexual Aggression in Dating Situations: Incidence and Risk Factors', *Journal of Counseling Psychology*, vol. 34, pp. 186-96.

Murnen, S. K., Perot, A. and Byrne, D. (1989), 'Coping with Unwanted Sexual Activity: Normative Responses, Situational Determinants, and Individual Differences', *The Journal of Sex Research*, vol. 26, pp. 85-106.

Mynatt, C. R. and Allgeier, E. R. (1990), 'Risk Factors, Self-Attributions, and Adjustment Problems among Victims of Sexual Coercion', *Journal of Applied Social Psychology*, vol. 20(2), pp. 130-53.

Parrot, A. (1986), *Acquaintance Rape and Sexual Assault Prevention Training Manual* (2nd ed), Cornell University Press, New York.

Rada, R. T. (ed) (1978), *Clinical Aspects of the Rapist*, Grune and Stratton, New York.

Rapaport, K. and Burkhart, B. R. (1984), 'Personality and Attitudinal Characteristics of Sexually Coercive College Males', *Journal of Abnormal Psychology*, vol. 93, pp. 216-21.

Roscoe, B. and Benaske, N. (1985), 'Courtship Violence Experienced by Abused Wives: Similarities in Patterns of Abuse', *Family Relations*, vol. 34, pp. 419-24.

Russell, D. E. H. (1975), *The Politics of Rape*, Stein & Day, New York.

Russell, D. E. H. (1982), *Rape in Marriage*, Stein & Day, New York.

Russell, D. E. H. (1984), *Sexual Exploitation: Rape, Child Sexual Abuse, and Workplace Harassment*, Sage, Beverly Hills, CA.

Ryan, K. M. (1995), 'Do Courtship Violent Men Have Characteristics Associated with a

"Battering" Personality?', *Journal of Family Violence*, vol. 10(1), pp. 99-111.

Scher, D. (1984), 'Sex Role Contradictions: Self-perceptions and Ideal Perceptions', *Sex Roles: A Journal of Research*, vol. 10, pp. 651-56.

Scully, D. (1990), *Understanding Sexual Violence: A Study of Convicted Rapists*, Unwin Hyman, Boston.

Scully, D. and Marolla, J. (1985), 'Riding the Bull at Gilley's: Convicted Rapists Describe the Rewards of Rape', *Social Problems*, vol. 32, pp. 251-63.

Shields, W. M. and Shields, L. M. (1983), 'Forcible Rape: An Evolutionary Perspective', *Ethnology and Sociobiology*, vol. 4, pp. 115-36.

Shotland, R. and Hunter, B. A. (1995), 'Women's "Token Resistance" and Compliant Sexual Behaviors are Related to Uncertain Sexual Intentions and Rape', *Personality and Social Psychology Bulletin*, vol. 21(3), pp. 226-37.

Sorenson, S. B., Stein, J. A., Siegel, J. M. and Burnam, M. A. (1987), 'The Prevalence of Sexual Assault: The Los Angeles Epidemiologic Catchment Area Project', *American Journal of Epidemiology*, vol. 126, pp. 1154-64.

Stets, J.E. and Pirog-Good, M.A. (1989), 'The Marriage License as a Hitting License: A Comparison of Assaults in Dating, Cohabiting, and Married Couples' in M.A. Pirog-Good and Stets, J.E. (eds), *Violence in Dating Relationships: Emerging Issues* (pp. 33-52), Praeger, New York.

Storr, A. (1970), *Human Aggression*, Penguin, Harmondsworth, England.

Story, M.D. (1982), 'A Comparison of University Students Experience with Various Sexual Outlets in 1974 and 1980', *Adolescence*, vol. 17, pp. 737-47.

Stuntz, E. C. (1975), 'Women's Reactions to Rape', *Smith College Studies in Social Work*, vol. 46, pp. 35-6.

Sweet, E. (1985, October), 'Date Rape: The Story of an Epidemic and Those Who Deny It', *Ms./Campus Times*, pp. 56-9, 84-5.

Tarvis, C. and Wade, C. (1985), *The Longest Way: Sex Differences in Perspective*, Harcourt Brace Jovanovich, New York.

Tetreault, P. A. and Barnett, M. A. (1987), 'Reactions to Stranger and Acquaintance Rape', *Psychology of Women Quarterly*, vol. 11, pp. 353-8.

Thompson, W.W.E. and Buttell, A.J. (1984), 'Sexual Deviance in America', *Emporia State Research Studies*, vol. 33, pp. 6-47.

Thornhill, R. and Thornhill, N. W. (1983), 'Human Rape: An Evolutionary Analysis', *Ethnology and Sociobiology*, vol. 4, pp. 137-73.

Tieger, T. (1981), 'Self Rated Likelihood of Raping and the Social Perception of Rape', *Journal of Clinical Psychology*, vol. 15, pp. 147-58.

Tong, R. (1984), *Women, Sex, and the Law*, Rowman and Allanheld, Totowa, NJ.

Veronen, L.J., Kilpatrick, D.G. and Resick, P.A. (1983), 'Treatment of Fear and Anxiety in Rape Victims: Implications for the Criminal Justice System', in W.H. Parsonage (ed), *Perspectives on Victimology* (pp. 148-159), Sage, Beverly Hills, CA.

Walby, S. (1990), *Theorizing Patriarchy*, Blackwell, Oxford.

Warshaw, R. (1988), *I Never Called it Rape*, Harper and Row, New York.

Weis, K. and Borges, S. S. (1973), 'Victimology and Rape: The Case of the Legitimate Victim', *Issues in Criminology*, vol. 8, pp. 71-115.

Weis, K. and Weis, S. (1975), 'Victimology and Justification of Rape', in I. Drapkin and E. Viano (eds), *Victimology: A New Focus*, vol. 5, Heath, Lexington, MA.

Williams, J. E. (1984), 'Secondary Victimization: Confronting Public Attitudes about Rape',

Victimology: An International Journal, vol. 9, pp. 66-81.

Wyatt, E.G. (1992), 'The Sociocultural Context of African American and White American Woman's Rape', *Journal of Social Issues*, vol. 48(1), pp. 77-91.

Yegidis, B.L. (1986), 'Date Rape and Other Forced Sexual Encounters Among College Students', *Journal of Sex Education and Therapy*, vol. 12, pp. 51-4.

5   Public Perceptions of Sexual Intercourse

Attitudes toward Date Rape

Attitudes toward victims, offenders, and the act of forced sexual intercourse have been measured extensively in recent research. Some of these studies have focused on the perception of victims and offenders regarding the labeling of their own behavior but most have focused on attitudes held by various groups regarding the justifiability of the use of force in dating and courtship. Most of these studies find that women and men hold varying perceptions of coerciveness. Many of the differences in perceptions appear to be due to social values and role differentiation between the sexes.

There is clearly a lack of clarity in this area, with many studies indicating that both men and women are critical of women who can be defined as contributing to their victimization. While most subjects are opposed to rape, many do not define all instances of forced sexual intercourse as rape.

Fischer (1986b, 1987) has conducted research evaluating the impact of exposure to course material designed to change student attitudes toward forcible date rape. The findings from the pretest suggested that, before exposure to the course content, persons who are more accepting of forcible date rape are less likely to define the behavior as really rape, have more traditional attitudes toward women, are more sexually permissive, have less accurate sexual knowledge, and, among the minority who do not blame the man, are slightly more inclined to blame society or the situation (1986b, p. 457). After exposure to these issues in class, the students became more rejecting of date rape, more sure that it was definitely rape, and slightly more liberal in attitudes toward women (p. 462). Less rejecting attitudes toward forcible date rape were related to more traditional attitudes toward women. When asked under what circumstance it was acceptable for a man to hold down a woman and force her to have intercourse, 82 percent of the students said "never" (Fischer, 1987); however, when rationalizations such as "He spent a lot of money on her" and "She led him on" are introduced, the percentage of subjects who answered "definitely unacceptable" dropped to 44 percent of the women and 24 percent of the men (p. 94).

College students tend to view date rape as different from rape; both men and women see contributing or mediating actions from both the man and the woman involved in the assault.   According to Korman (1983): "Typically, progression through the stages of sexual intimacy by males has been seen as legitimized in exchange for the amount of money spent by a male on a date" (p. 576).

Attitudes when the victim of sexual coercion is a man are different than attitudes held when the victim is a woman.   According to Garcia, Milano, and Quijano's (1989) study of heterosexual interactions between acquaintances found that male victims of sexual coercion may not be perceived as "real victims", thus suggesting that all men would welcome or enjoy aggressive sexual advances from women (Smith, Pine, & Hawley, 1988).   Male victims seem to receive little or no support from other men regardless of the degree of severity of their sexual experiences.   This unsupportive attitude may be attributed to masculine sex role identification whereby men are supposed to be the initiators of sexual encounters and women are supposed to be the resistors.   Therefore, men may find it difficult to understand why a man would want to resist the sexual advances of a woman (Garcia, Milano, & Quijano, 1989).

While the categories are not discrete, the studies which address public attitudes toward the use of forced sexual intercourse between people who know each other will be examined from five perspectives in this chapter. These categories are the degree of force used, the nature of the relationship between the victim and the offender, situational factors, characteristics of the victim, sex role socialization and stereotyping, and rape myth acceptance.

Degree of Force

Virtually all studies of public attitudes toward the use of force to gain sexual access focus on the extent to which the subjects will label the use of force as rape; however, relatively few empirical studies have directly measured this variable.   The constructed consent argument appears frequently in the literature, with the suggestion that some believe that the woman is consenting unless she actively and forcefully resists.   In this context, "minimal" force is perceived as acceptable or expected in a normal relationship as the couple approaches sexual intimacy.

The labeling of an incident as rape often varies with the degree of force used. Data suggest that as the amount of force used in forced sexual intercourse increases, the incident is more likely to be perceived as rape and the victim is less likely to be perceived as responsible for her victimization (Krulewitz & Payne, 1978; Shotland & Goodstein, 1983, 1992).

Garcia, Milano, and Quijano (1989) examined subjects' perceptions of degree of coercion in sexual behavior. Their measure of coercion ranged from several forms of verbal pressure to the use of physical force, with sexual behavior ranging from an invitation to go to the man's apartment to fondling and unwanted kissing. They found that women tended to label the acts as more coercive than men but that all subjects label the acts as more coercive when a member of the opposite sex was the victim than when a member of their own sex was the victim.

The degree to which the general public, victims, and offenders define forced sexual intercourse as rape based on the degree of force used, the extent to which these groups believe that it is normal for women to resist mild force when they are consenting, and the extent to which these groups accept the concept of constructed consent must be evaluated empirically. At present, these factors often are incorporated into a more general category of rape myth acceptance and will be considered in that context.

Nature of the Relationship between the Offender and the Victim

A number of studies have assessed the extent to which the degree of social distance between the offender and the victim influences the labeling of the offense as rape. In most studies, social distance is operationalized as a two or three category nominal variable: stranger and various types of dating, courtship, or acquaintance. Koss, Dinero, Seibel, and Cox (1988) noted that most published studies of the victim-offender relationship have dichotomized the relationship variable into stranger-versus-acquaintance categories, and that few rapes placed in the acquaintance category of these studies involved victims who were dating or who were married to their offender while the acquaintance category tended to consist of offenders who had non-intimate and non-romantic relationships with the victim (pp. 3-4).

Some studies focused on the victim-offender relationship and the amount or degree of violence/force used (Amir, 1971; Bart & O'Brien, 1981, 1985; Ellis, Atkeson, & Calhoun, 1981; Stuntz, 1975; Weis & Borges, 1973). Studies have shown that subjects interpret rape differently when rapists and victims are strangers than when they are acquaintances (Bridges & McGrail, 1989; Fenstermaker, 1988; Kormos & Brooks, 1994; L'Armand & Pepitone, 1982; Stacy, Prisbell, & Tollefsrud, 1992; Tetreault & Barnett, 1987) and that victims of rape between acquaintances feel more self blame than victims of stranger rape (Katz & Burt 1986).

Bridges and McGrail (1989) examined the effects of the victim-perpetrator relationship on college students' attributions of responsibility for rape by asking both men and women subjects to read one of six scenarios that depicted a rape as a proposition that varied according to the victim-perpetrator relationship (steady dating partners, acquaintances on a first date, strangers). Seven responsibility attributions were rated for the rape or propositions. The authors stated that most forms of victim responsibility were stronger for rape on a date than for the incidents between strangers. The findings concerning the perpetrator's responsibility were mixed. In addition, male subjects gave higher ratings to several responsibility attributions, and these were also linked to sex role and sexual considerations.

L'Armand and Pepitone (1982) measured subjects' judgments of rape as influenced by the variables of victim-rapist relationship and victim sexual history. The results show that the relationship between the victim and rapist significantly affected all judgments of the rape, with acceptance of the rape increasing as the degree of association increased.

Tetreault and Barnett (1987) conducted a study of 80 undergraduates (40 men and 40 women) enrolled in a general psychology course to elicit their reactions to a woman who presumably had been raped by a stranger or an acquaintance. The subjects read one of two rape descriptions prior to watching a videotape of the woman who they were told had been the rape victim. They found that the victim-offender relationship may be one variable influencing perceptions of rape victims. Univariate analyses of variance showed that women respondents who attributed less responsibility to the victim of a stranger rape than an acquaintance rape were more certain that a rape had occurred in the stranger than in the acquaintance condition, and tended to view stranger rape as more serious than acquaintance rape, while the opposite was found for men on these three variables (p. 356). The authors stated that no significant main effect of sex of subject or type of rape was found in any analysis. The authors also found that the men rated the rape victim as markedly less likable when she had been raped by a stranger than an acquaintance (Tetreault & Barnett, 1987, p. 356). These findings would fit with the traditional view in our society that men are the aggressors and women the recipients of this aggressiveness (Weis & Borges, 1973).

A study of 170 students at a midwestern urban university conducted to determine the differences in attitudes toward sexual violence committed by strangers and by acquaintances found that while college men and women consider rape by a stranger more serious than rape by a date, they differed in their perceptions of the seriousness of acquaintance rape (Stacy, Prisbell, & Tollefsrud, 1992). In the study, women considered acquaintance rape more serious than the male college students. Men were less likely to believe that men are always responsible for the rape, and more likely to believe that, in some cases, the woman asked to be raped.

A more recent study (Kormos & Brooks, 1994) reported different results. In their study of college students and prison inmates, Kormos and Brooks found no difference in the assignment of blame by college students for stranger vs. acquaintance incidents of forced sexual intercourse, but prison inmates assigned more blame to the victim in the acquaintance condition.

Research conducted on the authors' campus investigated a number of factors related to forced sexual intercourse. Subjects were asked to define a set of 11 characterizations of forced sexual intercourse as rape, date rape, or not rape and to identify criminal penalties for the same set of characterizations (see Chart 5.1). The characterizations ranged from stranger rape to forced marital intercourse. Section six also measured preferences for penalties for forced sexual intercourse. The eleven characterizations of acts of forced sexual intercourse were developed with differing degrees of association. For this study degree of association was operationalized along three dimensions: level of prior interaction (none to married), degree of intimacy (none to regular sexual exchange), and degree of permitted intrusion into personal space (none to living together). In addition, degree of resistance was included as a variable in five characterizations. The characterizations were designed to permit analysis of the data with the characterizations used as points on an ordinal scale. Subjects were asked to identify the characterizations as rape, date rape, and not rape and to identify an appropriate penalty for each characterization.

For the total sample, all characterizations were labeled as rape or date rape by over 70 percent of the subjects; all characterizations except for those in which a fairly permanent relationship exists were labeled as a form of rape by more than 80 percent of the subjects. The percentage of subjects who labeled the characterizations as rape declined as the degree of association increased until the level of association reached living together (see Table 5.1), at which point the trend reversed.

Chart 5.1   Illustrative items

Offensive Behavior
Women
11. How many times in the past 12 months have you had a young man continue to move on you after you have told him that you were not interested? (If none, write 0.) _____
12. Why do you think young men don't stop in cases like this?
Men
11. How many times in the past 12 months have you continued to move on a young woman after she told you that she was not interested? (If none, write 0.)
_____
12. Why do you think young men don't stop in cases like this?

Resistance Techniques
Women
22a. When the young man was trying to force you to have sex, did you

tell him to stop? Yes ___ No ___
b. If yes, was it successful in making him stop? Yes ___ No ___
c. Why would a young man not stop if a young woman asked him to?
Men
22a. When you tried to get your date to have sex, did she tell you to stop? Yes ___ No ___
b. If yes, did you stop? Yes ___ No ___
c. Why would a young man not stop if a young woman asked him to?

Type of Forced Sexual Intercourse
and Preferred Penalties

52. Someone the girl meets for the first time at a party gives her a ride home. She invites him into her room for a Coke. Before leaving, he forces her to have sex.

Table 5.1   Characterization of selected acts of forced sexual intercourse as rape, date rape, or not rape (in percentages)

	Rape	Date Rape	Not Rape	No.
Stranger on street				
All	100			202
Men	100			97
Women	100			104

Table 5.1 Continued

	Rape	Date Rape	Not Rape	No.
Fraternity/sorority	100			76
Non fraternity/sorority	100			124
Known-On Street-Talk				
All	85.4	14.6		199
Men[2]	90.6	8.3	1.0	96
Women	79.6	20.4		103
Known-On Street-Talk				
Fraternity/sorority[3]	74.7	24.0	1.3	75
Non fraternity/sorority	91.9	8.1		123
First meet-Party-Take home Stop				
All	84.1	15.9		201
Men	83.5	16.5		97
Women	84.5	15.5		200
Fraternity/sorority[1]	76.3	23.7		76
Non fraternity/sorority	88.6	11.4		123
First meet-Party-Invite in for a Coke				
All	70.3	28.7	1.0	202
Men	71.1	27.8	1.0	97
Women	69.2	29.8	1.0	104
Fraternity/sorority[2]	60.5	36.8	2.6	76
Non fraternity/sorority	76.6	23.4		124
Dating-Take home-Stop				
All	24.0	74.0	2.0	200
Men[2]	31.3	66.7	2.1	96
Women	17.5	80.6	1.9	103
Fraternity/sorority[2]	14.7	80.0	5.3	75
Non fraternity/sorority	30.1	69.9		123
Dating-Her room				
All	24.9	72.6	2.5	201
Men[3]	34.4	65.6		93
Women	17.6	82.4		102
Fraternity/sorority[2]	16.9	83.1	2.0	71
Non fraternity/sorority	30.9	69.1		123

Table 5.1 Continued

	Rape	Date Rape	Not Rape	No.
Dating-Her room-Hit				
All	23.9	74.6	1.5	202
Men[3]	32.3	66.7	1.0	96
Women	16.3	81.7	1.9	104
Fraternity/sorority[3]	13.3	85.3	1.3	75
Non fraternity/sorority	30.6	67.7	1.6	124
Dating-Her room-No hit				
All	16.5	71.0	12.5	200
Men[2]	21.1	65.3	13.7	95
Women	12.5	76.9	10.6	104
Fraternity/sorority[2]	8.0	78.7	13.3	75
Non fraternity/sorority	22.0	66.7	11.4	123
Dating-Her room-Prior sex-Kiss				
All	16.7	64.6	18.7	198
Men[2]	21.1	55.8	23.2	95
Women	12.7	73.5	13.7	102
Fraternity/sorority	9.3	69.3	21.3	75
Non fraternity/sorority	21.5	62.0	16.5	121
Live with-Regular sex				
All	26.9	47.7	25.4	197
Men	24.2	44.2	31.6	95
Women	29.7	51.5	18.8	101
Fraternity/sorority[3]	12.3	57.5	30.1	73
Non fraternity/sorority	36.1	41.8	22.1	122
Husband				
All	40.5	28.7	29.7	193
Men[2]	36.2	25.5	38.3	94
Women	45.9	32.7	21.4	98
Fraternity/sorority[2]	30.1	35.6	34.2	73
Non fraternity/sorority	48.3	24.6	27.1	118

[1] Not rape was combined with date rape for sex and fraternity/sorority comparisons when the number of subjects choosing not rape was too small to permit appropriate statistical analysis.

[2] Pearson's for chi square significance $< .05$.

[3] Pearson's for chi square significance $< .01$.

Table 5.2 Preferred penalties for selected types of forced sexual intercourse (in percentages)

	5+ Years	1-5 Years	0-1 Years	Academic[1] Affairs	No Crime[1]	No.
Stranger on street						
All	94.5	4.0	.5	1.0		201
Men	92.8	4.1	1.0	2.1		97
Women	97.1	2.9				103
Fraternity/sorority	96.1	1.3		2.6		76
Non fraternity/sorority	94.3	4.9	.8			123
Known-On Street-Talk						
All	80.0	16.0	2.5	1.0	.5	201
Men	76.3	18.6	4.1		1.0	97
Women	84.3	12.7	1.0	2.0		102
Fraternity/sorority	76.3	18.4	2.6	1.3	1.3	76
Non fraternity/sorority	82.8	13.9	2.5	.8		122
First meet-Party-Take home-Stop						
All	82.5	14.0	2.5	1.0		200
Men	78.1	15.6	5.2	1.0		96
Women	87.4	11.7		1.0		103
Fraternity/sorority	77.6	15.8	5.3	1.3		76
Non fraternity/sorority	86.1	12.3	.8	.8		122
First meet-Party-Invite in for a Coke						
All	63.1	29.8	5.1	1.5	.5	198
Men[2]	58.3	29.2	9.4	2.1	1.0	96
Women	68.3	29.7	1.0	1.0		101
Fraternity/sorority	53.3	37.3	6.7	2.7		75
Non fraternity/sorority	70.2	24.0	4.1	.8	.8	121
Dating-Take home-Stop						
All	51.0	33.0	12.5	2.0	1.5	200
Men[2]	42.3	36.1	17.5	2.1	2.1	97
Women	59.8	29.4	7.8	2.0	1.0	102

Table 5.2 Continued

	5+ Years	1-5 Years	0-1 Years	Academic[1] Affairs	No Crime[1]	No.
Dating-Take home-Stop						
Fraternity/sorority	42.7	34.7	14.7	5.3	2.7	75
Non fraternity/sorority	56.9	31.7	10.6		.8	123
Dating-Her Room						
All	48.7	33.2	12.1	4.0	2.0	199
Men	41.2	34.0	17.5	5.2	2.1	97
Women	56.4	31.7	6.9	3.0	2.0	102
Fraternity/sorority[2]	37.3	36.0	17.3	6.7	2.7	75
Non fraternity/sorority	55.7	32.0	8.2	2.5	1.6	123
Dating-Her room-Hit						
All	46.7	34.7	11.6	5.0	2.0	199
Men	41.2	34.0	16.5	6.2	2.1	97
Women	52.5	34.7	6.9	4.0	2.0	101
Fraternity/sorority	41.3	32.0	17.3	6.7	2.7	75
Non fraternity/sorority	50.0	36.1	8.2	4.1	1.6	122
Dating-Her room-No hit						
All	37.1	33.5	18.8	7.6	3.0	197
Men[3]	32.3	27.1	28.1	8.3	4.2	96
Women	42.0	40.0	9.0	7.0	2.0	100
Fraternity/sorority	29.3	32.0	22.7	12.0	4.0	75
Non fraternity/sorority	41.7	35.0	15.8	5.0	2.5	120
Dating-Her room-Prior sex-Kiss						
All	23.1	35.7	21.1	11.1	9.0	197
Men[3]	18.6	27.8	25.8	14.4	13.4	7
Women	27.7	43.6	15.8	7.9	5.0	101
Fraternity/sorority	20.2	30.7	22.7	18.7	8.0	75
Non fraternity/sorority	24.6	39.1	20.5	6.6	9.0	122
Live with-Regular sex						
All	23.2	29.3	22.2	10.1	15.2	198
Men[3]	18.8	20.8	25.0	14.6	20.8	96
Women	27.7	37.6	18.8	5.9	9.9	101
Fraternity/sorority	20.2	33.1	20.7	16.6	16.0	75
Non fraternity/sorority	25.6	33.1	20.7	6.6	14.0	121

Table 5.2 Continued

	5+ Years	1-5 Years	0-1 Years	Academic[1] Affairs	No Crime[1]	No.
Husband						
All	22.6	24.6	16.9	8.2	27.7	198
Men[3]	16.0	17.0	14.9	12.8	39.4	94
Women	29.0	32.0	18.0	4.0	17.0	100
Fraternity/sorority	18.9	23.0	16.2	14.9	27.0	74
Non fraternity/sorority	25.2	26.1	16.8	4.2	27.7	119

[1] Not a crime and referrals to academic affairs were combined or added to less than one year for sex and fraternity/sorority comparisons when the number of subjects choosing these was too small to permit appropriate statistical analysis.
[2] Pearson's for chi square significance < .05.
[3] Pearson's for chi square significance < .01.

The subjects were more likely to label forced sexual intercourse as rape in marital or cohabitating characterizations than in characterizations in which dating is occurring with some degree of intimacy (kissing and hugging). This finding is similar to that found in a study of the general public (Sigler & Haygood, 1987). In general, the willingness to label a specific aggressive sexual act as rape declines as the degree of intimacy increases, with one exception. It appears that wives are accorded more sympathy or right to refuse than a woman who lives with a man without marriage. It should be noted that the not rape category is chosen by a very small number of subjects until the degree of association reaches dating with prior intimacy and increases as the degree of association increases from that point on.

Shotland and Goodstein (1992) conducted an experiment assessing the extent to which prior sexual intimacy influences the perceived legitimacy of forced sexual intercourse. They found that both men and women were less likely to label an act of forced sexual intercourse as rape when the couple had had consensual sexual intercourse on several prior occasions.

It is possible that the concept of "date rape" is not acceptable when a fairly permanent relationship exists. Thus, there appears to be a tendency to label these characterizations as either rape or not rape. A more precise measure of association and greater specificity of the range of labeling options will be required to clarify the confusion in the patterns observed here.

The pattern for preferred penalty is more evident. As the degree of association increased, the severity of the penalty endorsed decreased. Not a crime was endorsed by a small number of subjects until the degree of association reached dating with intimacy and increased through living together and marriage (see Table 5.2). It is noted that referral to academic affairs was not seen as appropriate by over 90 percent of the subjects for all characterizations; that is, most subjects saw forced sexual intercourse as a justice system issue with differing levels of endorsed punishment. Men tended to select lower levels of punishment than women for six of the eight characterizations with higher levels of association (see Table 5.2).

When sex and fraternity or sorority affiliation were evaluated, several patterns emerged. The strongest pattern existed for fraternity or sorority affiliation and labeling of the characterizations as rape, date rape, or not rape. With the exception of stranger rape, members of fraternities or sororities were less likely to identify the characterizations as rape (see Table 5.1) (Dating in her room with prior sex and kissing approached significance: p=.0808). This pattern was not found for severity of sentence with a single significant relationship (severity of punishment and dating in her room) (see Table 5.2). These findings are compatible with some of the patterns reported by Boeringer, Shehan, & Akers, (1991). A similar but weaker pattern existed for sex; men were more likely than women to label some characterizations as rape (see Table 5.1). The opposite relationship is noted for marital rape. Women were more likely than men to label this characterization as rape. For the two characterizations with the greatest amount of association, men were more likely to select not rape than women. Differences by sex in terms of preferred penalty were fairly persistent and reached significance for six characterizations. Women endorsed stronger penalties than men for these characterizations (see Table 5.2).

Fraternity or sorority affiliation and sex were used as control variables to further explore the patterns observed. The lower rate of endorsement of most characterizations as rape disappeared for sorority women. Fraternity men were less likely to label the characterizations as rape than non-fraternity men for all but the two characterizations with lower levels of association (stranger rape and meeting someone she knows on the street), but the differences between sorority women and non-sorority women were not significant, with the exception of the living with-regular sex characterization, with sorority women less likely than non-sorority women to endorse the label of rape. A difference in preferred sentence emerged, with fraternity men endorsing lower penalties than non-fraternity men for six of the characterizations.

When fraternity or sorority affiliation was the control variable, fraternity men were significantly more likely to label some characterizations as rape than sorority women. These were: dating-take home-stop, dating-her-room, dating her room-hit, dating-her room-no hit, live with-regular sex, and husband; however, sorority women endorsed more severe penalties than fraternity men for some characterizations. These were: dating-take home-stop, dating-her room, dating-her room-no hit, dating-her room-prior sex-kiss, and live with-regular sex.

The degree to which the victim and the offender are intimately involved prior to the assault appears to be a pervasive factor in the willingness of subjects to label forced sexual intercourse as rape and in the degree of sanctions which subjects are willing to impose. Future research should focus on refinement of the nature and strength of the prior relationship as to permit closer examination of the relationship between prior relationship and the definition of the nature of the interaction between the victim and the offender.

Situational Factors

One of the most pervasive sets of attitudes which are held to influence the labeling of the use of forced sexual intercourse as rape is related to the nature of the situation in which the offense occurs. These attitudes tend to define situations in which the use of force is justifiable or in which the responsibility of the man for the offense is decreased and the responsibility of the woman for the offense is increased. Factors which influence the labeling of an incident as date rape include type of clothing, money spent, and type of date (Johnson, 1995).

Giarrusso, Johnson, Goodchilds, and Zellman (1979), in a study of high school students, found that 82 percent of the subjects said it was never acceptable for a boy to hold a girl down and force her to have intercourse. However, when given circumstances were described, the percentage considering the action unacceptable dropped to 44 percent for the female subjects and 24 percent for male subjects. Fischer (1986a) reported finding an even lower percentage of college students who answered definitely unacceptable. The influencing circumstances described were such factors as whether the woman "led on" her date and whether her date spent money on her. Fischer (1986a) found that students who did not consider the man's behavior definitely unacceptable had more traditional attitudes toward women.

Muehlenhard, Friedman, and Thomas (1985), in two related studies of 268 male undergraduates, assessed the perceived justifiability of date rape, finding that rape was rated as significantly more justifiable under the following conditions: (a) if the couple went to the man's apartment rather than to a religious function, (b) if the woman asked the man out rather than the man asking the woman out, and (c) if the man paid all the dating expenses rather than splitting them with the woman (p. 306). Further, the researchers predicted that the men who were classified as having traditional attitudes toward women would see date rape as more justifiable than nontraditional men. Muehlenhard (1988) reported similar findings in a subsequent study and suggested that a man may overestimate his date's interest in sex and may later feel that he has been led on and that his use of force was justified. A study conducted by Korman and Leslie (1982) also found a relationship between expense paying by the man and identification of an incident of forced sexual intercourse as rape.

Much of the material considered under other categories can be defined as situational factors. At some point theoretical models will need to be developed which will attempt to integrate the various factors which influence the perceptions of incidents of forced sexual intercourse held by the general public.

Characteristics of the Victim

Studies which have focused on public perceptions of characteristics of the victim have either focused on the perceived impact of the act on the victim or on characteristics of the victim which may be seen as having precipitated the attack. In the latter case, responsibility again is shifted from the offender to the victim for the attack. Interest in the attribution of blame to a protected group is a relatively new endeavor (Felson, 1991) which can be productively applied to the assignment of blame to victims of forced sexual intercourse for their victimization.

A number of factors have been advanced which increase the likelihood that the victim will be blamed for her victimization. Intoxication has been shown to increase attribution of responsibility (Richardson & Campbell, 1982) while physical attractiveness has been shown to reduce recommended punishments (Deitz, 1980) and reduction of the labeling of a act of forced sexual intercourse as rape (Kanekar & Kolsawalla, 1980; Seligman, Brickman, & Koulack, 1977). Johnson and Jackson (1988) examined the nature of the interaction between the offender and the victim, focusing on the degree of ambiguity in the woman's communication of her willingness to engage in sexual intercourse and social distance. As ambiguity in the woman's willingness to engage in sexual intercourse increased, favorable assessment of the offender increased and favorable assessment of the victim decreased.

Gerdes, Dammann, and Heilig (1988) focused on perceptions of rape victims and assailants and the effects of physical attractiveness, acquaintance, and subject gender. They found that both women and men treated the rape as a serious crime, but women saw the crime as more debilitating for the victim and warranting greater punishment. The authors stated that there was some evidence that the tendency for women to blame rape victims less than men is limited to certain rape circumstances. The probability of the victim's having contributed to the crime was low in all conditions, but was rated higher by men reading the acquainted version than by men reading the unacquainted version or by women reading either version (p. 149). The authors suggested that because of their greater identification with the victim, women may be less open than men to the belief that rapists have been provoked by their victims (p. 150).

Other studies (Krulewitz & Payne, 1978; Kanekar & Kolsawalla, 1980; Yarmey, 1985) found that women who are emotionally uncontrolled and sexually inexperienced are more likely to be perceived as innocent victims and there is a relationship between sexual attractiveness and perceptions of victim blame. When the victim is perceived as having experienced sexual pleasure, or if the forced sexual intercourse is perceived as foreseeable, victim-blaming increases (McCaul, Veltum, Boyechko, & Crawford, 1990).

Blaming the victim is a common reaction in cases of date rape (Burgess & Holmstrom, 1983, 1974; Holmstrom & Burgess, 1978). Victims themselves are less likely to define their victimization as date rape when a relationship exists between the victim and assailant, even when the relationship is casual (Klemmack & Klemmack, 1976). Prior acquaintance between the victim and assailant becomes more of an issue in a rape incident when the victim has engaged in some type of voluntary social contact and when the rape itself occurs in an intimate setting (the assailant's apartment or house). One important factor in date rape is the degree of individual choice. If a victim has free choice in deciding whether or not to go the assailant's apartment on the first date and she does, and is raped, then she is often perceived as responsible (Loh, 1980).

The victim's blameworthiness for the incident is more pronounced when the victims are acquainted with their assailants, have voluntary social contact with their assailants prior to the date rape, have been victimized in the assailant's residence, and the offenders have used relatively little force. These factors reinforce the perception held by many victims that the criminal justice system, family, friends, and society will hold victims responsible for their victimization.

L'Armand and Pepitone (1982) measured subjects' judgments of rape as influenced by the variables of victim-rapist relationship and victim sexual history. The results show that sexual history was significantly related to all judgments of the rape, with no greater tendency to mitigate the rape where a limited (47.7 percent) or extensive (51.2 percent) victim sexual history was described than when no description was offered (46.7 percent).

Assigning blame to victims of forced sexual intercourse is broad with a wide variety of both active and passive responses identified as providing a basis for shifting blame from the offender to the victim. These finding lend support to the feminist perspective though many of these studies are not reported from a feminist perspective.

Sex Role Socialization and Stereotyping

Several studies have indicated that forced sexual intercourse occurs because men and women learn roles which make the use of force in intimate situations acceptable. Collateral values regarding things such as male dominance and female submissiveness reinforce the acceptability of the use of force by men.

It has been suggested (Field, 1978; Burt, 1980; Kanin, 1985; Muehlenhard, Friedman, & Thomas, 1985) that there is a relationship between traditional sex role stereotyping and the acceptability of the act of rape. A number of studies have addressed attitudes toward rape (Giarrusso, Johnson, Goodchilds, & Zellman, 1979; Fischer, 1986a, 1987).

Griffin (1971) directed attention to the cultural supports for rape, leading to assertion that rape results from normal socialization processes (Weis & Borges, 1973; Medea & Thompson, 1974; Russell, 1975, 1982; Weis & Weis, 1975; Jackson, 1978). Warshaw (1988) addressed heterosexual rituals, suggesting sexual assertiveness on the part of the man and gatekeeping behaviors on the part of the woman may play a role in date rape. Parrot (1986) and Parrot & Bechhofer (1991) asserted that women who demonstrate the traditional female role of being passive, gentle, and sacrificing are more likely to be victims of rape than those who are assertive. Bridges and McGrail (1989) suggested that the model of rape which has been proposed by several writers (e.g., Burt, 1980; Cherry, 1983) (rape is an extension of the traditional behaviors and motives that operate in heterosexual situations) is particularly applicable to date rape.

Any consideration of the perceptions of date rape must take into account expectations which are held for women's behavior (Bourque, 1989; Tetreault & Barnett, 1987). Male-female interactions are viewed differently by men and women. Men are more likely than women to interpret friendly behavior as indicating sexual interest (Abby, 1982). Women are held accountable for these male interpretations of their behavior. Any type of suggestive behavior (the woman being "a teaser" or "loose") leads to an increase in the acceptance of justification for a rape in many studies (Muehlenhard, Friedman, & Thomas, 1985). Women are held accountable for such things as choosing to go to a certain place on a date, initiating a date, or allowing the date to pay the expenses. Meeting in a public place and going somewhere together is held to be suggestive, or at least subject to misinterpretation. The man's misinterpretation of the woman's desire for sex is attributed to her. When the women says no, he may feel she has been leading him on. This feeling leads to the rapist regarding the rape (or date rape) as justifiable.

Jenkins & Dambrot (1987) suggested that sex role socialization leads to a value system which supports rape in that the use of coercion and physical force to obtain sex is seen as normative rather than as deviant behavior (p. 877). Within our society, there are hidden norms that condone this type of sexual violence as part of our courtship culture (Dull & Giacopassi, 1987; Gordon & Riger, 1989). Studies conducted on college campuses suggest that persons relatively more accepting of forcible sexual intercourse are less likely to define forced sexual intercourse as rape, have more traditional attitudes toward women, are more self-sexually permissive and are slightly more inclined to blame society or the situation for the rape (Fischer, 1986b).

As was the case with victim characteristics, much of the research addressing sex roles is compatible with the feminist perspective. Socialization and sex role stereotyping as causes or mediators of offensive sexual behavior need to be more closely examined.

Rape Myth Acceptance

The issues raised in studies which assess attitudes toward rape myth acceptance tend to overlap other categories, particularly the sex role socialization and victim blaming perspectives. Rape myth acceptance positions tend to be more ideological in nature but have generally measured the defined variables effectively.

Rape myths are defined as "prejudicial, stereotyped, or false beliefs about rape, rape victims, and rapists" (Burt, 1980, p. 271). Rape myths are common and they are usually grounded in patriarchal attitudes and values (Brinson, 1992). Patriarchal attitudes and values reflect the inferiority of women while at the same time assert the superiority of males. The internalization of these patriarchal attitudes by individuals and society eventually leads to these values becoming institutionalized in laws. It appears that the definition of rape and rape myths are intertwined in cultural sexist stereotypes of women in society (Burt, 1980). Such myths support the patriarchal notion that women are not injured physically, socially, or psychologically by the rape. Thus, the blame shifts from the offender to the victim or to external factors like drugs, alcohol, or the dress and mannerism of the victim. The ultimate blame for the occurrence of the rape lies with the victim.

Rape myths allow society to accept patriarchal attitudes and values which rationalize the existence of rape. Many people who rationalize the existence of rape and internalize rape myths tend to hold traditional views of the woman's role in society (Burt, 1980). Rape myths assert that women are naturally sexual and that they welcome any form of sexual intercourse, including forced sexual intercourse. They further suggest that controlling and dominating women is acceptable, even if violence has to be used. Such myths only sustain a type of violence that is fundamental to the established male power structure.

Rape myths are widespread in society and are generally accepted by many people. There are numerous misconceptions about the crime of rape. One of the most commonly held rape myths is that the "victim asked for it" or that "she wanted to be raped". This myth blames the victim for the rape and excuses the rapist.

Consistent with the myth that the victim is responsible for the rape is the belief that there is no such phenomenon as a "real rape". The more people believe that the victim acted in some way to encourage the sexual assault, the less likely they are to label the behavior as a real rape and to acknowledge that a rape actually occurred (Burt & Alkin, 1981; Check & Malamuth, 1981). The internalization of traditional attitudes toward the roles of men and women, distrust of the opposite sex, and acceptance of interpersonal violence make it easy to place the blame upon the woman.

The myth that a woman wants to be raped is usually supported by the assertions that a woman cannot be raped against her will and that when a woman is willing to engage in sexual intercourse she will say "no" to sex to maintain her status as a "good girl". It is suggested that a reasonable, independent, strong-willed, and healthy woman can get away from the rapist or prevent the rape if she desires. If for some reason she does not prevent the rape from occurring by fighting back, it is assumed that the act was not rape but an acceptable form of sexual intercourse. Giacopassi and Dull (1986; Dull & Giacopassi, 1987) conducted a self-report study of college students designed to measure attitudes toward sex, dating, and rape. Seventeen percent of the respondents agreed with the statement "A female cannot be forced to have intercourse against her will", and 56 percent agreed with the statement, "For some females, physical aggressiveness by the male is a necessary prelude to the acceptance of love and affection" (p.181). While differences among racial and sexual groups were not consistent, men tended to be slightly more accepting of rape myths than women, with black women tending to see both the victim and the offender more blameworthy than did white females (Foley, Evancic, Karnik, King, & Parks, 1995). In her study of receptiveness of subjects to attempts to modify their acceptance of rape myths, Jensen (1993) also found that men were more accepting of rape myths than women.

The perceptions of and attitudes toward rape are, in many cases, shaped by the presence of these rape myths. Examples of rape myths include, but are not limited to, the beliefs that prior sexual activity indicates a willingness to participate in other sexual acts, women say "no" when they really mean "yes", women desire and want to be raped, and women provoke rape by their appearance and/or behavior (Muehlenhard & Hollabaugh (1988).

Koss and Leonard (1984) define the following beliefs as supportive of rape:

(1) rape is not a serious crime,
(2) women are responsible for rape prevention,
(3) women provoke and want men to use force in sexual interactions,
(4) relationships between men and women are adversarial and manipulative,

(5) a man's role is to convince a reluctant woman to have sex,

(6) some amount of force is a legitimate strategy to get sex, and

(7) women do not find offensive the forceful strategies that men use to obtain sex.

A survey of college students (Sandberg, Jackson, & Petretic-Jackson, 1987) found that a majority of males respondents believed that dating partners said "no" to sexual activity when they really meant "yes", suggesting poor communication skills. As Koss, Gidycz, and Wisniewski (1987) pointed out, "It may be that some men fail to perceive accurately or to acknowledge the degree of force and coerciveness that was involved in a particular sexual encounter" (p. 169).

Gender role expectations and cultural norms dictate that males in society be naturally aggressive, dominant, detached, and independent. This myth facilitates the belief that a woman is to blame for the rape because of her dress, mannerism, or presence in an unacceptable place at an unacceptable time. A woman's clothing may be viewed as being sexually provocative or suggestive, such as wearing a mini skirt, short shorts, or a transparent top. Furthermore, women who are viewed as independent and initiators of sexual encounters by kissing or petting a man or allowing themselves to be kissed or petted are viewed as asking for sexual intercourse. These types of mannerisms reflect prior sexual knowledge and send out clear signs that they want sex. Lastly, women who frequent bars or are unescorted by a man are seen as being in the wrong place at the wrong time for decent and proper women. In each instance of dress and mannerism it is assumed that the victim asked to be raped because she did not conform to traditional gender role expectations.

Margolin, Miller, and Moran (1989) examined the relationship between rape attitudes and violations of consent in kissing. Subjects to whom questionnaires were administered were 49 undergraduate men and 162 undergraduate women taking a psychology course in a large Eastern university. The distribution was heavily skewed in favor of women due to the low enrollment of men at that particular college. The results indicated that the association between rape myth acceptance and responses to violations of consent in kissing was significant regardless of whether the violations took place within the context of a first date, long-term dating, or marriage. In addition, the study showed that male subjects had higher rape myth acceptance than women and were more supportive of a man's right to violate a woman's consent in kissing, and the association between gender and responses to forced kissing was significant independent of the context in which the forced kiss occurred.

Although rape myths are pervasive and widely accepted, there has been some opposition to these myths by a number of feminists (Brownmiller, 1975). During the past two decades, feminist writers and researchers have dispelled some of the myths surrounding rape by replacing the myths with facts. Complete abolishment of rape myths will be slow in coming because rape myths are so interwoven with other attitudes of sex roles and violence. It has been well documented that individuals who do not hold the traditional values of women are likely to reject rape myths (Burt, 1980; Check & Malamuth, 1981). Such individuals are sensitive to rape related issues. The responsibility for the rape is placed upon the rapist and not upon the victim.

Rape myths are especially dangerous to the victim and society as a whole when they are internalized in the belief systems of lay people and professionals who interact with rape victims and rapists (Barber, 1974; Burt, 1980; Field, 1978). Professionals who internalize rape myths and who work with rape victims on a day-to-day basis cannot provide the victim with the help she needs. Rape myths have the tendency to reduce a very complex crime to a phenomenon that is simple and easy. In understanding the fact and reality of rape, one has to confront the complex interrelated entities that encompass rape. Internalizing and believing rape myths may be perceived as easier to accept than reality or fact.

Summary

Public attitudes are important for several reasons, the most important of which is the extent to which these attitudes provide a context in which victims and offenders act. Public attitudes which shift blame for victimization to female victims or which hold forced sexual intercourse as natural because that is the nature of men, socialization, or society may increase the rates of forced sexual intercourse in all circumstances.

The issue is confused in many cases by the manner in which key variables are operationalized. Subjects state that it is never right to force a women to engage in intimate behavior, then modify their position when presented with specific examples. It is possible that operationalization in the examples produced different conditions than the operationalization of the general condition. While the emphasis in many scenarios tends to be on factors such as degree of social distance, the operationalization of force is often very broad. Force varies in studies from physical damaging force to verbal intimidation. Generally speaking, as the degree of force applied increases, the labeling of the act as rape increases.

Related to the use of force is the issue of resistance. Implied consent is a subtle underlying factor in many studies of public attitudes - implied in that it is not directly operationalized but underlies the variables of primary interest. A few studies have assessed resistance and find that when the woman strongly and physically resists, forced sexual intercourse is rape. When resistance is not physical, not strong, and not persistent, forced sexual intercourse is perceived by some as something other than rape. A number of studies have focused on the "real" meaning of no, suggesting that simply saying no is implied consent.

Most beliefs which assess victim behavior or characteristics as reasons for justifying offensive sexual behavior have an underlying implied consent basis. If a woman goes to a man's apartment, allows him to pay for dating activities, drinks alcohol, dresses provocatively, is friendly, or is attractive, then she is perceived as consenting to intimate behavior. Even in the most passive of factors (being attractive) implied consent is held to be a potential condition. When these beliefs exist, men can justify offensive behavior and rates of victimization can increase.

Social values change slowly. In most cases of social change there is cultural lag. In the simplest terms, the belief that no action or condition of a woman implies consent to sexual intimacy is preferable and accepted by many, but, in the foreseeable future, many in our society will be operating from a different perspective. Research, development of theoretical perspectives, and prevention and treatment program development must be based in a firm accurate assessment of public attitudes. Having said that, it should also be noted that in most studies, those who hold regressive attitudes tend to be in the minority.

References

Abby, A. (1982), 'Sex Differences in Attributions for Friendly Behavior: Do Males Misperceive Females' Friendliness?', *Journal of Personality and Social Psychology*, vol. 42, pp. 830-8.

Amir, M. (1971), *Patterns in Forcible Rape*, University of Chicago Press, Chicago.

Barber, R. (1974), 'Judge and Jury Attitude toward Rape', *Australia and New Zealand Journal of Criminology*, vol. 7, pp. 157-72.

Bart, P. B. and O'Brien, P. H. (1981), 'A Study of Women Who Were Both Raped and Avoided Rape', *Journal of Social Issues*, vol. 37, pp. 123-37.

Bart, P. B. and O'Brien, P. H. (1985), *Stopping Rape: Successful Survival Strategies*, Pergamon, New York.

Boeringer, S. B., Shehan, C. L. and Akers, R. L. (1991), 'Severity of Sentence, Social Contexts, and Sexual Labeling in Sexual Coercion and Aggression: Assessing the Contribution of Fraternity Membership', *Family Relations*, vol. 40(1), pp. 58-65.

Bourque, L. B. (1989), *Defining Rape*, Duke University Press, Durham, NC.

Bridges, J. S. and McGrail, C. A. (1989), 'Attributions of Responsibility for Date and Stranger Rape', *Sex Roles*, vol. 21(3/4), pp. 273-86.

Brinson, S. L. (1992), 'The Use and Opposition of Rape Myths in Prime Time Television Dramas', *Sex Roles: A Journal of Research*, vol. 27, pp. 359-76.

Brownmiller, S. (1975), *Against Our Will: Men, Women, and Rape*, Simon and Schuster, New York.

Burgess, A. W. and Holmstrom, L. L. (1974), 'Rape Trauma Syndrome', *American Journal of Psychiatry*, vol. 131, pp. 981-6.

Burgess, A.W. and Holmstorm, L. L. (1983), 'The Rape Victim in the Emergency Ward', *American Journal of Nursing*, vol. 73(10), pp. 1740-5.

Burt, M. R. (1980), 'Cultural Myths and Supports for Rape', *Journal of Personality and Social Psychology*, vol. 38, pp. 217-34.

Burt, M. R. and Alkin, R. S. (1981), 'Rape Myths and Support for Rape', *Journal of Personality and Social Psychology*, vol. 38, pp. 217-30.

Check, J. V. and Malamuth, N. M. (1981), 'Feminism and Rape in the 80's: Recent Research Findings', in P. Caplan, C. Larson and L. Cammaert (eds), *Psychology Changing for Women*, Eden Press Women's Publications, Montreal.

Cherry, F. (1983), 'Gender Roles and Sexual Violence', in E. R. Allgeier and N. B. McCormick (eds), *Changing Boundaries: Gender Roles and Sexual Behavior*, Mayfield, Palo Alto, CA.

Deitz, S. R. (1980, fall), 'Double Jeopardy: The Rape Victim in court', *Rocky Mountain Psychologist*, pp. 1-11.

Dull, R. T. and Giacopassi, D. J. (1987), 'Demographic Correlates of Sexual and Dating Attitudes: A Study of Date Rape', *Criminal Justice and Behavior*, vol. 14(2), pp. 175-193.

Ellis, E. M., Atkeson, B. M. and Calhoun, K. S. (1981), 'An Assessment of Long-term Reaction to Rape', *Journal of Abnormal Psychology*, vol. 90, pp. 263-6.

Felson, R. B. (1991), 'Blame Analysis: Accounting for the Behavior of Protected Groups', *The American Sociologist*, vol. 22, pp. 5-23.

Fenstermaker, S. (1988), 'Acquaintance rape on campus: Attributions of Responsibility and Crime', in M. Pirog-Good and J. Stets (eds), *Violence in Dating Relationships* (pp.

257-71), Praeger, New York.

Field, H. S. (1978), 'Attitudes toward Rape: A Comparative Analysis of Police, Rapist, Crisis Counselors, and Citizens', *Journal of Personality and Social Psychology*, vol. 36, 156-179.

Fischer, G. J. (1986a), 'College Student Attitudes toward Forcible Date Rape: Changes After Taking a Human Sexuality Course', *Journal of Sex Education and Therapy*, vol. 12(1), pp. 42-6.

Fischer, G. (1986b), 'College Student Attitudes toward Forcible Rape. I. Cognitive Predictors', *Archives of Sexual Behavior*, vol. 15, pp. 457-66.

Fischer, G. J. (1987), 'Hispanic and Majority Student Attitudes toward Forcible Date Rape as a Function of Differences in Attitudes toward Women', *Sex Roles*, vol. 17(1 / 2), pp. 93-101.

Foley, L. A., Evancic, C., Karnik, K., King, J. and Parks, A. (1995), Date rape: Effects of Race of Assailant and Victim and Gender of Subjects on Perceptions', *Journal of Black Psychology*, vol. 21, pp. 6-19.

Garcia, L. T., Milano, L. and Quijano, A. (1989). 'Perceptions of Coercive Sexual Behavior by Males and Females, *Sex Roles*, vol. 21, pp. 569-77.

Gerdes, E. P., Dammann, E. J. and Heilig, K. E. (1988), Perceptions of Rape Victims and Assailants: Effects of Physical Attractiveness, Acquaintance, and Subject Gender, *Sex Roles*, vol. 19(3/4), pp. 141-53.

Giacopassi, D. J. and Dull, R. T. (1986), 'Gender and Racial Differences in the Acceptance of Rape Myths within a College Population', *Sex Roles*, vol. 15(1 / 2), pp. 63-75.

Giarrusso, R., Johnson, P., Goodchilds, J. and Zellman, G. (1979, April), 'Adolescents' Cues and Signals: Sex and Assault', in Acquaintance Rape and Adolescent Sexuality Symposium, presented at the meeting of the Western Psychological Association, San Diego (P. Johnson, Chair).

Gordon, G. and Riger, S. (1989), *The Female Fear*, The Free Press, New York.

Griffin, S. (1971), 'The All-American Crime', *Ramparts*, vol. 10, pp. 26-35.

Holmstrom, L. L. and Burgess, A. W. (1978), *The Victim of Rape: Institutional Reactions*, Wiley, New York.

Jackson, S. (1978), 'The Social Context of Rape: Sexual Scripts and Motivation', *Women's Studies International Quarterly*, vol. 1, pp. 27-38.

Jenkins, M. and Dambrot, F. (1987), 'The Attribution of Date Rape: Observers' Attitudes and Sexual Experiences and the Dating Situation', *Journal of Applied Social Psychology*, vol. 17, pp. 875-95.

Jensen, L. A. (1993), *College Student's Attitudes toward Acquaintance Rape: The Effects of a Prevention Intervention Using Cognitive Dissonance Theory*, Unpublished doctoral dissertation, University of Alabama, Tuscaloosa, AL.

Johnson, J. D. and Jackson, L. A., Jr. (1988), 'Assessing the Effects of Factors that Might Underlie the Differential Perception of Acquaintance and Stranger Rape', *Sex Roles*, vol. 19(1 / 2), pp. 37-45.

Johnson, K. (1995), 'Attributions about Date Rape: Impact of Clothing, Sex, Money Spent, Date Type, and Perceived Similarity', *Family and Consumer Sciences Research Journal*, vol. 23 (3), pp. 293-11.

Kanekar, S. and Kolsawalla, M. (1980), 'Responsibility of a Rape Victim in Relation to her Respectability, Attractiveness, and Provocativeness', *Journal of Social Psychology*, vol. 112, pp. 153-4.

Kanin, E. J. (1985), 'Date Rapists: Differential Sexual Socialization and Relative Deprivation', *Archives of Sexual Behavior*, vol. 14(3), pp. 219-31.

Katz, B. L. and Burt, M. R. (1986, August), *Effects of Familiarity with the Rapist on Postrape Recovery*, presented at the annual meeting of the American Psychological Association, Washington, DC.

Klemmack, S. H. and Klemmack, D. L. (1976), 'The Social Definition of Rape', in *Sexual Assault* (pp. 135-147), Lexington Books, Lexington, MA.

Korman, S. K. (1983), 'Nontraditional Dating Behavior: Date-Initiation and Date Expense-sharing among Feminists and Nonfeminists', *Family Relations*, vol. 32, pp. 575-81.

Korman, S. K. and Leslie, G. (1982), 'The Relationship of Feminist Ideology and Date Expense Sharing to Perceptions of Sexual Aggression in Dating', *Journal of Sex Research*, vol. 18 (2), 114-129.

Kormos, K. C. and Brooks, C. I. (1994), 'Acquaintance rape: Attributions of Victim Blame by College Students and Prison Inmates as a Function of Relationship Status of Victim and Assailant', *Psychological Reports*, vol. 74, pp. 545-6.

Koss, M., Dinero, T., Seibel, C. and Cox, S. (1988), 'Stranger and Acquaintance Rape: Are There Differences in the Victim's Experience?', *Psychology of Women Quarterly*, vol. 12(1 / 2), pp. 1-24.

Koss, M. P., Gidycz, C. A. and Wisniewski, N. (1987), The Scope of Rape: Incidence and Prevalence of Sexual Aggression and Victimization in a National Sample of Higher Education Students', *Journal of Counseling and Clinical Psychology*, vol. 55, pp. 162-70.

Koss, M. P. and Leonard, K. E. (1984), 'Sexually Aggressive Men: Empirical Findings and Theoretical Implications', in N. M. Malamuth and E. Donnerstein (eds), *Pornography and Sexual Aggression*, Academic Press, Orlando, FL.

Krulewitz, J. and Payne, E. (1978), 'Attributions about Rape: Effects of Rapist Force, Observer Sex, and Sex Role Attitudes', *Journal of Applied Social Psychology*, vol. 8, pp. 291-305.

L'Armand, K. L. and Pepitone, A. (1982), 'Judgments of Rape: A Study of Victim-rapist Relationship and Victim Sexual History', *Personality and Social Psychology Bulletin*, vol. 8(1), pp. 134-9.

Loh, W. (1980), 'The Impact of Common Law and Reform Rape Statutes on Prosecutions: An Empirical Study', *Washington Law Review*, pp. 552-613.

Margolin, L., Miller, M. and Moran, P. (1989), 'When a Kiss is Not Just a Kiss: Relating Violations of Consent in Kissing to Rape Myth Acceptance', *Sex Roles*, vol. 20(5/6), pp. 231-43.

McCaul, K. D., Veltum, L. G., Boyechko, V., and Crawford, J. J. (1990), 'Understanding Attributions of Victim Blame for Rape: Sex, Violence, and Foreseeability', *Journal of Applied Social Psychology*, vol. 20(1), pp. 1-26.

Medea, A. and Thompson, K. (1974), *Against Rape*, Farrar, Straus & Giroux, New York.

Muehlenhard, C. L. (1988), 'Misinterpreted Dating Behaviors and the Risk of Date Rape', *Journal of Social and Clinical Psychology*, vol. 6(1), pp. 20-37.

Muehlenhard, C. L., Friedman, D. E. and Thomas, C. M. (1985), 'Is Date Rape Justifiable? The Effects of Dating Activity, Who Initiated, Who Paid, and Men's Attitudes toward Women, *Psychology of Women Quarterly*, vol. 9(3), pp. 297-310.

Muehlenhard, C. L. and Hollabaugh, L. C. (1988), 'Do Women Sometimes Say No When They Mean Yes? The Prevalence and Correlates of Women's Token Resistance to Sex', *Journal of Personality and Social Psychology*, vol. 54, pp. 872-878.

Parrot, A. (1986), *Acquaintance Rape and Sexual Assault Prevention Training Manual* (2nd ed), Cornell University Press, New York.

Parrot, A. and Bechhofer, L. (1991), *Acquaintance Rape: The Hidden Crime*, John Wiley & Sons, Inc., New York.

Richardson, D. C. and Campbell, J. C. (1982), 'Alcohol and Rape: The Effect of Alcohol on Attribution of Blame for Rape', *Personality and Social Psychology Bulletin*, vol. 8, pp. 468-476.

Russell, D. E. H. (1975), *The Politics of Rape*, Stein & Day, New York.

Russell, D. E. H. (1982), *Rape in Marriage*, Stein & Day, New York.

Sandberg, G. G., Jackson, T. L. and Petretic-Jackson, P. (1987), 'College Students Attitudes Regarding Sexual Coercion and Aggression: Developing Educational and Preventive Strategies', *Journal of College Student Personnel*, vol. 28, pp. 302-11.

Seligman, C., Brickman, J. and Koulack, D. (1977), 'Rape and Physical Attractiveness: Assigning Responsibility to Victims', *Journal of Personality*, vol. 45, pp. 555-63.

Shotland, R. L. and Goodstein, L. (1983), 'Just Because She Doesn't Want to Doesn't Mean it's Rape: An Experimentally Based Causal Model of the Perception of Rape in a Dating Situation', *Social Psychology Quarterly*, vol. 46, pp. 222-32.

Shotland, R. L. and Goodstein, L. (1992), 'Sexual Precedence Reduces the Perceived Legitimacy of Sexual Refusal: An Examination of Attributions Concerning Date Rape and Consensual Sex', *Personality and Social Psychology Bulletin*, vol. 18(6), pp. 756-65.

Sigler, R. T. and Haygood, D. (1987), 'The Criminalization of Forced Marital Intercourse', *Marriage and Family Review*, vol. 12(1-2): pp. 71-86.

Smith, R. E., Pine, C. J. and Hawley, M. E. (1988), 'Social Cognitions about Adult Male Victims of Female Sexual Assault', *Journal of Sex Research*, vol. 24, pp. 101-12.

Stacy, R. D., Prisbell, M. and Tollefsrud, K. (1992), 'A Comparison of Attitudes among College Students toward Sexual Violence Committed by Strangers and by Acquaintances: A Research Report', *Journal of Sex Education and Therapy*, vol. 18, pp. 257-63.

Stuntz, E. C. (1975), 'Women's Reactions to Rape', *Smith College Studies in Social Work*, vol. 46, pp. 35-6.

Tetreault, P. A. and Barnett, M. A. (1987), 'Reactions to Stranger and Acquaintance Rape', *Psychology of Women Quarterly*, vol. 11, pp. 353-8.

Warshaw, R. (1988), *I Never Called it Rape*, Harper and Row, New York.

Weis, K. and Borges, S. S. (1973), 'Victimology and Rape: The Case of the Legitimate Victim', *Issues in Criminology*, vol. 8, pp. 71-115.

Weis, K. and Weis, S. (1975), 'Victimology and Justification of Rape', in I. Drapkin and E. Viano (eds), *Victimology: A New Focus*, Vol. 5, Heath: Lexington, MA.

Yarmey, A. D. (1985), 'Older and Younger Adults' Attributions of Responsibility toward Rape Victims and Rapists', *Canadian Journal of Behavioral Science*, vol. 17, pp. 327-38.

6 Theories and Models Addressing Forced Sexual Intercourse

Introduction

Forced sexual intercourse has been growing steadily in importance as an area of concern for scholars, social service personnel, and criminal justice personnel. The definition of women's roles and the social values which define the relationships between men and women have been changing. These changes have been a result of the contemporary feminist movement, which has identified cultural and legal precedents that have reduced a woman's freedom and made her dependent upon and under the control of the males in her environment (Brownmiller, 1975). This control includes the use of reasonable physical force (Dobash & Dobash, 1979). In the process of creating an atmosphere for change, proponents of women's rights sought to introduce accountability into the social service and justice systems for dealing effectively with complaints addressing physical and sexual abuse of women (Dobash & Dobash, 1979). These agencies responded to these concerted challenges by moving to adopt policies and practices which were more sympathetic to female victims of domestic violence, courtship violence, and forced sexual intercourse. In the process, rape, the intentional or planned use of physical force to obtain sexual access against the wishes of a woman who was not intimately involved with her assailant, has been redefined to the extent that rape is no longer an accurate characterization of the behaviors which can be addressed by the justice system on the complaint of a victim.

The definition of rape which was common in the first half of this century has been expanded to include types of forced sexual intercourse which, in the past, were held to be of no interest to the justice system and to include offensive sexual behaviors less than intercourse. Sexual assault, the emerging concept, is broad, has been widely accepted, and specifies degrees of offensiveness. There is some recognition that offensive sexual behavior

103

and forced sexual intercourse can be placed on a continuum based on degree of unacceptability of the offensive behavior. The perspective which will be presented here suggests that the continuum is broader than generally accepted and may include offensive sexual behaviors which are tolerated by some of the victims. That is, some offensive sexual behavior occurs in the context of courtship and dating and is accepted to some degree by some of the victims.

Prior to the 1980s, theories which sought to explain rape were based on those cases in which a stranger forcibly attacked and sexually assaulted a relatively unknown victim. These theories tended to explain sexual assaults in terms of mental illness and generally asserted that rape was more a matter of dominance and control of women than a matter of gaining sexual access.

In the 1980s, three major works addressed the broader range of behaviors which had emerged as behaviors that were sufficiently unacceptable that they should be subjected to the control of the justice system. Sunday and Tobach (1985) addressed the sociobiological approach to violence against women, including rape. Ellis (1989) shifted the emphasis from predatory stranger rape to acquaintance rape and recognized the influence of the feminist perspective as originally advanced by Brownmiller (1975). He grouped explanations for forced sexual intercourse into three general theoretical perspectives: feminist theory, learning theory, and evolutionary theory. At the same time, Baron and Straus (1989) also sought to present theories which reflected the broader definition of rape which had emerged by the 1980s. They grouped explanations for sexual assault into four general theoretical perspectives: gender inequality, pornography, social disorganization, and legitimate violence. Readers who seek more comprehensive coverage of these perspectives should review these three earlier works as well as Brownmiller's 1975 book, *Against Our Will: Men, Women, and Rape.*

This chapter will briefly review the theoretical perspectives advanced by these and other authors. In addition, theories of aggression and violence will be reviewed, as the foundation for most theories of sexual assault appears to assume some level of aggression and/or acceptance of violence. The chapter will conclude with the presentation of a preliminary model which the authors' advance as one basis for model development which can be used to frame continuing research in this area. The model assumes that the use of force in sexual intercourse is not a single type of phenomena and that forced sexual intercourse can be understood best if conceptualized as related sets of phenomena which are substantially different in terms of definition of the situation by men and women, psychological damage, and controlling factors.

The Definition of Violence

Most approaches to the explanation of forced sexual intercourse assume that the events can be characterized as violent and/or aggressive acts. Violence and aggression tend to be linked in most theoretical approaches. In spite of this, or perhaps because of it, definitions of aggression and violence are often unclear (Siann, 1985). First, the term aggression is more a part of the common vocabulary than a part of the scientific vocabulary and has considerable common usage. As is frequently the case with terms in social science, the colloquial uses vary from the technical definitions, introducing confusion when terms are not defined clearly in specific reports. In addition, questions as to intent, affective orientation, and motivation introduce additional confusion.

The most common usages of aggression involve concepts of power, dominance, defense of territory, or the imposition of the will of one person on another. Siann's (1985) definitions are suitable for placing aggression and violence in context. She suggests that "aggression involves the intention to hurt or emerge superior to others, does not necessarily involve physical injury and may or may not be regarded as being underpinned by different kinds of motives" (p 12). She goes on to define violence as involving "the use of great physical force or intensity" and says that "while it is often impelled by aggressive motivation, [it] may be used occasionally by individuals engaged in a mutual violent interaction which is regarded by both parties as intrinsically rewarding" (p 12). In these definitions, the use of physical force may be an instrument of aggression, but violence can occur outside of the context of aggression, and aggression can occur without violence. In much the same way, sexual assault can be an act of aggression; however, it may be non-aggressive. In the context of sexual assault, it is possible, in some cases, that the use of physical force or violence in sexual interaction can be understood better as a ritual exchange or as being a "normal" process for the actors rather than as aggression.

Perspectives on Violence through History

It can be argued that the use of physical force (violence) is commonly and widely accepted as appropriate behavior, which reduces the ability of victims of sexual assault to seek redress whenever physical force is used against them. Whether a specific act or the use of physical force is "right" or "wrong" is determined by the context and by the intent of the actor(s). Support for this position can be found in historical as well as contemporary perspectives (Brown, 1969). It is also obvious that even the most extreme forms of violence have been justified in the name of the greater good. Organized violence in the form of war generally is accepted, whether the target be Hitler in World War II or the American Indians in the Indian wars. The support for these activities is and has been used to justify other organized acts of violence committed in the name of the stabilization of the frontier and the establishment of the rights of the laborer (Brown, 1969). The use of extreme physical violence by posses, vigilantes, and unions has been both praised and condemned, depending on the times. Group violence is good or bad depending on the beliefs of the public at the time.

It has been argued that the immigrant nature of our society has produced a condition in which violent resolution of differences between different immigrant groups, including newcomers and established groups, could be expected and has been so common that it is accepted as normal (Graham & Gurr, 1969). During a 300-year process of settlement of our country, the Indians were defeated, European presences were forced to withdraw, some Mexicans were forcibly annexed, and immigrant minorities were forced into fierce competition. The result has been a legacy of nativism, vigilantism, and ethnic aggression (Gurr & Graham, 1969, pp. 80-81).

The frontier created a condition which fostered a legitimization of violence. The frontier extended beyond civilization and beyond the control of established law and order. Social control was essentially informal, and individuals protected their persons and their property with their own resources. The use of force was commended when those property rights had to be protected from Native Americans who expressed competing rights and extended to protecting property rights from other new Americans. When concerted community action was required, vigilante committees, courts, or posses were formed and justice was dispensed (Frantz, 1969).

Vigilantism is an established American tradition which existed in the early colonies as well as in the western frontier and continuously has been held in high regard (Brown, 1969). The level of physical force authorized in this context was extreme but was usually held to be good or justifiable even when poorly supported by the facts of the situation (Brown, 1969). These acts of vigilantism consistently have been characterized in this manner in popular literature (Lynn, 1969). Outlaws, marshals, posses, miners' courts, and their adventurous activities have been immortalized in film and print. Stories stress the courageous, independent, self-justifying nature of the American character and provide unending examples in which violence is good if the cause is good and if the actor is good.

The emergence of labor in the United States has been more violent than in other parts of the world (Taft & Ross, 1969). Most of the violence has been directed toward strikebreakers or striking employees, with acts against employers tending to be characterized as acts against property. Conflicts between strikers and strikebreakers have been particularly violent. In one instance, striking miners ambushed a train which was bringing strikebreakers to open a mine closed by the strikers. Almost all of the strikebreakers were killed, with only a few of those who were fleet of foot successfully escaping (Angle, 1952). This ambush is still excused as an appropriate response in the communities surrounding the site, even though it occurred so long ago that none of those involved are still alive. The use of violence to gain labor goals began with the emergence of the labor movement in the late 1800s and continues today. Each year there are stories in the news of shots fired and occasional deaths of strikebreakers in a labor dispute. This violence is accepted as legitimate by the general public and justified as necessary and appropriate by representatives of organized labor. Efforts to separate the organizations themselves from the violence have more to do with liability than with a belief that the acts themselves are wrong.

An acceptance of violence as appropriate behavior is rooted in ample historical precedent. While much of the material presented here reports the approved use of violence by groups, the underlying values created support individual use of violence. If violence is acceptable if the reasons for the violence can be characterized as acceptable and individual initiative and independence are valued, then individuals should be able to decide to use violence if that use is justified by the circumstances. This reasoning can be seen most clearly in the self-defense argument and other collateral defenses in our legal system. That is, the use of force is justified in a number of circumstances, with diminished capacity and the heat of passion included in the list of rationales which mediate responsibility. The position is embedded sufficiently in our culture that the question is not should force be used but, rather, what are the circumstances under which force can be used. Every

American believes that he or she has the right to use force to deal with his or her problems. The differences between those who believe that they have the right to use force to protect their lives, those who believe that they have the right to use force to protect their property, and those who believe that they have the right to use force to gain publicity for their political beliefs or to meet their personal needs is simply a matter of degree. That is, each of these individuals would assert that his or her cause is right, therefore, her or his use of force is right.

While the level of violence tolerated has varied from time to time and from place to place, the use of violence in intimate relationships has been tolerated persistently throughout history. Tolerance is not and should not be equated with approval. While violent acts among intimates have been defined as private family matters, they have not been prescribed in most cases. Until quite recently, the use of force to gain sexual access in intimate relationships was not controlled by the justice system. Although society's tolerance for the use of force in intimate relationships has declined, it should not be assumed that the "new" definitions are universally accepted. That is, there are still those who accept or define the use of violence in intimate relationships as private, not criminal, behavior.

In this context, the use of physical force in intimate relationships can be seen as acceptable by some actors and by some in society who argue that these matters are private and of no interest to the justice system. As society's recognition of the rights of women has matured, willingness to accept the use of physical force by men to control women has come to be defined more and more as a public matter and legally unacceptable. However, as was indicated in Chapter 5, attitudes which have been measured in recent studies involving victims, offenders, and the general public accept the use of physical force to gain sexual access in specific situations. While we may decry this argument as regressive and completely unacceptable, we must recognize that the general acceptance of violence and the limited acceptance of the use of force in specific situations in intimate relations exists and influences the behavior of those whom we study and whose behavior we seek to understand.

Explanations for Violent Acts

Explanations for the occurrence of violent acts are exceptionally varied, ranging from explanations which are based in the biological make-up of human beings to those which are based in various learning theories.

Biological theories tend to link tendencies to violence with a biological dysfunction. They generally are concerned only with extreme acts of violence and, at times, assume that aggression and lesser violence is relatively normal. The list of factors which can cause a person to exhibit violent behavior include: genetics or the "bad seed", including the XYY factor; dysfunctions of the limbic areas of the brain; epilepsy related disorders; head injuries; and biochemical and endocrinal imbalances (Siann, 1985). Many of the earlier theories of rape, which focused on explaining cases of predatory stranger rape, tended to accept the assumptions of one or more of these perspectives.

Ethnological and sociobiological approaches link violence with aggression, treating violence as an extension or consequence of aggression. Lorenz (1966) developed the theoretical perspective which was subsequently adapted by the sociobiologists which links violence and aggression to instinctual behavior. The sociobiologists posit an instinct for aggression (the fighting instinct) which is directed against other members of the same species and results from natural selection (the survival of the fittest) and protecting one's territory. A variation of this perspective was developed by Ardrey (1966) who suggested that man exhibits violence because he has an instinct to develop increasingly efficient weapons which, as a territorial animal, he uses to defend his territory. While Ardrey's work is less rigorous than that of Lorenz, both perspectives can be seen to have influenced the work of Wilson (1975) and other sociobiologists (Siann, 1985). Wilson's (1975) work attempts to apply the concepts of evolution to social behavior. Aggression and the attendant violence are instinctual responses which have been selected for their survival value as man struggled for survival in his environment. These instincts are expressed in terms of emotions which are determined by genetic predispositions.

The psychoanalytic perspective holds that aggression is an instinctual drive. Freud asserted that aggression was related to sadism. In his later work, aggression emerged as an element in the resistance of *thanatos* or the striving for death (Siann, 1985). The mechanism works by directing self-destructive forces outward. Aggression is related to both sadism (turning the destructive forces outward) and masochism (turning the destructive forces inward). Freud's work in aggression was a minor part of his overall work and had little impact until it was expanded by Storr (1968) and Fromm (1977).

Storr (1968) suggested that aggression is essential for survival and is broad, encompassing many different behaviors. Storr's model of aggression includes inquisitiveness, controversy, and competition. Storr is consistent with traditional psychoanalytic theory in that he holds that the manner in which the individual handles this basic instinct is determined by early development and can be distorted to form psychopathology. Aggression can be normal or can appear in distorted or extreme forms which are mental illnesses. While Fromm's (1977) work is more complex and differs in detail from Storr's, he also accepts these basic psychoanalytic principles. Fromm does have several categories of benign or positive aggression which are related to defense, unintentional harm, conformist aggression, or self-assertive aggression. Fromm's perspective identifies most aggression as normal, with pathological aggression occurring less frequently.

Siann (1985, p. 130) has summarized the psychoanalytic perspective regarding aggression and violence. Aggression is seen as instinctual, involving either hurting or dominance, potentially non-physical, having both positive and negative aspects, potentially normal, and, when problems occur in development, potentially psychopathological.

Violence, in the psychoanalytical perspective, involves the use of great or intense physical force. With the exception of Fromm, psychoanalysts see violence as motivated by a drive for aggression. Violence can be used in mutually rewarding exchanges, with acts occurring in the sexual context emphasized.

Bandura (1973) has focused on aggression from the modeling perspective, a drive-based, psychoanalytic, social learning theory. His research indicates that aggression is learned by observing others perform aggressive acts. The observer learns or models the behavior of the actor. From this perspective, a drive exists which is channeled by the environment in which all behaviors are learned responses for drive reduction and are environment specific. As his work matured, Bandura moved from a focus on drive to a focus on learning and reinforcement.

Baron (1977) developed the concept of social determinants by combining the work of the social learning theorists with other psychological perspectives. He argued that aggressive behavior is a drive response mediated by factors such as frustration, emotional arousal, experience of physical pain, modeling, and pressures toward conformity. Baron stressed that aggression is learned and suggested that the treatment of aggression involves controlled exposure to violence and aggression and reinforcement of non-violent behaviors in the child-rearing process. The environment needs to be reshaped so that children are not exposed to aggression and violence and so that they are exposed to non-aggressive and non-violent models. The environment must also provide positive or acceptable outlets for dissipating arousal responses.

Sociologists generally have been less inclined than other social scientists to address violence and aggression directly. In sociological theory, violence and aggression often are addressed in terms of broader theory or from a descriptive perspective. An exception has been the work of Wolfgang and Ferracuti (1967) who asserted that violence occurs in a subculture which is supportive of violence. That is, violence is more likely to occur in some subcultures than in others. Values, norms, roles, and expectations establish a condition which predisposes the members of the subculture to the use of physical force in some situations. In low income subcultures, commitment to subcultural values commits young men, in particular, to regard the exchange of physical force as illustrating daring and courage and the avoidance of fighting as non-masculine behavior leading to ostracization from the group. For these young men, most violent behavior is caused by adherence to cultural values that endorse or prescribe violence as appropriate in a particular context. From this perspective, violence is normal, not pathological.

Toch (1977) and Sutherland and Cressey (1974) accept the influence of the cultural context but place the violence in a broader context. While Sutherland and Cressey focus on the acquisition of criminal behavior, they suggest that all behaviors are learned based on differential exposure to expectations and behaviors in the environment. From this perspective, aggression and violence are learned behaviors which are seen as correct, appropriate, or right in a particular context.

Toch (1977) focused on violent individuals rather than on violence as a general behavior. While he accepted the importance of the social context in which the individual is immersed as a determinant in the development of violent behavior, he focused on attitudes toward violence and the expectations held for violent behavior by violent offenders. Toch's analysis focused on the perceptions of violent exchanges held by both criminals and police officers who had a history of use of physical force. From the analysis of his interviews ten types emerged based on the dimensions of maintaining a reputation, conformity, enhancement of self-esteem or self-concept, self-defense, conflict resolution or problem solving, bullying, exploitation, self-satisfaction or pleasure, and catharsis. Violence can be habitual or occur without thought or planning when environmental circumstances provide the appropriate cues. The tendency toward violence varies from man to man, with some men identified as having a violence-prone orientation. Toch recommends that men who are violence prone should be exposed to treatment programs designed to change their orientation toward violence.

For most criminologists with a sociological orientation, violence is another dimension of the broader field of deviance. Research and theory tends to focus on general explanations of sets of behavior which are unacceptable to society. Criminality is linked with anomie (Merton, 1957), subcultural values (Cohen, 1955; Cloward & Ohlin, 1960), youthful alienation (Matza, 1964), social expectations (Lemert, 1951; Becker, 1963), or culture conflict (Miller, 1976). Most of these perspectives consider violence as a peripheral issue or product of a social condition or don't consider violence at all. Crime is regarded by most of these theorists as a natural result of the social context in which it occurs. While there may be differences of opinion about what is right and wrong, for the actor, his or her criminal behavior (violence) is an acceptable or expected behavior.

Discussions which focus on differences between men and women in aggression and violence consistently stress that excessive aggression and violence tend to be primarily a male phenomena. A review of the preceding section will reveal that frequently when the theorist speaks of the violent man, he or she is using the term in the sexual sense, not in the sense of mankind. The difference in aggression between men and women has been attributed to chemical differences occurring at puberty (Moyer, 1976) with some support for those who argue for castration as a treatment (Mazur, 1983); however, the experimental evidence generally does not support such a course of action. Sex differences in animals, in terms of aggression, have been used to explain this difference between males and females in aggression; nevertheless, there are exceptions in the animal kingdom, particularly in primates (Siann, 1985). The psychoanalysts base their definition of men as aggressive and women as passive in psychosexual development and in differing drives and drive levels in men and women (Siann, 1985). Experimental evidence regarding different levels of violence in the laboratory is also inconclusive. The areas in which there is consistent support for the differences between men and women include crime statistics (and this is changing), observational field studies, and ethnographies. It is possible that any differences between men and women in terms of aggression and violence are created during the socialization process. That is, they are learned.

Explanations for violence are varied, identifying causes ranging from biological agents to social pressure. The one thing that all of these explanations have in common is an acceptance of the normality of violence.

That is, violence in the right amounts and in the right context is either good, acceptable, or to be expected. The rightness or wrongness of violence in each case is determined by factors such as degree, nature of the intent, social setting, expectations, the need for self-protection, or for the protection of property. It is in this framework that scholars and practitioners work, and it is a framework that contributes additional confusion to an already confusing situation.

Explaining Forced Sexual Intercourse

The Feminist Perspective

Much of the reform in the manner in which society relates to women has been and should be attributed to the feminist movement. The feminist movement is addressed here in its broader sense rather than in the restricted negative advocacy sense that it is frequently addressed. In this sense, the feminist movement is a relatively broad, loosely-centralized set of groups which seek to document the manner in which women are disadvantaged and abused by the existing social systems and value systems. These groups seek to change the laws, rules, procedures, and practices that limit the ability of women to function at their full potential. At times, the feminist movement is characterized by the more disturbing attributes of the more radical groups which form this loosely structured movement.

To some extent, it can be said that feminists argue that sexual assault is defined as legitimate or normal in male-dominated societies. It is possible, however, to argue that the behaviors themselves are not defined as acceptable but, rather, they are defined as personal or private and not of interest to those outside the family. That is, men who abuse their wives are not defined as good, but the offensive behavior which they exhibit is defined as beyond the control of society. From this perspective, the infamous rule of thumb reported by Brownmiller (1975) and persistently repeated in the literature can be defined as feminist reform rather than as a definition of wife abuse as prescribed behavior. Laws of this type, as unacceptable as they might be seen today, were designed to place limits on male abuse of the women under their control. The ability to abuse had been unlimited prior to the enactment of the various laws/court decisions and might have reflected an early movement toward recognizing/redefining women's rights.

Feminist theorists argue that patriarchal societies define men as dominant over women. Women are assigned inferior social status, with relatively little power, while men are socially superior and dominate and control women (Dobash & Dobash, 1979; Friedan, 1963). Men's power over women historically was defined as not subject to control by society in even the most severe of instances, thus came to be perceived as a right or, at least, as a privilege exercised by men. In this context, forced sexual intercourse becomes more a matter of dominance and control than a matter of sex (Brownmiller, 1975; Goth, 1979; Holmstrom & Burgess, 1980; Riger & Gordon, 1981; Scarpitti & Scarpitti, 1977). Men (male dominated society) use the fear of rape to allow men to assert their dominance over women and rape to control non-conforming women as a means of maintaining the patriarchal system of male dominance (Adamec & Adamec, 1981; Barry, 1979; Brownmiller, 1975; Goth, 1979; Persell, 1984; Riger & Gordon, 1981; Russell, 1975; Thompson & Buttell, 1984; Weis & Borges, 1977). Studies supporting the feminist perspective have tended to measure the incidence of rape in relation to incidents of violence in general (Benderly, 1982; Baron & Straus, 1984; Kutchinski, 1988; Sanday, 1981; Schwendinger & Schwendinger, 1985; Sigelman, Berry, & Wiles, 1984). Self-report studies which ask rapists to report their motivation tend to contradict the feminist model. They find that rapists report motivation by desire for excitement, risk taking, and sex (Scully & Marolla, 1984) and report high levels of deviant sexual fantasies (Walker & Meyer, 1981), with high levels of sexual arousal reported by date rapists (Yegidis, 1986).

To some extent, the feminist perspective can be seen as an application of social learning theory. Some authors suggest that traditional gender roles and expectations define forced sexual intercourse as a normal aspect of male-female interaction, thus encourage rape (Burt, 1980; Check & Malamuth, 1983a; Cherry, 1983; Curtis, 1975; Russell, 1975; Weis & Borges, 1977). Norms which define masculinity in terms of dominance and control and femininity in terms of passivity and submission define the use of force by men to control women as gender role expectations which support or encourage forced sexual intercourse (Gagnon & Simon, 1973).

Pornography has been advanced as a cause of rape by both feminists and non-feminists. There are two bases for arguing that pornography increases the incidence of forced sexual intercourse. First, the influence of pornography can be subtle and subjective. The mere presence of pornography as an acceptable medium of recreation/entertainment emphasizes the sexual nature of women, which is related to dominance by men and reinforces the patriarchal male-dominated social and value systems that permit men to use force in their intimate relationships with women and perpetuate attitudes that are supportive of forced sexual intercourse (Allen, M., Emmers, Giery, 1995; Barry, 1979; Brownmiller, 1975; Diamond, 1980; Dworkin, 1981; MacKinnon, 1986; Morgan, 1980; Wheeler, 1985). Some feminist and non-feminist learning theorists argue that exposure to pornography which depicts the use of violence in sexual relationships increases the incidence of forced sexual intercourse (Barry, 1979; Donnerstein & Barrett, 1978a, 1978b; Donnerstein & Hallman, 1978; Dworkin, 1981; Longino, 1980; MacKinnon, 1986; Malamuth, Fesback, & Jaffe, 1977; Morgan, 1980; Schmidt & Sigusch, 1970; Schmidt, Sigusch, & Schafer, 1973; Tannenbaum, 1971).

Social Learning Theory

As was noted earlier, much of what is identified as a feminist explanation of forced sexual intercourse and much of the research and theory reported regarding the impact of pornography also can be identified as learning theory. Learning theory perspectives are relatively straightforward - forced sexual behavior is learned in the same ways that other behaviors are learned. Men who force women to have sex do so because they (and in some perspectives their victims) have learned that this is appropriate behavior. For the feminists, this learning is related to or associated with the set of values which supports the socioeconomic and political exploitation of women by men; non-feminist social learning theorists see forced sexual intercourse as related to or associated with cultural traditions linked with interpersonal aggression, masculine roles, and sexuality.

While learning theory is frequently a general term encompassing theories developed in a number of traditions including symbolic interaction and cognitive attitude theory, much of the work which addresses rape is derived from Bandura's (1973) drive-based, psychoanalytic modeling theory addressing aggression. Ellis (1989, pp. 12-13) states that social learning theories of rape which assert that rape is a form of aggression posit that these behaviors are learned in four ways: by imitating or modeling aggressive sexual behaviors which the learner has observed in real life or in media presentations (Nelson, 1982; Huesman & Malamuth, 1986b); by observing sex and violence in the same context or presentation (Check & Malamuth, 1986b; Malamuth 1980, 1984, 1986, 1988; Malamuth, Briere, & Check,

1986); by repeating or portraying rape myths that make rape acceptable (Burt, 1980); and by the desensitization of the learner to the victim's perspective through repetition of exposure to incidents of sex and violence or of violent sex (Donnerstein, Linz, & Penrod, 1987).

The Sociobiological Perspective

In its simplest form, the sociobiological perspective asserts that humanity is a product of evolution in which both physical and social traits conducive to survival are selected and survive through a process of natural selection. Propagation is key to survival of a trait as genetic predispositions only can be passed on through offspring. The linkage of sexual selection and rape with trait survival was first made by Deutsch (1944). Social traits which have been selected include female emphasis on child care and male emphasis on mating with as many partners as possible (Bateman, 1948; Chamove, Harlow, & Mitchell, 1967; Daly & Wilson, 1978; Hagen, 1979; Leshner, 1978; Smith, 1978; Symons, 1979; Trivers, 1972; Williams, 1975). From a sociobiological perspective, men have a lower commitment to gestation than women (Quinsey, 1984) but have a disadvantage in that they can not definitely identify their children (Daly & Wilson, 1978; Dawkins, 1976; Durden-Smith & deSimone, 1983), thus, an inclination to impregnate many females has gene survival value. From this it can be argued that forced sexual intercourse would increase the survival of a male's genes, selecting a tendency to rape (Gibson, Linden, & Johnson, 1980; Hagen, 1979; Quinsey, 1984; Symons, 1979). On the other hand, females who resist males who impregnate them and move on to other females are more likely to pass on their genes. The use of force to gain sexual access reduces the ability of a female to choose a mate who will stay with her after insemination. The absence of a male partner decreases the likelihood of survival of her children (Mellen, 1981; Richard & Schulman, 1982; Symons, 1979; Thornhill, 1980; Wilder, 1982). From this, rape would be particularly effective in modern times for men who have limited resources with which to attract a mate (Shields & Shields, 1983; Thornhill & Thornhill, 1983).

Social Disorganization and Legitimate Violence

Baron and Straus (1989) advanced two additional theoretical perspectives for explaining rape: social disorganization and legitimate violence. Social disorganization occurs when social institutions and norms that regulate social conduct become ineffective (Blumer, 1937; Martindale, 1957; Mower, 1941; Thomas & Zaniecki, 1927; Wirth, 1940). When society's social control is weakened, deviant behavior and crime, including rape, are more likely to occur. Baron & Straus (1989) constructed a social disorganization index and discovered that when their measure of social disorganization is high, rates of rape are high.

Legitimate violence begins with the recognition that some theoretical perspectives define rape as normatively permitted rather than as beyond the control of society as suggested earlier in this chapter. Baron and Straus (1989) noted that the feminists argue the presence of such norms (Brownmiller, 1975; Scully & Marolla, 1985).

Baron and Straus (1989) also noted that a number of perspectives suggest that the legitimacy of rape might be supported indirectly. They cited violent subculture theories (Gastil, 1971; Hackney, 1969; Messner, 1983; Wolfgang & Ferracuti, 1967) and cross-cultural theories which demonstrate a link between types of violence (Lambert, Triandis, & Wolf, 1959; Archer & Gartner, 1984; Huggins & Straus, 1980) and between violence and sexual violence (Sanday, 1981) as well as between violence and sexual violence in the United States (Amir, 1971). These findings were taken by Baron and Straus to support a cultural spillover theory of criminal violence. As the extent to which society approves the legitimate use violence in some areas increases, the use of violence in collateral areas, such as personal assault, and rape increase.

State of the Art

The theories which have been advanced to date treat forced sexual intercourse as a single type of behavior. As forced sexual intercourse is seen as a single thing, scholars have sought a single theory. The theories that have been developed tend to be most effective in explaining incidents of forced sexual intercourse in which a man intends to force a woman to have sex when she doesn't want to have sex, when physical force is used, and when the woman defines her victimization as rape. If the nature of the interaction between the victim and offender is such that forced sexual intercourse produces different sets of phenomena, then a single model theory will not be sufficient to describe accurately the phenomena under study.

Limited attention has been directed toward the development of theoretical models which address forced sexual intercourse in dating or courtship settings. Most studies with a theoretical base attempt to identify factors which make types of assault or adjustment more or less likely to occur. One recent effort (Shotland, 1992) developed a basic typology of date rape. Five different types of date rape are characterized, based on time, courtship violence, and degree of development of a relationship. Felson (1992) has developed a model which seeks to explain sexual assaults in terms of motives and goals. He identified five paths using factors, such as social identity, bodily pleasure, personal justice, domination, sexual relations, and harm to target.

The present theories which focus on rape are not effective in describing all of the events which presently are included under the terms date rape, acquaintance rape, and marital rape. In some incidents which are identified as date rape, a man intentionally forces a woman to have sex when she doesn't want to, using substantial force, and the woman defines her victimization as rape. In other instances which are identified as date rape, the man may not intend to force the woman to have sex, the degree of force may be less substantial, and the woman may not define her victimization as rape. In the first instance, a rape has occurred which can be explained with one or more of the existing models; the incident just happened to occur in a dating context. In the second instance, the behavior is offensive and unacceptable by standards which are emerging today, but the behavior can not be accurately explained with existing theories. The inability to describe the nature of the phenomena accurately reduces the ability to effectively address what is clearly a contemporary social problem.

The data available from studies of forced sexual intercourse consistently have identified sets of incidents in which the forced sexual intercourse reported by victims is not identified as rape, beginning with Russell's (1984) early study. About one-half of the women who indicated that they had experienced incidents which met the legal definition of rape in use at that time did not respond affirmatively when asked if they had been raped. Similar results were reported by a leading study in the area of date rape. Koss, Dinero, Seibel, and Cox (1988) reported 23.1 percent of the women victimized by men they knew labeled their victimization as rape, and 62 percent of these victims indicated that they did not view their victimization as any type of crime. Similar results have been reported by Johnson, Palileo, and Gray (1992), Doyle and Burfeind (1994), and other studies which report findings for women's characterizations of their victimization.

Similar findings have appeared in the authors' research. The contention that some incidents of forced sexual intercourse can be different from incidents codified in law as rape is supported by the perception of the incidents reported by both the victims and the offenders (see Table 6.1). One-half of the victims stated that they were not raped, 88 percent reported that they did not believe that the offender (their date) believed that he was raping them, and only 14 percent believed that their assailant planned to rape them when he made the date. Almost 80 percent of the offenders chose not to characterize their action as rape, about 9 percent reported that their dates believed that they had been raped, and only one reported that he had planned to rape his date at the time he made the date.

The victims were less likely to trust their assailants after the incident (92 percent to 26 percent), but about one-third of the victims continued to date their assailants. Offenders report less loss of trust (88 percent, 44 percent) and higher rates of continued dating (55 percent). More victims believed that their assailants planned to rape them than offenders reported planning to rape (see Table 6.1). Both men (86.5 percent) and women (84 percent) reported that a man could use force and believe that he was not committing rape. Victims were more likely to make positive statements (48.9 percent) when describing their assailants than negative statements (17.8 percent) or negative and mixed statements (26.7 percent). Men's statements describing their victims tended to be predominately positive (64.3 percent all positive statements) (see Table 6.2).

Table 6.1 Perceptions of the incident for most recent incident of forced sexual intercourse

Perception	Victims No.	Victims Percent	Offenders No.	Offenders Percent
Subject thinks rape*	35	48.3	2	8.7
Other thinks rape	8	11.1	5	20.8
Planned to rape*	6	14.0	1	10.0
Trust before	45	91.8	15	88.2
Trust after	14	25.9	8	44.4
Continue to date	17	32.1	10	55.6
Force not always rape	64	86.5	21	84.0

*p < .05 for Pearson's test for chi square.

Table 6.2 Perceptions of the other person in the most recent incident of forced sexual intercourse

Status	Positive statements No.	Percent	Mixed statements No.	Percent	Negative statements No.	Percent	Neutral statements No.	Percent	Total
Victim	22	48.9	4	8.9	8	17.8	11	24.4	45
Offender	9	64.3	3	21.4	1	7.1	1	7.1	14

Women frequently agree to engage in sexual intercourse when they don't want to do so. Both men (52.1 percent) and women (65.2) recognize that at times women agree when they would rather not, or because they feel threatened (men 16.2 percent, women 20.4) or coerced (men 15.7 percent, women 17.9 percent) (see Table 6.3).

Table 6.3 Willingness of women to engage in sexual intercourse

	Men			Women		
	Subjects Endorsing		Degree of Influence	Subjects Endorsing		Degree of Influence
Degree of Willingness	No.	Percent	Percent	No.	Percent	Percent
She wanted to *	313	83.2	88.2	359	81.2	82.6
Didn't want to but agreed	196	52.1	37.9	288	65.2	42.1
Didn't want to but felt threatened	61	16.2	79.4	90	20.4	75.0
Didn't want to but felt forced	59	15.7	83.0	79	17.9	85.3

*p < .00l for t for degree of influence.

The most common reason for a woman to agree to unwanted sexual intercourse given by both men and women is A Desire to Make Her Date or Boyfriend Happy (see table 6.4). The second most common reason given by women was To Maintain the Relationship; for men the second most frequent reason was Things got Out of Control. Both men and women selected There Was No Good Reason Not to Engage in Sex as the third most frequent reason for a woman to agree to sexual intercourse when she didn't want to have sex. Coercive strategies were the least frequently selected reasons of those available to the subjects. Both men and women appear to believe that women do agree to have sex when they don't want to but that this agreement is caused by a willingness to please rather than because of coercion.

Both men and women recognize that, at times, women participate in sexual intercourse when they really don't want to do so, a decision often influenced by a desire to make their partner happy and/or to maintain a relationship which is pleasurable/beneficial for them.

Table 6.4   Reasons why women agree to have sexual intercourse when they don't really want to

Reasons given	Men Endorsing		Women Endorsing	
	No.	Percent	No.	Percent
Make date/friend happy	125	44.3	161	45.1
Keep man as boyfriend**	67	23.6	44	12.3
Date had shown her a good time**	43	15.2	22	6.1
Date had spent a lot of money*	25	8.9	11	3.1
Things got out of control	40	14.1	67	18.6
She thought something wrong with her	13	4.6	21	5.8
No good reason not to	48	16.9	61	16.9
Date threatened to leave and not date again	6	2.1	6	1.7
Man wanted her to prove her love	11	3.9	24	6.7
She didn't want to be labeled frigid	7	2.5	16	4.4
Other	37	13.1	46	12.7

*p < . 01 for t.
**p < .001 for t.

A Beginning Model

It has been suggested that all instances of forced sexual intercourse are not the same - that there are substantial differences between various sets of sexually offensive behaviors. While existing theories provide an effective basis for dealing with those cases in which the man intends to rape a woman who realizes that she is being raped, they are less effective in explaining many of the victimizations which are presently included under the labels of date or acquaintance rape.

While the dynamics of these situations have not been made clear by contemporary efforts to examine forced sexual intercourse, sufficient information has been gleaned to permit the development of a tentative model that can be used to guide further research. The model only addresses behavior which is generally characterized as date or acquaintance rape and does not address stranger rape, marital rape, or blitz/predatory rape.

Chapters Two, Three, and Four discussed forced sexual intercourse in the context of courtship, dating, and dating violence. The model advanced here suggests that some forms of forced sexual intercourse can be understood best in the context of courtship or dating. Courtship is defined as activities which are undertaken with the intent of establishing a fairly permanent relationship. While some undetermined portion of dating is primarily temporary and recreational in nature, much of dating has a courtship function. That is, participants in recreational dating are, in many instances, evaluating their partners in terms of potential suitability as long-term partners. Dating is an activity which leads to courtship when a potential partner is identified. While this shift in emphasis is usually not formally noted, most of those who actively date are aware of the potential in their activity.

The process of moving from casual dating partners to a committed, long-term, relatively permanent relationship is a process of increasing intimacy. In most cases, both partners assume that, at some point, sexual intimacy will become a part of the relationship as the relationship matures. This assumption is not overtly recognized, the stages through which a relationship moves to maturity are not specified, and the circumstances under which sexual intimacy will occur are not overtly addressed. The process, in terms of increasing commitment, is one of advancing and retreating as the relationship moves towards the development of a relatively permanent relationship. Forced sexual intercourse can occur when the process of relationship formation gets out of control.

Women control the degree of sexual intimacy at each stage in the development of the relationship. Men are expected to seek increasing degrees of sexual intimacy. Women are expected to resist male pressure until the relationship matures. Women have personal standards which must be met before they are willing to engage in increased sexual intimacy, particularly sexual intercourse. These standards are not overt - couples generally do not discuss the conditions which must be met before complete sexual intimacy becomes a part of the relationship. While these standards are individual, they can include such things as a determination with a high degree of certainty by the woman that this man is the person with whom she wishes to establish a permanent relationship, he will not abuse her at some later date, he is as committed to her as she is to him, and he (as well as her friends, his friends, and other significant others) will not label her negatively if she agrees to complete sexual intimacy. Men who are aware that such standards exist are not aware of the standards held by the person with whom they are seeking to establish a relatively permanent relationships.

Men are expected to be aggressive if they are to be identified as masculine. Aggression by men in the courtship process produces a situation in which men assertively attempt to move the courtship process forward while women resist these efforts in favor of a more deliberate and cautious development of the relationship. In some cases, men are placing pressure on women to move forward with commitment to the relationship while women want to move forward but not as fast as the men are requesting. Moving toward sexual intimacy is an interactive process; it is frequently a trial and error process of advancing and retreating from complete sexual intimacy as the couple works to develop a long-term, relatively permanent relationship. An out-of-control situation can develop which can produce forced sexual intercourse when unclear expectations produce unacceptable behavior, biological arousal reduces rational behavior for one or for both parties, or the level of male aggression is greater than the woman anticipated.

On occasion, some women consent to sexual intimacy when they don't really want to be intimate. There are a number of circumstances under which unwilling consent is given. Once a relationship has moved to a level including sexual intimacy, the man may desire sexual intimacy when the woman does not or more frequently than the woman. Women sometimes will agree to sexual intimacy when they would rather not in order to meet the man's needs. At times a women may hesitate to commit to complete sexual intimacy although she has decided that she will become sexually intimate at some point in the relationship with the man she is dating. On the other hand, she may respond to a man's pressure to agree to sexual intimacy before she is certain that she is ready for the relationship to move to that particular level of intimacy. Men generally are aware that, if they are persistent, some women will consent when they are uncertain about their decision. Some men are not sufficiently sensitive to realize that they are forcing the women with whom they have a relationship to be sexually intimate.

The factors which have been advanced as important to a model which seeks to explain incidents of non-predatory forced sexual intercourse include: (1) the relationship formation process in which couples become increasingly intimate, (2) role expectations for aggressive behavior in courtship (more rapid development of the relationship), (3) role expectations for women to resist male aggression in courtship (less rapid development of the relationship), (4) women control (decide) when the relationship will move to more intense levels of sexual intimacy, (5) women have standards (conditions) which must be satisfied before they agree to sexual intimacy, (6) some women will consent to sexual intimacy when they don't really want to be sexually intimate, and (7) men are aware that women will consent at times when they don't want to be sexually intimate, but men are usually not aware of/sensitive to the existence of or of the nature of the standards/conditions which women hold for their own commitment to sexual intimacy. When these factors are applied to instances of forced sexual intercourse in courtship and dating, a number of patterns emerge.

In some situations, both the man and the woman anticipate and are moving toward eventual intense sexual intimacy. They engage in preliminary sexually intimate behavior, and, at a point in the relationship, the situation gets out of control. The man forces the woman to have sex while they are engaging in consensual sexual activity. In these cases it is probable that neither the man nor the woman will label the behavior as rape, psychological damage will be minimal, and both the man and the woman may choose to continue to develop a long-term relationship and have positive images of each other.

In some instances, the woman considers intense sexual intimacy a possibility at some point, but she has not committed to the development of permanent relationship at that point in the relationship. She engages in some exploratory sexual activity even thought she does not anticipate a permanent relationship. During a period of intimacy the man forces the woman to have intercourse. In these cases, both the woman and the man might or might not define the incident as rape. If the woman defines the incident as rape, she will terminate the relationship and have mixed or negative opinions of the man. Psychological damage will be moderate to high. If the woman does not define the incident as rape, she may continue the relationship and have mixed opinions of the man. Psychological damage will be low to moderate.

In some situations, the women will hold a value which prohibits sexual intercourse before a firm permanent relationship is established, but she engages in some intimate sexual behavior in the process of seeking a relationship. During a period of consensual sexual activity the man forces the woman to have sexual intercourse. In these cases, the woman will define the incident as rape and the man may or may not define the incident as rape. The woman will terminate the relationship and have mixed but predominately negative opinions of the man in that there are characteristics which she found attractive which were not related to his sexual aggression. She will not continue the relationship and psychological damage, in most cases, will be high.

This model suggests that the development of an agreement to engage in consensual sexual intercourse in a dating or courtship setting is a negotiated process in which the woman grants sexual access to the man when specific personal conditions (personal standards) are met. It is acceptable for men to actively pursue sexual intercourse, and this pursuit is not channeled by the woman's conditions for agreeing to sexual intimacy because these conditions (woman's expectations) frequently are not clear.

The process of moving forward in a relationship involves exploratory sexual behavior in which the couple approaches but does not necessarily engage in sexual intercourse. If this process gets out of control, forced sexual intercourse might occur because the man is larger and stronger and/or because the woman can not manage to withdraw without permanently damaging a relationship she may want to preserve. When forced sexual intercourse occurs in this context, the woman may accept responsibility for the outcome, and the man might see this as an acceptable/anticipated outcome.

This model only addresses forced sexual intercourse which occurs during a legitimate pursuit of a relatively long-term relationship and does not address forced sexual intercourse labeled as predatory, blitz, or confidence rape. In the latter, a male predator engages in dating or courtship behavior to gain a position from which he can relatively safely force a women to submit to sexual intercourse. He does not intend to develop a long-term relationship but pretends to pursue a relationship in order to gain sexual access by trick or fraud. If his efforts to gain consensual sexual access are not successful, he might use whatever degree of force is necessary to gain sexual access. The characterization of this behavior as courtship behavior provides some protection from sanctioning for the offender. It should be noted that research to date has not indicated that a woman has the ability to distinguish between the predatory rapist and the legitimate suitor until after she has been successfully victimized, and it is possible that she may not be certain after her victimization. This behavior can be explained more successfully by traditional theories of rape than by a courtship model of rape.

The model will not effectively address marital rape or rape that occurs in relatively stable relationships in which sexual intercourse has been accepted as a normal part of the relationship. While sufficient empirical attention has not been devoted to an examination of this phenomena to permit preliminary model development, it is probable that models which stress dominance and control rather than sexual access are more appropriate than other models.

The courtship model advanced here will not effectively address situations in which sexual intercourse is a potential form of recreation rather than an activity that occurs in a relatively permanent relationship. In situations in which both the man and the woman define sexual intercourse as a recreational option in casual dating, the behavioral patterns might be similar but accelerated, with different interpretations of expectations and processes held by the actors. If a man forces a woman to have sex in this setting, traditional theories of rape may be more effective in understanding and investigating the behavior. Little empirical attention has been directed toward this phenomena, so any assessment is pure speculation at this point.

The model advanced here is a simplification of a very complex system of interactions which comprise dating and courtship. There is a need for extensive further research directed toward increasing our understanding of all forms of forced sexual intercourse. An effort must be made to determine if different types of phenomena are addressed under the labels of date rape and under the more general category of rape. If there are differences, are they such that, if they were fully understood, effective strategies to protect women could be developed? The questions which must be addressed are extensive. What are the factors in the individual settings that are more likely to precipitate the use of physical force? What are the interactional characteristics of these situations? What are the factors which cause some people to be more likely to use physical force in intimate situations than others. When the relevant variables are identified, patterns can be defined and resources can be allocated effectively and efficiently. The rudimentary model presented here can provide a focus for this research.

Summary

All forms of forced sexual intercourse have been defined as parts of a social problem which has emerged because changing social values regarding the roles of women and men in society and in intimate settings have created a change in the orientation toward the degree of public interest in women's victimization. As the value system has changed, the social institutions that are responsible for dealing with pathology have had to adapt, frequently while under attack for being insensitive, ineffective, and possibly guilty of misfeasance. The resulting response has been somewhat unfocused, because these agencies have moved to satisfy the critics and complete their assigned tasks.

Before effective responses to all forms of forced sexual intercourse can be developed, this phenomena must be understood. A first step in increasing understanding of the phenomena is to recognize that some forms of forced sexual intercourse occur between relatively intimate partners and that this form of forced sexual intercourse might be substantially different from other forms of rape. That is, types of forced sexual intercourse must be examined in the social context in which they occur.

Rape consistently has been evaluated in terms of aggression, dominance, control, and violence rather than in terms of sexual access. The use of force to obtain goals has a lengthy history of legitimacy in the United States. This society is presented as having a high tolerance for violence. That is, the use of physical force is acceptable behavior in some social situations. A review of violence in history provides virtually unlimited examples. The frontier experience, combined with the pressures of assimilating diverse immigrant groups, led to direct citizen action in the protection of person and property and in maintaining social order and expansion by defeating and displacing Native Americans, controlling outlaws, and settling disputes. This direct action frequently involved violence on the part of individuals acting for the "right reasons" and on the part of vigilante groups. These groups were perceived as positive when they took the form of posses, miner's courts, or semi-formal committees and have been held to be appropriate to settle labor disputes, pursue noble goals, or to maintain personal privilege or status. They were perceived as negative when the targets were innocent and/or pursued and punished primarily for their race, religion, politics, or ethnic origin. To this day, citizens of the United States assert their right to use physical force to protect themselves and their property and to achieve their goals.

Theoretical explanations which have addressed aggression and the commission of violent acts are as broad and varied as the social sciences themselves. Violence has been addressed from psychological, sociological, and anthropological perspectives, as well as having been explained by biological explanations. Violent behavior can be caused by organic pathology, psychological or emotional pathology, diminished capacity, or any of a variety of learning contingencies. Common to all of these approaches is the assumption that violence and aggression are normal conditions which are pathological only when they are excessive.

Historically, rape has been a crime which has been condemned, if not effectively prosecuted. Reforms in the past decade have introduced changes in the law that create different levels of sexual assault and that make cases of sexual assault easier to prosecute successfully. Social concern which accompanied reform efforts on intimate violence as well as on forced sexual intercourse has focused attention on the prevalence and nature of forced sexual intercourse.

Traditional theories of rape treat it as a single phenomenon. That is, all forms of forced sexual intercourse are seen as the same thing. The feminist perspective argues that rape is a characteristic of male-dominated patriarchal societies. Threat of rape functions to control and dominate women, forcing them into passive submissive roles. Pornography is interpreted as a cause of rape in two ways. First, it perpetuates the definition of women as passive sexual objects and reinforces the male-dominated patriarchal system. Second, from a learning theory perspective, consumers exposed to violent sexual pornography or to pornography in which both violent acts and sexual acts occur are more likely to use force in sexual encounters.

Learning theories from a number of perspectives specify that the use of force in sexual encounters is learned in the same way that other behaviors and/or values are learned. The most prominent of these are drive-based, psychoanalytic theories which are related to the work of Bandura (1973). Most other learning theorists, sociologists, and criminologists have not applied their perspectives directly to the explanation of forced sexual intercourse.

Sociobiologists argue that the use of force in sexual intercourse is functional for males in that access to the greatest number of partners maximizes gene survival. Women maximize the transmission of their genes to future generations by resisting males who use force and by attracting males who will remain with them after insemination to care for the children.

Baron and Straus (1989) added models based on social disorganization and on legitimate use of violence to other existing traditional models to advance an integrated model to explain rape. While their model effectively combines the elements of many of the traditional theories, it still treats rape as a single phenomenon in which a male intends to use force to obtain sex from an unwilling resisting female who sees herself as being raped.

The argument advanced in this chapter is that there are types or sets of related forms of forced sexual intercourse which are sufficiently different as to require separate models to be effectively understood and examined. A tentative model for one of these sets - the use of force in intimate sexual encounters in the context of courtship - has been developed and can be used to frame future research in this area. This model assumes that the process of establishing a relatively permanent or long-term relationship involves progressively more intimate interaction as the relationship matures with sexual intercourse anticipated at some point in the relationship. The point at with sexual intercourse becomes a part of the relationship and the conditions which must be met before this level of commitment to the relationship is accepted is determined by the woman. The likelihood that the woman will define the use of force in sexual intercourse as rape or criminal, the likelihood that the woman will continue the relationship, and the degree of psychological damage which occurs will vary according to the manner in which the woman defines the situation.

As this model is refined and assessed through empirical examination, a more thorough and accurate understanding of the use of force in intimate relationships will emerge. As conceptualization of the phenomena becomes more thorough and accurate, more effective responses will be developed for the justice system, and more effective educational materials can be developed to reduce the victimization of women at the hands of those with whom they seek to develop long-term relatively, permanent relationships.

References

Adamec, C. S. and Adamec, R. E. (1981), 'Aggression by Men Against Women: Adaptation or Aberration', *International Journal of Women's Studies*, vol. 1, pp. 1-21.

Allen, M., Emmers, T. and Giery, M. A. (1995), 'Exposure to Pornography and Acceptance of Rape Myths', *Journal of Communication*, vol. 45(1), pp. 5-26.

Amir, M. (1971), *Patterns in Forcible Rape*, University of Chicago Press, Chicago.

Angle, P. M. (1952), *Bloody Williamson: A Chapter in American Lawlessness*, Alfred A. Knopf, New York.

Ardrey, R. (1966), *The Territorial Imperative*, Antheneum, New York.

Archer, D. and Gartner, R. (1984), *Violence and Crime in Cross-National Perspective*, Yale University Press, New Haven, CT.

Bandura, A. (1973), *Aggression: Social Learning Analysis*, Prentice Hall, Englewood Cliffs, NJ.

Baron, L. and Straus, M. A. (1984), 'Sexual Stratification, Pornography, and Rape in the United States', in M. N. Malamuth and E. Donnerstein (eds), *Pornography and Sexual Aggression* (pp. 185-209), Academic Press, Orlando, FL.

Baron, L. and Straus, M. A. (1989), *Four Theories of Rape in American Society: A State Level Analysis*, Yale University Press, New Haven, CT.

Baron, R. A. (1977), *Human Aggression*, Plenum, New York.

Barry, K. (1979), *Female Sexual Slavery*, Prentice Hall, Englewood Cliffs, NJ.

Bateman, A. J. (1948), 'Introsexual Selection in Drosophila', *Heredity*, vol. 2, pp. 349-68.

Becker, H. (1963), *Outsiders: Studies in the Sociology of Deviance*, Free Press, New York.

Benderly, B. L. (1982), 'Rape Free or Rape Prone', *Science*, vol. 82(3), pp. 40-3.

Blumer, H. (1937), 'Social Organization and Individual Disorganization', *American Journal of Sociology*, vol. 42, pp. 871-7.

Brown, R. M. (1969), 'Historical Patterns of Violence in America', in H. D. Graham and T. R. Gurr (eds), *Violence in America: A Staff Report to the National Commissions on the Causes and Prevention of Violence*, U.S. Government Printing Office, Washington, DC.

Brownmiller, S. (1975), *Against Our Will: Men, Women, and Rape*, Simon and Schuster, New York.

Burt, M. R. (1980), 'Cultural Myths and Supports for Rape', *Journal of Personality and Social Psychology*, vol. 38, pp. 217-34.

Chamove, A., Harlow, H. F. and Mitchell, G. D. (1967), 'Sex Differences in the Infant Directed Behavior of Preadolescent Rhesus Monkeys', *Child Development*, vol. 38, pp. 329-55.

Check, J. V. P. and Malamuth, N. M. (1983), 'Sex-role Stereotyping and Reactions to Stranger vs. Acquaintance Rape', *Journal of Personality and Social Psychology*, vol. 45, pp. 344-56.

Check, J. V. P. and Malamuth, N. M. (1983), 'Can Participation in Pornography Experiments have Positive Effects?', *Journal of Sex Research*, vol. 20, pp. 14-31.

Cherry, F. (1983), 'Gender Roles and Sexual Violence', in E. R. Allgeier and N. B. McCormick (eds), *Changing Boundaries: Gender Roles and Sexual Behavior* (pp. 245-60), Mayfield Publishing Company, Palo Alto, CA.

Cloward, R. A. and Ohlin, L. E. (1960), *Delinquency and Opportunity*, The Free Press, Glencoe, IL.

Cohen, S. (1955), *Delinquent Boys: The Culture of the Gang*, The Free Press, Glencoe, IL.

Curtis, L. A. (1975), *Violence, Race, and Culture*, Lexington Press, Lexington, MA.

Daly, M. and Wilson, M. (1978), *Sex, Evolution, and Behavior*, Duxbury Press, North Scituate, MA.

Dawkins, R. (1976), *The Selfish Gene*, Oxford University Press, New York.

Deutsch, H. (1944), *The Psychology of Women: Vol. 1. Girlhood*, Bantam Books, New York.

Diamond, I. (1980), 'Pornography and Repression: A Reconsideration', *Signs*, vol. 5, pp. 686-701.

Dobash, R. E. (1979), *Violence Against Wives: A Case Against the Patriarchy*, The Free Press, New York.

Donnerstein, E. and Barrett, G. (1978a), 'Eroticism and Aggression', *Journal of Personality and Social Psychology*, vol. 36, pp. 180-8.

Donnerstein, E. and Barrett, G. (1978b), 'The Effects of Erotic Stimuli on Male Aggression toward Females', *Journal of Personality and Social Psychology*, vol. 36, pp. 180-8.

Donnerstein, E. and Hallman, J. (1978), 'Facilitating Effects of Erotica on Aggression toward Females', *Journal of Personality and Social Psychology*, vol. 36, 1270-7.

Donnerstein, E., Linz, D. and Penrod, S. (1987), *The Question of Pornography*, Free Press, New York.

Doyle, D. P. and Burfeind, J. W. (1994), *The University of Montana Sexual Victimization Survey Executive Summary*, Author, Missoula, Montana.

Durden-Smith, J. and deSimone, D. (1983), *Sex and the Brain*, New York, Warner Publishing Company.

Dworkin, A. (1981), *Pornography: Men Possessing Women*, Perigee Press, New York.

Ellis, L. (1989), *Theories of Rape: Inquiries into the Causes of Sexual Aggression*, Hemisphere Publishing Corporation, New York.

Felson, R. B. (1992), *Motives for Sexual Coercion*, Annual Meeting of the American Society of Criminology, Tucson, AZ.

Frantz, J. B. (1969), 'The frontier tradition: An invitation to violence', in D. Graham and T. R. Gurr (eds), *Violence in America: Historical and Comparative Perspectives*, vol. 1, U.S. Government Printing Office, Washington, DC.

Friedan, B. (1963), *The Feminine Mystique*, W. W. Norton Publishing Company, New York.

Fromm, E. (1977), *The Anatomy of Human Destructiveness*, Penguin, Harmondsworth, England.

Gagnon, J. H. and Simon, W. (1973), *Sexual Conduct: The Sources of Sexuality*, Chicago, Aldine Press.

Gastil, R. D. (1971), 'Homicide and a Regional Culture of Violence', *American Sociological Review*, vol. 36, pp. 412-27.

Gibson, L., Linden, R. and Johnson, S. (1980), 'A Situational Theory of Rape', *Canadian Journal of Criminology*, vol. 22, pp. 51-63.

Goth, A. N. (1979), *Men Who Rape: The Psychology of the Offender*, Plenum Press, New York.

Graham, D. G. and Gurr, T. R. (1969), *Violence in America: Historical and Comparative Perspectives*, vols. I and II, U.S. Government Printing Office, Washington, DC.

Hackney, S. (1969), 'Southern Violence', *American Historical Review*, vol. 74, pp. 906-25.

Hagen, R. (1979), *The Bio-social Factor*, Doubleday, Garden City, NJ.

Holmstrom, L. L. and Burgess, A. W. (1980), 'Sexual Behavior of Assailants During Reported Rapes', *Archives of Sexual Behavior*, vol. 9, pp. 427-39.

Huesman, L. R. and Malamuth, N. M. (1986), Media Violence and Antisocial Behavior: An Overview, *Journal of Social Issues*, vol. 42, pp. 1-6.

Huggins, M. D. and Straus, M. A. (1980), 'Violence and the Social Structure as Reflected in Children's Books From 1850 to 1970', in M. A. Strauss and G. T. Hotaling (eds), *The Social Causes of Husband Wife Violence* (pp. 51-67), University of Minnesota Press, Minneapolis, MN.

Johnson, D. G., Palileo, G. J. and Gray, N. B. (1992), 'Date Rape on a Southern Campus: Reports from 1991', *Sociology and Social Research*, vol. 76(2), pp. 37-41.

Koss, M. P., Dinero, T. E., Seibel, C. A. and Cox S. (1988), 'Stranger and Acquaintance Rape: Are There Differences in the Victim's Experience?', *Psychology of Women Quarterly*, vol. 12, pp. 1-24.

Kutchinski, B. (1988), 'Towards an Exploration of the Decrease in Registered Sex Crimes in Copenhagen', *Technical Report of the Commission on Obscenity and Pornography*, vol. 7., U.S. Government Printing Office, Washington, DC.

Lambert, W. W., Triandis, L. M. and Wolf, M. (1959), 'Some Correlates of Beliefs in the Malevolence and Benevolence of Supernatural Beings: A Cross Cultural Study', *Journal of Abnormal and Social Psychology*, vol. 58, pp. 162-9.

Lemert, E. M. (1951), *Social Pathology*, McGraw-Hill.

Leshner, A. L. (1978), *An Introduction to Behavioral Endocrinology*, Oxford University Press, New York.

Longino, H. E. (1980), 'Pornography, Oppression, and Freedom: A Closer Look', in L. Lederer (ed), *Take back the night: A closer look*, pp. 26-41, William Morrow Company, New York.

Lorenz, K. (1971), *On Aggression*, Bantam Books, New York.

Lynn, K. (1969), 'Violence in American Literature and Folk Lore', in H. G. Graham and T. R. Gurr (eds), *Violence in America: Historical and Comparative Perspectives*, vol. I, U.S. Government Printing Office, Washington, DC.

MacKinnon, C. (1986), *Feminism Unmodified*, Harvard University Press, Cambridge, MA.

Malamuth, N. M. (1981), 'Rape Proclivity Among Males', *Journal of Social Issues*, vol. 37(4), pp. 138-157.

Malamuth, N. M. (1984), 'Aggression Against Women', in N. A. Malamuth and E. Donnerstein (eds), *Pornography and Sexual Aggression*, Academic Press, Orlando, FL.

Malamuth, N. M. (1986), 'Predictors of Naturalistic Sexual Aggression', *Journal of Personality and Social Psychology*, vol. 50, pp. 953-62.

Malamuth, N. M. (1988), 'Predicting Laboratory Aggression Against Female and Male Targets: Implications for Sexual', vol. 22, pp. 47-495.

Malamuth, N., Briere, J. and Check, J. V. P. (1986), 'Sexual Arousal in Response to Aggression: Ideology, Aggressive, and Sexual Correlates', *Journal of Personality and Social Psychology*, vol. 50, pp. 330-40.

Malamuth, N., Fesback, S. and Jaffe, Y. (1977), 'Sexual Arousal and Aggression: Recent Experiments and Theoretical Issues', *Journal of Social Issues*, vol. 33, pp. 110-33.

Martindale, D. (1957), 'Social Disorganization: The Conflict of Normative and Empirical Approaches', in H. Becker and A. Boskoff (eds), *Modern Sociological Theory in Continuity and Change* (pp. 340-367), Rinehart & Winston, New York.

Matza, D. (1964), *Delinquency and Drift*, Wiley, New York.

Mazur, A. (1983), 'Hormones, aggression and dominance in humans', in B. B. Svare (ed), *Hormones and Aggressive Behavior*, Plenum, New York.

Mellen, S. L. (1981), *The Evolution of Love*, Freeman Press, San Francisco.

Merton, R. K. (1957), *Social Theory and Social Structure*, Free Press of Glencoe, New York.

Messner, S. F. (1983), 'Regional and Racial Effects on the Urban Homicide Rate: The Subculture of Violence Revisited', *American Journal of Sociology*, vol. 88, pp. 997-1007.

Miller, W. (1976), 'Youth Gangs in the Urban Crisis Era', in J. F. Short (ed), *Delinquency, Drime, and Society*, University of Chicago Press, Chicago.

Morgan, R. (1980), 'Theory and Practice: Pornography and Rape', in L. Lwederer (ed), *Take Back the Night: A Closer Look*, William Morrow Company, New York.

Mower, E. R. (1941), 'Methodological Problems in Social Disorganization', *American Sociological Review*, vol. 6, pp. 639-49.

Moyer, K. E. (1976), *The Psychobiology of Aggression*, Harper and Row, New York.

Nelson, E. (1982), 'Pornography and Sexual Aggression', in M. Yaffee and E. Nelson (eds), *The Influence of Pornography on Behavior*, Academic Press, London.

Persell, C. H. (1984), *Understanding Society*, Harper and Row, New York.

Quinsey, V. L. (1984), 'Sexual Aggression: Studies of Offenders Against Women', in D. Weisstub (ed), *Law and Mental Health: International Perspectives*, vol. 1, Pergamon Press, New York.

Richard, A. F. and Schulman, S. R. (1982), 'Sociobiology: Primate Field Studies', *Annual Review in Anthropology*, vol. 11, pp. 231-55.

Riger, S. and Gordon, M. T. (1981), The Fear of Rape: A Study in Social Control', *Journal of Social Issues*, vol. 37(4), pp. 71-92.

Russell, D. E. (1975), *The Politics of Rape: The Victim's Perspective*, Stein and Day, New York.

Russell, D. E. H. (1984), *Sexual Exploitation: Rape, Child Sexual Abuse, and Workplace Harassment*, Sage, Beverly Hills, CA.

Sanday, P. R. (1981), 'The Socio-cultural Context of Rape: A Cross-cultural Study', *The Journal of Social Issues*, vol. 37, pp. 5-27.

Scarpitti, F. and Scarpitti, E. (1977), 'Victims of Rape', *Transaction*, vol. 14, pp. 29-32.

Schmidt, G. and Sigusch, V. (1970), 'Sex Differences in Responses to Psychosexual Stimulation by Films and Slides', *Journal of Sex Research*, vol. 6, pp. 268-83.

Schmidt, G., Sigusch, V. and Schafer, S. (1973), 'Responses to Erotic Stories: Male Female Differences', *Archives of Sexual Behavior*, vol. 2, pp. 181-99.

Schwendinger, J. and Schwendinger, H. (1985), 'Homo Economics as the Rapist in Sociobiology', in S. R. Sanday and E. Toch (eds), *Violence Against Women* (pp. 85-114), Gordian Press, New York.

Scully, D. and Marolla, J. (1984), 'Convicted Rapists' Vocabulary of Motives: Excuses and Justifications', *Social Problems*, vol. 32, pp. 530-44.

Scully, D. and Marolla, J. (1985), 'Riding the Bull at Gilly's: Convicted Rapists Describe the Rewards of Rape', *Social Problems*, vol. 32, pp. 251-62.

Shields, W. M. and Shields, L. M. (1983), 'Forcible Rape: An Evolutionary Perspective', *Ethnology and Sociobiology*, vol. 4, pp. 115-36.

Shotland, R. L. (1992), 'A Theory of the Causes of Courtship Rape', *Journal of Social Issues*, vol. 48, pp. 127-44.

Siann, G. (1985), *Accounting for Aggression and Violence*, Allen & Unwin, London.

Sigelman, C. K., Berry, C. J. and Wiles, K. A. (1984), 'Violence in College Students' Dating Relationships', *Journal of Applied Social Psychology*, vol. 14, pp. 530-48.

Smith, J. M. (1978), *The Evolution of Sex*, Cambridge Press, New York.

Storr, A. (1970), *Human Aggression*, Penguin, Harmondsworth, England.

Sunday, S. R. and Tobach, E. (1985), *Violence Against Women: A Critique of the Sociobiology of Rape*, Gordian Press, New York.

Sutherland, E. H. and Cressey, D. R. (1974), *Criminology* (9th ed), Lippincot, Philadelphia.

Symons, D. (1979), *The Evolution of Human Sexuality*, Oxford University Press, New York.

Taft, P. and Ross, P. (1969), 'American Labor Violence: Its Causes, Character and Outcome', in H. G. Graham and T. R. Gurr (eds), *Violence in America: Historical and Comparative Perspectives*, vol. I, U.S. Government Printing Office, Washington, DC.

Tannenbaum, P. H. (1971), 'Emotional Arousal as a Mediator of Erotic Communication Effects', in *Technical Report of the Commission Obscenity and Pornography*, vol. 1, U.S. Government Printing Office, Washington, DC.

Thomas, W. I. and Zaniecki, F. (1927), *The Polish Peasant in Europe and America*, Knopf & Company, New York.

Thompson, W. W. E. and Buttell, A. J. (1984), 'Sexual Deviance in America', *Emporia State Research Studies*, vol. 33, pp. 6-47.

Thornhill, R. (1980), 'Rape in Panorpa Scorpionflies and a General Rape Hypothesis', *Animal Behavior*, vol. 28, pp. 55-9.

Thornhill, R. and Thornhill, N. W. (1983), 'Human Rape: An Evolutionary Analysis', *Ethnology and Sociobiology*, vol. 4, pp. 137-73.

Toch, H. (1977), *Police, Prisons, and the Problem of Violence*, National Institute of Mental Health, Rockville, MD.

Trivers, R. (1972), 'Parental Investment and Sexual Selection', in B. Campbell (ed), *Sexual Selection and the Descent of Man* (pp. 136-179), Aldine Publishing Company, Chicago.

Walker, P. A. and Meyer, W. J. (1981), 'Medroxyprogesterone Acetate Treatment for Paraphiliac Sex Offenders', in J. R. Hays (ed), *Violence and the Violent Individual*, Spectrum, New York.

Weis, K. and Borges, S. S. (1977), 'Victimology and Rape: The Case of the Legitimate Victim', in D. R. Nass (ed), *The Rape Victim* (pp. 35-75), Kendall/Hunt, Dubuque, IO.

Wheeler, H. (1985), 'Pornography and Rape: A Feminist Perspective', in A. W. Burgess (ed), *Rape and Sexual Assault* (pp. 374-412), Garland Publishing Company, New York.

Wilder, R. (1982, July), 'Are Sexual Standards Inherited?' *Science Digest*, p. 69.

Williams, G. C. (1975), *Sex and Evolution*, Princeton University Press, Princeton, NJ.

Wilson, E. O. (1975), *Sociobiology: The New Synthesis*, Belknap Press of Harvard University, Cambridge, MA.

Wirth, L. (1940), 'Ideological Aspects of Social Disorganization', *American Sociological Review*, vol. 5, pp. 472-82.

Wolfgang, M. and Ferracuti, F. (1967), *The Subculture of Violence*, Tavistock, London.

Yegidis, B. L. (1986), 'Date Rape and Forced Sexual Encounters among college students', *Journal of Sex Education and Therapy*, vol. 12, pp. 51-4.

7 Understanding and Addressing

Introduction

As is the case with most research, more questions have been raised than answered by the data in this study. While the need for further research is pressing, the information available permits the development of a tentative theoretical model and the presentation of some recommendations for addressing the social problem which is generally identified in the literature as date or acquaintance rape. These products must be considered in the context of courtship and dating if they are to be useful.

Courtship is defined as a set of activities in which men and women engage for the purpose of identifying and selecting a mate. Courtship is not a concept which occurs frequently in describing contemporary relationships between men and women. Today, the term or concept which applies to activities occurring between men and women who engage in shared activities of a personal or intimate nature as couples is dating. While courtship rituals have changed greatly over time and from place to place, in most cases in the United States today, men and women associate together through dating to get to know one another well enough to decide whether or not to marry or enter a relatively long-term relationship. While dating has other more visible functions, finding someone with whom to have a fairly permanent intimate relationship is still a goal for most men and women.

Protection of young women from both forced sexual intercourse and from seduction has been consistently important throughout history, particularly during courtship. Before the late 1800s, courtship rituals limited interaction to relatively well supervised settings with a narrowness of purpose. That is, the only reason for engaging in activities as a couple was to approach marriage. During the latter part of the nineteenth century and the early part of the twentieth century, these activities became both recreational in nature and less supervised.

The risks to which women were exposed from sexual exploitation increased as women gained more freedom and left home for work or study before marriage. Activities which had taken place within the safety of supervised courtship began to take place in the context of recreation and dating, and a set of activities in which couples engaged for recreation emerged. Recreational dating increased in popularity and appears to be the dominant purpose for dating today. While dating is now primarily recreational, courtship is never very far away. That is, recreational dating leads to attraction, which leads to an exclusive relationship (going steady), which leads to a relatively permanent and exclusive relationship. If the relationship dissolves, a new cycle of dating begins. In this context, women are vulnerable to sexual exploitation, including both sexual and non-sexual violence. Forced sexual intercourse in intimate relationships involving non-married couples occurs in a dating/courtship context and is a form of what is commonly addressed as courtship violence in the literature. Courtship violence is similar in many ways to other forms of violence. Violence is often linked with aggression; however, aggression can occur without violence, and violence can occur without aggression.

As is the case with other forms of violence, intimate violence can be explained in terms of aggression. Courtship violence also can be produced by environmental pressures, by the actor's "personality", or by mutually accepted rituals or accepted patterns of behavior for some groups. Our frontier history, ethnic diversity, and history of the labor movement have produced a set of beliefs which supports the belief that violence is acceptable if the circumstances justify it. Violence is an option which can be exercised if the cause is just. These values can and are used to support the decision to resolve disputes in intimate relationships. Women and children traditionally have been at a disadvantage in that men as husbands or fathers were expected to discipline their wives and children. This responsibility justified the use of physical force. The first reforms were designed to limit this force to force which would not cause death or great bodily harm and did not challenge the use of force to gain sexual access if the man had reason to expect the woman to submit.

Intimate violence is continuously in the process of redefinition. Several cases are in the process of being adjudicated which will sharpen the boundaries between legally tolerable behavior and criminal behavior. News coverage of these and other cases continues to influence public opinion and administrators of organizations which provide services or opportunities to women. During the twentieth century child abuse, spouse abuse, and, most recently, elder abuse have been targets of social concern. Extreme cases have been documented and special interest groups have lobbied successfully for changes in the law and in the orientation of the justice system to spouse, child, and elder abuse as well as to rape and sexual aggression. Behaviors which in the past were considered to be private matters are now public matters and are addressed by social institutions.

As a part of this process, forced sexual intercourse has undergone substantial redefinition. Laws regarding rape have been expanded to criminalize a broad range of sexually offensive behavior with sexual assault and changes in the application of the rules of evidence permitting the successful prosecution of types of forced sexual intercourse which were not prosecutable in the past. There are still areas in which the application of public interest is limited, but these limits are not well defined. These areas include forced sexual intercourse among spouses and forced sexual intercourse among intimates (date or acquaintance rape). That is, some still consider this behavior as wrong but not a public/criminal matter, and some still consider the behavior as justifiable, if not acceptable, under certain conditions.

While substantial research has addressed forced sexual intercourse and other forms of offensive behavior between intimates or friends, it tends to be broadly focused on secondary issues. Some of the research in all types of intimate violence focuses on the factors which are related to the use of or justification for the use of physical force. Attitudes toward women, attitudes toward the use of force, perceived provocative behavior of the victim, implied consent, perceived character of the victim, organizational membership, environmental pressure, masculine stereotypes, dominance, and financial investment have all been considered factors relevant to the use of force in intimate relationships. While the evaluation of these factors is worthy and provides useful insights, it does not focus on the behaviors of interest in the context in which it occurs, limiting the development of effective explanatory models.

In the context provided by research to date and in the public arena, date rape and rape frequently are perceived as being the same. The confusion which results in both practice and research can be more clearly understood and taken into account if viewed in the context of a number of differences in historical perspective and in contemporary orientation. An understanding of these differences can reduce the confusion and should be understood before proceeding with an examination of forced sexual intercourse in an intimate or friendship relationship. First, it should be noted that there are many similarities in instances of forced sexual intercourse. While the focus of the research reported in this work is on forced sexual intercourse in friendship and intimate relationships, there is much in common among the various forms of forced sexual intercourse.

Historically, women had few rights; they did not have the right to control their own sexual behavior. In centuries past, women were legally treated as property to be controlled by the dominant male rather than as individuals. As a result, rape was treated as a crime of theft and the owner (male) was compensated for his loss. It was not until the twentieth century that rape began to be defined as an act of violence committed against the women who were the victims and that punishment was directed toward the male offender and not to the female victim. From the woman's perspective, a broader range of behaviors which have little to do with her "property value" are offensive and should be actionable. These interests are being recognized and, in the process, laws condemning these behaviors are being broadened and trial procedures are being modified to remove irrelevant damaged property defenses. The concept of sexual assault has emerged, and procedures which put the victims on trial have been restricted.

Even the simple counting of the incidents of forced sexual intercourse is difficult. The prevalence and incidence of forced sexual intercourse among intimates has been difficult to assess because of confusion in the definition of the phenomena, inconsistent time frames, and differing methodologies. While estimates vary widely, it appears certain that the rates of rape are considerably greater than those based on reports of rape to the police. The prevalence of rape consistently has been underestimated due to the choice of many victims to avoid reporting forced sexual intercourse. At times, victims do not define their victimization as rape, are too embarrassed to come forward, have little faith in the ability of the justice system to prosecute the offender successfully, or fear the negative labeling that frequently is directed toward victims of rape. To some extent, society damages the victim as much as the offender, affecting reluctance to report attacks, influencing all estimates. Estimates of the rate of victimization range from 1 percent to 24 percent for rape. Rape damages the victims psychologically and emotionally as well as physically. It is probable that, in many cases, the psychological damage is greater than the physical damage. At this point, relatively little is known about stranger rapists; even less is known about men who force their dates and intimate partners to have sex regardless of how it is labeled.

The norms which define appropriate behavior for men and women continuously are changing in such a way as to give both men and women more freedom in their personal behavior. As orientation toward appropriate behavior for men and women has changed, orientation toward sexual freedom and sexual offenses has changed. The definition of rape has been broadened to include all forms of forced sexual intercourse and other offensive sexual behaviors. In the process a new class of behaviors, sexual assault has been created which, to some extent, has replaced rape. The definition of forced sexual intercourse as rape or sexual assault still is influenced by historical factors in orientation toward rape. The most pervasive of these is perceived consent, the right (property) of men to sexual access in intimate relationships, and holding women accountable for their victimization in cases of sexual assault.

The definitions of rape and of the nature of relationships between boys and girls and between men and women presently are undergoing substantial change. The trend today is toward labeling all instances of forced sexual intercourse as criminal; however, some ambiguity exists in the area of the use of force in marital or co-habitation relationships. The legal definition does not appear to match reality in that many of the victims have not identified their victimization as criminal.

Studies of attitudes held by subjects tend to focus on the acceptability of forms of forced sexual intercourse and the linkage of acceptability to underlying attitudes toward women. While these studies consistently find that men are less likely to identify types or characterizations of forced sexual intercourse as rape than women, both men and women tend to decline to identify forced sexual intercourse as rape when the woman engages in risky behaviors or behaviors which imply that she has an obligation to the man. Those who hold traditional attitudes toward women are more likely to decline to label acts of forced sexual intercourse in friendship and intimate relationships as rape.

It is difficult to identify differences between victims and non-victims and offenders and non-offenders. Victims and offenders both tend to hold the woman responsible for her own victimization and tend to come from violent families or families which can be characterized as using harsh parenting techniques.

The findings reported here indicate that forced sexual intercourse occurs sufficiently frequently to warrant continued and increased attention. About 18.5 percent of the women in this study reported that they had been forced to have sex by a stranger or on a date in their lifetime, estimates which are similar to those reported by a number of other studies. This study did not include older men and women; the sample is essentially composed of relatively young university women and men. The rates for the prior year were smaller, with about 4.7 percent of the women reporting victimizations (3.6 percent on a date). The numbers of victims and offenders with severe patterns of experience were relatively small. There does appear to be a small number of male predators in this sample, only one of whom identifies himself as a rapist.

These subjects reported a relatively high level of sexual activity. Both men and women reported that sex is an activity in which both men and women engage for mutual pleasure. Both men and women recognized that women sometimes participate in sexual intercourse when they really don't want to. Usually, this decision was influenced by the woman's desire to make her partner happy and/or to maintain a relationship which was pleasurable/beneficial for her.

The question raised in this analysis suggests that forced sexual intercourse is not always rape. This contention is supported by the perception of the incidents reported by both the victims and the offenders. About half of the victims (80 percent of the offenders) did not define their victimization as rape. That is, these women said that they had been forced to have sex but that the use of force in their case was not rape and 80 percent stated that they did not believe that their assailant intended to rape them.

The victims were less likely to trust their assailants after the incident (92 percent to 26 percent), but about one-third of the victims continued to date their assailants. Offenders reported less loss of trust (88 percent, 44 percent) and higher rates of continued dating (55 percent). Both men and women (86.5 percent) reported that a man (84 percent) could use force and believe that he was not committing rape. Victims were more likely to make positive statements (48.9 percent) when describing their assailants than negative statements (17.8 percent) or negative and mixed statements (26.7 percent). Men's statements describing their victims were predominately positive (64.3 percent).

The victims reported that severe force was not used. The most frequently reported degree of force for both women (54.8 percent) and men (77.8 percent) was the man holding the woman down, with about 30 percent of the victims reporting that no physical force was used. Perhaps as a result, low levels of physical damage were reported by both victims (90 percent) and offenders (78 percent). Both men (53 percent) and women (72 percent) reported that relatively high levels of psychological damage occurred.

There are several possible explanations for these results. It is possible that forced sexual intercourse in a dating environment is one dimension of courtship conflict/violence. That is, some of the participants accept this behavior as relatively normal. It is possible that victims are in denial. That is, by accepting the behavior as legitimate, they deny their victim status and the potential for negative labeling which accompanies being a victim of a sexual assault. It is also possible that some men use the cover of courtship and a presumed normality of some types of forced sexual intercourse as a cover for their predatory behavior.

Investigation and analysis of these phenomena is clouded by our history of systematic and persistent discrimination against women, the forces which are redefining acceptable roles for both men and women, and the growing lack of tolerance for violence in "private" relationships. It is probable that the ideal, completely open consensual sex is not common. It is also probable that many women choose to remain sexually inactive or to become sexually active only when specific limited conditions are met. Dating serves many functions, including courtship and recreation. When forced sexual intercourse occurs in the context of dating or courtship, all of the dimensions of these dynamic relationships must be considered.

A complete and accurate understanding of these phenomena is necessary for practical as well as for theoretical purposes. There is general acceptance among activists and other informed parties that the only requirement for control of a woman's personal involvement in any intimate relationship is saying no to unwanted advancements of any type. While this standard is logically sound and ethically preferred, conducting research as if this standard were reality will prevent accurate understanding of the nature of the interactions, motivations, and consequences of the use of force in interactions between dating men and women. It will be difficult to develop effective prevention and treatment programs unless well articulated explanations for the use of force in dating and courtship interactions which match to some extent the reality which the men and women experience are developed. Inadequate information can create unreasonable fear and inadequate defensive strategies, leading to increased victimization by predatory men or denial of opportunities to develop healthy relationships with intimidated women.

A Preliminary Model

Theory development in the area of forced sexual intercourse among intimates has been relatively limited. Several typologies have been advanced, and some models link risk or offending behavior with traditional attitudinal sets. There is clearly a need for continued research and for the development of models which link specific behaviors, attitudes, and situational factors to the various degrees/types of forced sexual intercourse among friends and intimates.

The subjects in this study reported a relatively high level of sexual activity. Both men and women reported that sex is an activity engaged in by both men and women for mutual pleasure. Both men and women recognized that, at times, women participate in sexual intercourse when they really don't want to do so, a decision often influenced by a desire to make their partner happy and/or to maintain a relationship which is pleasurable/beneficial for them.

The development of sound theoretical models which address forced sexual intercourse among intimates has tended to be limited. Those explanatory frameworks which have been developed generally do not differentiate among various types of forced sexual intercourse and tend not to recognize that there are some fundamental differences in the factors which influence the occurrence and nature of the phenomena. When theoretical issues are pursued, they tend to be secondary to the explanation of date rape and tend to focus on issues such as the existence of traditional orientations toward women and the relationship between specific attitudinal perspectives and the use of force against women.

This study sought data that would clarify the nature of forced sexual assault in dating and courtship. While the dynamics of the situation are not clear, sufficient information has been gleaned to permit the development of a tentative model which can be used to guide further research.

Although forced sexual intercourse can be represented on a continuum based on social distance, some fundamental differences among types are formed by dividing the continuum. A three-category typology would group forced sexual intercourse by strangers, forced sexual intercourse by predators who use the appearance of dating or association to entrap their victims, and forced sexual intercourse among intimates or couples who are approaching intimacy. This grouping is based on the intent of the offender. Stranger rapists intend to rape and make no attempt to disguise their intention. Predatory rapists intend to gain sexual access through the use of trickery or force but attempt to disguise their intentions. Some instances of (probably most) predatory rape are classified as date or acquaintance rape. In cases of forced sexual intercourse among couples who are dating for recreation or for the purpose of finding a partner, the man does not intend to commit rape and will usually not label his behavior as rape. The model presented here only applies to the latter type of forced sexual intercourse and does not apply to stranger rape or predatory rape. This model flows from the data gathered in the two studies reported here, is interactional in nature, and is based on four assumptions underlying forced sexual intercourse among intimates: most young adults are sexually active, gaining/granting sexual access is a negotiated process, the rules of engagement are not clear, and gaining an understanding of the rules is not necessarily a part of the negotiation process. This model only addresses behavior which is generally characterized as date or acquaintance rape and does not address stranger rape or blitz/predatory rape. This rudimentary model can be expressed best as a series of propositions:

1. Participation in sexual intercourse is fairly common.

2. Women occasionally consent to sexual intercourse when they would prefer to abstain.

3. Men know that women occasionally consent to sexual intercourse when they would prefer to abstain.

4. The decision to engage in sexual intercourse is something women control.

5. Sexual intercourse is something men seek to gain from women.

6. Men are expected to actively pursue women's consent to sexual intercourse.

7. Women are expected to resist the efforts of men to gain sexual access until specific individual conditions exist, even though they plan to consent at some point in the relationship.

8. The presence and nature of these conditions is usually not explicit.

9. In the process of developing a relationship, men and women engage in exploratory sexual behavior.

10. Gaining/granting sexual access is an interactive process involving some degree of trial and error.

11. On occasion, the trial and error process produces an out-of-control situation that leads to forced sexual intercourse.

12. If both actors anticipate sexual access, the question is one

of timing; they engage in some exploratory sexual behavior leading to an out-of-control situation, neither the man nor the woman will define the incident as rape.

13. If the woman does not anticipate sexual access at that point in the relationship but engages in some exploratory sexual activity leading to an out-of-control situation, the woman and the man may or may not define the incident as rape.

14. If the woman chooses not to engage in sexual intercourse but engages in some exploratory sexual behavior in the process of seeking a relationship and the situation gets out of control, she will define the incident as rape; the man may or may not define the incident as rape. This model suggests that the development of an agreement to engage in sexual intercourse is a negotiated process in which the woman grants sexual access to the man when specific personal conditions (personal standards) are met. It is acceptable for men to actively pursue sexual intercourse, and this pursuit is not channeled by the woman's conditions for agreeing to sexual intercourse, as these conditions (woman's expectations) frequently are not clear.

As a couple approaches but does not necessarily engage in sexual intercourse as a relationship develops, forced sexual intercourse might occur if one or both of the participants loses control. In these cases, the woman may accept responsibility for the outcome, the man may see his behavior as acceptable, and both may choose to continue to pursue the development of a relatively permanent relationship.

This model is a simplification of a very complex system of interactions which comprise dating and courtship. There is a need for further research so that this rudimentary model can be clarified and expanded.

Addressing the Social Problem

From a practical perspective, it is possible that some of today's efforts to protect young women on campuses are misguided. Victimization rates for the studied campus were estimated to be as high as 60 percent. The actual rates, while high, are considerably less than the lowest estimate offered prior to this study. Overestimating and dramatizing a risk increases fear and reduces freedom without protecting. This study indicates that almost all unwanted sexual encounters occur in apartments (66.7 percent) or cars (26.6 percent), are committed by men with whom the women have at least casual relationships, and are preceded by behavior which causes sexual arousal (almost one-half of the women reported that they were biologically aroused, about two-thirds reported that one or the other had been aroused, and about one-third reported that both had been aroused). Educational materials should indicate that women who want to protect themselves should exercise care in situations in which they are alone with men (even though they know them) and should avoid behavior which is sexually arousing.

Women and men should be told that most forced sexual intercourse appears to arise out of an interactive situation in that men who commit these acts are not perceived by their victims to have planned their assaults. That is, they can not expect to be able to tell in advance which men are likely to become assailants, with perhaps one exception. The use of force in personal relationships appears to be correlated with incidence of forced sexual intercourse.

Experience with early attempts to develop educational drug prevention programs suggests that caution should be exercised in the development of prevention programs in the area of safe sexual behavior for young adults. Early drug prevention programs contained a great deal of information based on values and a great deal of information about drugs and drug use, some of which was not accurate. The young drug-using adults who were the targets of these programs were well informed about the nature of drugs and drug use. When they noted statements which were unrealistic or untrue, they rejected the program.

It appears that some of the date rape prevention programs developed in recent years suffer from misinformation and unrealistic statements. Some of these programs set standards for young women that are not realistic if the young women expect to remain socially active. Much more must be known about the nature of dating and courtship among young men and women today so that programs developed for prevention are both accurate in describing typical and risky behavior and realistic in terms of today's dating standards.

Looking to the Future

It appears at this point that future research must step back from the examination of prevalence, incidence, and individual factors and broaden the research frame to include the context in which these acts of violence occur. Date rape and acquaintance rape must be examined in the context of dating and courtship. There may be a relationship between the use of force or aggression in intimate relationships and the use of force to obtain sexual intercourse or sexual access. It is also possible that the values which define the appropriate behaviors for negotiating a dating, intimate, sexual relationship are unclear and may include the use of "acceptable" force. Such a situation would produce situations in which conflicting definitions would produce incidents of rape. If young women are to be adequately prepared to protect themselves, then accurate information must be available to inform the potential victims and their potential offenders of appropriate and inappropriate behaviors in dating and of the potential for confusion in situations in which the values are unclear.

The studies reported here were developed to add clarity to the effort to develop an understanding of the phenomena of date rape. Although care was taken to measure the variable of forced sexual intercourse rather than the label rape, it appears that the measures were not adequate. A more refined measure of the degree of association between the offender and the victim will be required to adequately explore the dynamics of forced sexual intercourse involving people who know each other. It is noted that few of the incidents reported here appear to approximate the "old" definition of rape - fear of great bodily harm and/or use of "physical force" (striking blows). This is not intended to reduce the seriousness of "lesser" forms of violation of personal rights. However, the behavior may be interpreted differently by different victims and different assailants, producing different levels of trauma and different labels of the behavior by the participants. In short, what may be rape to one victim may be unpleasant but acceptable behavior to another. There is more than ample room and a pressing need for extensive research in this area.

Bibliography

Abby, A. (1982), 'Sex Differences in Attributions for Friendly Behavior: Do Males Misperceive Females' Friendliness?', *Journal of Personality and Social Psychology*, vol. 42, pp. 830-8.

Abel, G.G., Bianchard, E.B. and Becker, J.V. (1978), 'An Integrated Treatment Program for Rapists', in R.T. Rada (ed), *Clinical Aspects of the Rapist* (pp.161-214), Grune and Stratton, New York.

Adamec, C.S. and Adamec, R.E. (1981), 'Aggression by Men Against Women: Adaptation or Aberration', *International Journal of Women's Studies*, vol. 1, pp. 1-21.

Adler, C. (1985), 'An Exploration of Self-Reported Sexually Aggressive Behavior', *Crime and Delinquency*, vol. 31 (2), pp. 306-31.

Ageton, S.S. (1983), *Sexual Assault among Adolescents*, Lexington Press, Lexington Press, MA.

Allen, M., Emmers, T. and Giery, M.A. (1995), 'Exposure to Pornography and Acceptance of Rape Myths', *Journal of Communication*, vol. 45(1), pp. 5-26.

Allison, J.A., Adams, D.L., Bunce, L.W., Gilkerson, T. and Nelson, K. (1992), 'The Rapist: Aggressive, Dangerous, Power Hungry, and Manipulative', paper presented at the Annual Meeting of Psychological and Educational Research, Emporia, KS.

Allison, J.A. and Wrightsman, L.S. (1993), *Rape: The Misunderstood Crime*, Sage, Newbury Park, CA.

Amick, A. and Calhoun, K. (1987), 'Resistance to Sexual Aggression: Personality, Attitudinal, and Situational Factors', *Archives of Sexual Behavior*, vol. 16, pp. 153-62.

Amir, M. (1971), *Patterns in Forcible Rape*, University of Chicago Press, Chicago.

Angle, P.M. (1952), *Bloody Williamson: A Chapter in American Lawlessness*, Alfred A. Knopf, New York.

Archer, D. and Gartner, R. (1984), *Violence and Crime in Cross-National Perspective*, Yale University Press, New Haven, CT.

Ardrey, R. (1966), *The Territorial Imperative*, Antheneum, New York.

Bailey, B.L. (1988), *From Front Porch to Back Seat: The History of Courtship in America*, The Johns Hopkins University Press, Baltimore, MD.

Bandura, A. (1973), *Aggression: A Social Learning Analysis*, Prentice Hall, Englewood Cliffs, NJ.

Bandura, A., Underwood, B. and Fromson, M.E. (1975), 'Disinhibition of Aggression through Diffusion of Responsibility and Dehumanization of Victims', *Journal of Research in Personality*, vol. 9, pp. 253-69.

Barber, R.   (1974), 'Judge and Jury Attitudes toward Rape', *Australia and New Zealand Journal of Criminology*, vol. 7, pp. 157-72.

Barnes, G.E., Greenwood, L. and Sommer, R.   (1991), 'Courtship Violence in a Canadian Sample of Male College Students', *Family Relations*, vol. 40, pp. 37-44.

Barnett, N.J. and Field, H.S.   (1977), 'Sex Differences in University Students' Attitudes toward Rape', *Journal of College Student Personnel*, vol. 18, pp. 93-6.

Baron, L. and Straus, M.A.   (1984), 'Sexual Stratification, Pornography, and Rape in the United States', in M.N. Malamuth and E. Donnerstein (eds), *Pornography and Sexual Aggression* (pp. 185-209), Academic Press, Orlando, FL.

Baron, L. and Straus, M.A.   (1989), *Four Theories of Rape in American Society: A State Level Analysis*, Yale University Press, New Haven, CT.

Baron, R.A.   (1977), *Human Aggression*, Plenum, New York.

Barry, K.   (1979), *Female Sexual Slavery*, Prentice Hall, Englewood Cliffs, NJ.

Bart, P.B. and O'Brien, P.H.   (1981), 'A Study of Women Who Were Both Raped and Avoided Rape', *Journal of Social Issues*, vol. 37, pp. 123-37.

Bart, P.B. and O'Brien, P.H.   (1985), *Stopping Rape: Successful Survival Strategies*, Pergamon, New York.

Bateman, A.J.   (1948), 'Introsexual Selection in Drosophila', *Heredity*, vol. 2, pp. 349-68.

Becker, H.   (1963), *Outsiders: Studies in the Sociology of Deviance*, Free Press, New York.

Becker, J.V., Abel, G.G., Blanchard, E.B., Murphy, W.D. and Coleman, E.   (1978), 'Evaluating Social Skills of Sexually Aggressives', *Criminal Justice and Behavior*, vol. 5, pp. 357-68.

Belenky, M.F., Clinchy, B.M., Goldberger, N.R. and Tarule, J.M.   (1986), *Women's Ways of Knowing*, Basic Books, New York.

Benderly, B.L.   (1982), 'Rape Free or Rape Prone', *Science*, vol. 82(3), pp. 40-3.

Berger, R.J., Searles, P. and Neuman, W.L.   (1988), 'The Dimensions of Rape Reform Legislation', *Law and Society Review*, vol. 22, pp. 329-57.

Bernard, M.L. and Bernard, J.L.   (1983), 'Violent Intimacy: The Family as a Model for Love Relationships', *Family Relations*, vol. 32, pp. 283-6.

Blackman, J.   (1985), 'The Language of Sexual Violence: More Than a Matter of Semantics', in S.R. Sunday and J. Tobach (eds), *Violence Against Women* (pp. 115-128), Gordian Press, New York.

Blumer, H.   (1937), 'Social Organization and Individual Disorganization', *American Journal of Sociology*, vol. 42, pp. 871-7.

Boeringer, S.B., Shehan, C.L. and Akers, R.L.   (1991), 'Social Contexts and Social Learning in Sexual Coercion and Aggression: Assessing the Contribution of Fraternity Membership', *Family Relations*, vol. 40, pp. 58-64.

Bourque, L.B. (1989), *Defining Rape*, Duke University Press, Durham, NC.

Brackman, R. (1993), 'Reporting of Rape Victimization: Have Rape Reforms Made a Difference?', *Criminal Justice and Behavior*, vol. 20, pp. 254-70.

Brackman, R. (1995), 'Is the Glass Half Empty or Half Full? A Response to Pollard', *Criminal Justice and Behavior*, vol. 22 (1), pp. 81-5.

Breines, W. and Gordon, L. (1983), 'The New Scholarship on Family Violence', *Signs*, vol. 8, pp. 491-531.

Brickman, J. and Briere, J. (1984), 'Incidence of Rape and Sexual Assault in an Urban Canadian Population', *International Journal of Women's Studies*, vol. 7, pp. 195-206.

Bridges, J.S. and McGrail, C.A. (1989), 'Attributions of Responsibility for Date and Stranger Rape', *Sex Roles*, vol. 21(3/4), pp. 273-87.

Brinson, S.L. (1992), 'The Use and Opposition of Rape Myths in Prime Time Television Dramas', *Sex Roles: A Journal of Research*, vol. 27, pp. 359-76.

Brown, R.M. (1969), 'Historical Patterns of Violence in America', in H.D. Graham and T.R. Gurr (eds), *Violence in America: A Staff Report to the National Commissions on the Causes and Prevention of Violence*, U.S. Government Printing Office, Washington, DC.

Brownmiller, S. (1975), *Against Our Will: Men, Women, and Rape*, Simon and Schuster, New York.

Burgess, A.W. (ed) (1988), *Rape and Sexual Assault*, vol. 2, pp. 193-220, Garland, New York.

Burgess, A.W. and Holmstrom, L.L. (1974), 'Rape Trauma Syndrome', *American Journal of Psychiatry*, vol. 131, pp. 981-6.

Burgess, A.W. and Holmstrom, L.L. (1980), 'Typology and the Coping Behavior of Rape Victims', in S.L. McCombie (ed), *The Rape Crisis Intervention Handbook*, Plenum, New York.

Burgess, A.W. and Holstorm, L.L. (1983), 'The Rape Victim in the Emergency Ward', *American Journal of Nursing*, vol. 73(10), pp. 1740-5.

Burkhart, B.R. and Fromuth, M.E. (1991), 'Individual and Social Psychological Understanding of Sexual Coercion', in E. Gruerholz and M.A. Koralewski (eds), *Sexual Coercion: A Sourcebook on Its Nature, Causes, and Prevention* (pp.75-89), Lexington Press, Lexington, MA.

Burt, M.R. (1980), 'Cultural Myths and Supports for Rape', *Journal of Personality and Social Psychology*, vol. 38, pp. 217-34.

Burt, M.R. and Alkin, R.S. (1981), 'Rape Myths and Support for Rape', *Journal of Personality and Social Psychology*, vol. 38, pp. 217-30.

Calhoun, K.S., Kelley, S.P., Amick, A. and Gardner, R. (1986), 'Research on Rape', paper presented at the Southeastern Psychological Association, Orlando, FL.

Carter, J.M. (1984), 'The Status of Rape in Thirteenth Century England: 1218-1276', *International Journal of Women's Studies*, vol. 7, pp. 248-59.

Cate, R.M., Henton, J.M., Koval, J.E., Christopher, F.S. and Lloyd, S.A. (1982), 'Premarital Abuse: A Social Psychological Perspective', *Journal of Family Issues*, vol. 3, pp. 79-90.

Chamove, A., Harlow, H.F. and Mitchell, G.D. (1967), 'Sex Differences in the Infant Directed Behavior of Preadolescent Rhesus Monkeys', *Child Development*, vol. 38, pp. 329-55.

Check, J.V. and Malamuth, N.M. (1981), 'Feminism and Rape in the 80's: Recent Research Findings', in P. Caplan, C. Larson, and L. Cammaert (eds), *Psychology Changing for Women*, Eden Press Women's Publications, Montreal.

Check, J.V.P. and Malamuth, N.M. (1983), 'Sex-role Stereotyping and Reactions to Stranger vs. Acquaintance Rape', *Journal of Personality and Social Psychology*, vol. 45, pp. 344-56.

Check, J.V.P. and Malamuth, N.M. (1983), 'Can Participation in Pornography Experiments Have Positive Effects?', *Journal of Sex Research*, vol. 20, pp. 14-31.

Cherry, F. (1983), 'Gender Roles and Sexual Violence', in E.R. Allgeier and B. McCormick (eds), *Changing Boundaries: Gender Roles and Sexual Behavior*, Mayfield, Palo Alto, CA.

Christie, R. and Geis, F.L. (1970), *Studies in Machiavellianism*, Academic Press, New York.

Clark, M.L., Beckett, J., Wells, M. and Dungee-Anderson, D. (1994), 'Courtship Violence among African American College Students', *Journal of Black Psychology*, vol. 20(3), pp. 264-80.

Clark, S.M. and Lewis, D.J. (1977), *Rape: The Price of Coercive Sexuality*, Women's Educational Press, Toronto.

Cloward, R.A. and Ohlin, L.E. (1960), *Delinquency and Opportunity*, The Free Press, Glencoe, IL.

Cohen, L.J. and Roth, S. (1987), 'The Psychological Aftermath of Rape: Long-term Effects and Individual Differences in Recovery', *Journal of Social and Clinical Psychology*, vol. 5, pp. 525-34.

Cohen, S. (1955), *Delinquent Boys: The Culture of the Gang*, The Free Press, Glencoe, IL.

Cornell, N. and Wilson, C. (1974), *Rape: The First Source Book for Women*, The New American Library, New York.

Curtis, L.A. (1975), *Violence, Race, and Culture*, Lexington Press, Lexington, MA.

Daly, M. (1978), *Gynecology: The Meta-ethics of Radical Feminism*, Beacon Press, Boston.

Daly, M. and Wilson, M. (1978), *Sex, Evolution, and Behavior*, Duxbury Press, North Scituate, MA.

Dawkins, R. (1976), *The Selfish Gene*, Oxford University Press, New York.

Degraw, D. and Ingram, J. (1990), 'Date Rape on Six College Campuses and the Issue of Consent', a paper presented to the Annual Meeting of the Academy of Criminal Justice Sciences, Denver, CO.

Deitz, S.R. (1980, fall), 'Double Jeopardy: The Rape Victim in Court', *Rocky Mountain Psychologist*, pp. 1-11.

DeKeseredy, W.S. (1988), *Woman Abuse in Dating Relationships: The Role of Male Peer Support*, Canadian Scholar's Press, Toronto.

Deutsch, H. (1944), *The Psychology of Women: Vol. 1. Girlhood*, Bantam Books, New York.

Diamond, I. (1980), 'Pornography and Repression: A Reconsideration', *Signs*, vol. 5, pp. 686-701.

Dilorio, J.A. (1989), 'Being and Becoming Coupled: The Emergence of Female Subordination in Heterosexual Relationships', in B.J. Risman and P. Schwartz (eds), *Gender in Intimate Relationships* (pp. 94-102), Wadsworth, Belmont, CA.

DiVasto, P.V., Kaufman, A., Rosner, L., Jackson, R., Christy, J., Pearson, S. and Burgett, T. (1974), 'The Relevance of Sexually Stressful Events among Females in the General Population, *Archives of Sexual Behavior*, vol. 13, pp. 59-67.

Dobash, R.E. and Dobash, R. (1979), *Violence Against Wives: A Case Against the Patriarchy*, Free Press, New York.

Donat, P.L.N. and D'Emilo, J. (1992), 'A Feminist Redefinition of Rape and Sexual Assault: Historical Foundations and Change', *Journal of Social Issues*, vol. 48, pp. 9-22.

Donnerstein, E. and Barrett, G. (1978a), 'Eroticism and Aggression', *Journal of Personality and Social Psychology*, vol. 36, pp. 180-8.

Donnerstein, E. and Barrett, G. (1978b), 'The Effects of Erotic Stimuli on Male Aggression toward Females', *Journal of Personality and Social Psychology*, vol. 36, pp. 180-8.

Donnerstein, E. and Hallman, J. (1978), 'Facilitating Effects of Erotica on Aggression toward Females', *Journal of Personality and Social Psychology*, vol. 36, pp. 1270-7.

Donnerstein, E., Linz, D. and Penrod, S. (1987), *The Question of Pornography*, Free Press, New York.

Dover, K.J. (1984), 'Classical Greek Attitudes to Sexual Behavior', in J. Peradotto and J. Sullivan (eds), *Women in the Ancient World: The Atrthusa Papers*, State University of New York Press, Albany, NY.

Doyle, D.P. and Burfeind, J.W. (1994), *The University of Montana Sexual Victimization Survey*, University of Montana, Missoula, MT.

Dull, R.T. and Giacopassi, D.J. (1987), 'Demographic Correlates of Sexual and Dating Attitudes: A Study of Date Rape', *Criminal Justice and Behavior*, vol. 14(2), pp. 175-193.

Durden-Smith, J. and deSimone, D. (1983), *Sex and the Brain*, Warner Publishing Company, New York.

Dworkin, A. (1981), *Pornography: Men Possessing Women*, Perigee Press, New York.

Ehrhart, J.K. and Sandler, B.R. (1985), *Campus Gang Rape: Party Games?* Association of American Colleges, Washington, DC.

Ellis, E.M., Atkeson, B.M. and Calhoun, K.S. (1981), 'An Assessment of Long-Term Reaction to Rape', *Journal of Abnormal Psychology*, vol. 90, pp. 263-6.

Ellis, L. (1989), *Theories of Rape: Inquiries into the Causes of Sexual Aggression*, Hemisphere Publishing Corporation, New York.

Eltzeroth, R., Charles, M.T., Kethineni, S. and Haghighi, B. (1994), *The Issues of Rape and Date Rape as Reported by Female and Male Students at the University of Illinois*, Police Training Institute, Champaign, IL.

Estrich, S. (1987), *Real Rape: How the Legal System Victimizes Women Who Say No*, Harvard University Press, Cambridge, MA.

Felson, R.B. (1991), 'Blame Analysis: Accounting for the Behavior of Protected Groups', *The American Sociologist*, vol. 22, pp. 5-23.

Felson, R.B. (1992), *Motives for Sexual Coercion*, paper presented at Annual Meeting of the American Society of Criminology, Tucson, AZ.

Fenstermaker, S. (1988), 'Acquaintance Rape on Campus: Attributions of Responsibility and Crime', in M. Pirog-Good and J. Stets (eds), *Violence in Dating Relationships* (pp. 257-71), Praeger, New York.

Field, H.S. (1978), 'Attitudes toward Rape: A Comparative Analysis of Police, Rapists, Crisis Counselors, and Citizens', *Journal of Personality and Social Psychology*, vol. 36, pp. 156-79.

Field, H.S. and Bienen, L.B. (1980), *Jurors and Rape: A Study in Psychology and Law*, Lexington Press, Lexington, MA.

Finkelhor, D. and Yllo, K. (1985), *License to Rape*, Rinehart and Winston, New York.

Fischer, G. (1986), 'College Student Attitudes toward Forcible Rape. I. Cognitive Predictors', *Archives of Sexual Behavior*, vol. 15, pp. 457-66.

Fischer, G.J. (1987), 'Hispanic and Majority Student Attitudes toward Forcible Date Rape as a Function of Differences in Attitudes toward Women', *Sex Roles*, vol. 17(1/2), pp. 93-101.

Foley, L.A., Evancic, C., Karnik, K., King, J. and Parks, A. (1995), Date Rape: Effects of Race of Assailant and Victim and Gender of Subjects on Perceptions', *Journal of Black Psychology*, vol. 21, pp. 6-19.

Follingstad, D.R., Rutledge, L.R., Polek, D.S. and McNeill- Hawkins, K. (1988), 'Factors Associated with Patterns of Dating Violence toward College Women', *Journal of Family Violence*, vol. 3, pp. 169-82.

Frantz, J.B. (1969), 'The Frontier Tradition: An Invitation to Violence', in D. Graham and T.R. Gurr (eds), *Violence in America: Historical and Comparative Perspectives*, vol. 1, U.S. Government Printing Office, Washington, DC.

Freeman, J. (ed) (1989), *Women: A Feminist Perspective*, Mayfield, Palo Alto, CA.

Friedan, B. (1963), *The Feminine Mystique*, W. W. Norton Publishing Company, New York.

Fromm, E. (1977), *The Anatomy of Human Destructiveness*, Penguin, Harmondsworth, England.

Gagnon, J.H. (1977), *Human Sexualities*, Scott Foresman, Glenview, IL.

Gagnon, J.H. and Simon, W. (1973), *Sexual Conduct: The Sources of Sexuality*, Aldine Press, Chicago.

Garcia, L.T., Milano, L. and Quijano, A. (1989), 'Perceptions of Coercive Sexual Behavior by Males and Females, *Sex Roles*, vol. 21, pp. 569-77.

Gastil, R.D. (1971), 'Homicide and a Regional Culture of Violence', *American Sociological Review*, vol. 36, pp. 412-27.

Gebhard, P.H., Gagon, J.H., Pomeroy, W.B. and Christenson, C.V. (1965), *Sex Offenders: An Analysis of Types*, Harper and Row, New York.

George, L.K., Winfield, I. and Blazer, D.G. (1992), 'Sociocultural Factors in Sexual Assault: Comparison of Two Representative Samples of Women', *Journal of Social Issues*, vol. 48 (1), pp. 105-25.

Gerdes, E.P., Dammann, E.J. and Heilig, K.E. (1988), 'Perceptions of Rape Victims and Assailants: Effects of Physical Attractiveness, Acquaintance, and Subject Gender', *Sex Roles*, vol. 19(3/4), pp. 141-53.

Getman, K. (1984), 'Sexual Control in the Slaveholding South: The Implementation and Maintenance of a Racial Caste System', *Harvard Women's Law Review*, vol. 7, pp. 115-53.

Giacopassi, D.J. and Dull, R.T. (1986), 'Gender and Racial Differences in the Acceptance of Rape Myths within a College Population', *Sex Roles*, vol. 15(1/2), pp. 63-75.

Giarrusso, R., Johnson, P., Goodchilds, J. and Zellman, G. (1979, April), 'Adolescents' Cues and Signals: Sex and Assault', in P. Johnson (Chair), Acquaintance Rape and Adolescent Sexuality Symposium presented at the Annual Meeting of the Western Psychological Association, San Diego, CA.

Gibson, L., Linden, R. and Johnson, S. (1980), 'A Situational Theory of Rape', *Canadian Journal of Criminology*, vol. 22, pp. 51-63.

Goodchilds, J.D. and Zellman, G.L. (1984), 'Sexual Signaling and Sexual Aggression in Adolescent Relationships', in N.M. Malamuth and E. Donnerstein (eds), *Pornography and Sexual Aggression* (pp. 233-43), Academic Press, Orlando, FL.

Goodchilds, J.D., Zellman, G., Johnson, P.B. and Giarrusso, R. (1988), 'Adolescents and Their Perceptions of Sexual Interaction Outcomes', in A.W. Burgess (ed),

Sexual Assault (vol. 2, pp. 245-70), Garland, New York.

Gordon, G. and Riger, S. (1989), *The Female Fear*, The Free Press, New York.

Graham, D.G. and Gurr, T.R. (1969), *Violence in America: Historical and Comparative Perspectives*, vol. 1, vol. 2, U.S. Government Printing Office, Washington, DC.

Griffin, S. (1971), 'The All-American Crime', *Ramparts*, vol. 10, pp. 26-35.

Groth, A.N. (1979), *Men Who Rape: The Psychology of the Offender*, Plenum Press, New York.

Groth, A.N. and Birnbaum, H.J. (1985), *Men Who Rape: The Psychology of the Offender*, Plenum Press, New York.

Gwartney-Gibbs, P.A., Stockard, J. and Brohmer, S. (1987), 'Learning Courtship Aggression: The influence of Parents, Peers, and Personal Experiences', *Family Relations*, vol. 36, pp. 276-82.

Hackney, S. (1969), 'Southern Violence', *American Historical Review*, vol. 74, pp. 906-25.

Hagen, R. (1979), *The Bio-Social Factor*, Doubleday, Garden City, NJ.

Hall, E.R. and Flannery, P.J. (1984), 'Prevalence and Correlates of Sexual Assault Experiences in Adolescents', *Victimology: An International Journal*, vol. 9, pp. 398-406.

Herman, J. (1989), 'The Rape Culture', in J. Freeman (ed), *Women: A Feminist Perspective* (pp. 20-44), Mayfield, Palo Alto, CA.

Hirsch, M. (1981), *Women and Violence*, Van Nostrand Reinhold, New York.

Holmstrom, L.L. and Burgess, A.W. (1978), *The Victim of Rape: Institutional Reactions*, Wiley, New York.

Holmstrom, L.L. and Burgess, A.W. (1980), 'Sexual Behavior of Assailants During Reported Rapes', *Archives of Sexual Behavior*, vol. 9, pp. 427-39.

Huesman, L.R. and Malamuth, N.M. (1986), Media Violence and Antisocial Behavior: An Overview, *Journal of Social Issues*, vol. 42, pp. 1-6.

Huggins, M.D. and Straus, M.A. (1980), 'Violence and the Social Structure as Reflected in Children's Books From 1850 to 1970', in M.A. Strauss and G.T. Hotaling (eds), *The Social Causes of Husband Wife Violence* (pp. 51-67), University of Minnesota Press, Minneapolis, MN.

Hursch, C. and Selkin, J. (1984), *Rape Prevention Research Project*, Annual Report of the Violence Research Unit, Division of Psychiatric Service, Department of Health and Hospitals, Denver Anti-Crime Council, Denver, CO.

Jackson, S. (1978), 'The Social Context of Rape: Sexual Scripts and Motivation', *Women's Studies International Quarterly*, vol. 1, pp. 27-38.

Jenkins, M. and Dambrot, F. (1987), 'The Attribution of Date Rape: Observers' Attitudes and Sexual Experiences and the Dating Situation', *Journal of Applied Social Psychology*, vol. 17, pp. 875-95.

Jensen, L.A. (1993), *College Students' Attitudes toward Acquaintance Rape: The Effects of a Prevention Intervention Using Cognitive Dissonance Theory,* unpublished doctoral dissertation, University of Alabama, Tuscaloosa, AL.

Johnson, A.G. (1980), 'On the Prevalence of Rape in the United States, *Signs: Journal of Women in Culture and Society*, vol. 6, pp. 136-46.

Johnson, G.D., Palileo, G.J. and Gray, N.B. (1992), '"Date Rape" on a Southern College Campus: Reports from 1991', *Sociology and Social Research*, vol. 76 (6), pp. 37-44.

Johnson, J.D. and Jackson, L.A., Jr. (1988), 'Assessing the Effects of Factors that Might Underlie the Differential Perception of Acquaintance and Stranger Rape', *Sex Role*, vol. 19(1/2), pp. 37-45.

Johnson, K. (1995), 'Attributions about Date Rape: Impact of Clothing, Sex, Money Spent, Date Type, and Perceived Similarity', *Family and Consumer Sciences Research Journal*, vol. 23 (3), pp. 293-311.

Jordon, W. (1968), *White Over Black: American Attitudes toward the Negro*, University of North Carolina Press, Williamsburg, VA.

Kanekar, S. and Kolsawalla, M. (1980), 'Responsibility of a Rape Victim in Relation to Her Respectability, Attractiveness, and Provocativeness', *Journal of Social Psychology*, vol. 112, pp. 153-4.

Kanin, E.J. (1957), 'Male Aggression in Dating-Courtship Relations', *American Journal of Sociology*, vol. 63, pp. 197-204.

Kanin, E.J. (1967), 'Reference Groups and Sex Conduct Norm Violations', *Sociological Quarterly*, vol. 8, pp. 495-504.

Kanin, E.J. (1984), 'Date Rape: Unofficial Criminals and Victims', *Victimology: An International Journal*, vol. 9(1), pp. 95-105.

Kanin, E.J. (1985), 'Date Rapists: Differential Sexual Socialization and Relative Deprivation', *Archives of Sexual Behavior*, vol. 14(3), pp. 219-31.

Katz, B.L. and Burt, M.R. (1986, August), *Effects of Familiarity with the Rapist on Postrape Recovery*, paper presented at the Annual Meeting of the American Psychological Association, Washington, DC.

Katz, S. and Mazur, M.A. (1979), *Understanding the Rape Victim: A Synthesis of Research Findings*, Wiley, New York.

Kirkpatrick, C. and Kanin, E. (1957), 'Male Sex Aggression on a University Campus', *American Sociological Review*, vol. 22, pp. 52-8.

Klemmack, S.H. and Klemmack, D.L. (1976), 'The Social Definition of Rape', in *Sexual Assault* (pp. 135-47), Lexington Books, Lexington, MA.

Knudsen, D.D. (1988), *Child Protective Services: Discretion, Decisions, Dilemmas*, Charles C. Thomas, Springfield, IL.

Koehler, I. (1980), *A Search for Power: The "Weaker Sex" in Seventeenth-century New England*, University of Illinois Press, Urbana, IL.

Kopp, S.P. (1962), 'The Character Structure of Sex Offenders', *American Journal of Psychotherapy*, vol. 16, pp. 64-70.

Korman, S.K. (1983), 'Nontraditional Dating Behavior: Date-Initiation and Date Expense-Sharing among Feminists and Nonfeminists', *Family Relations*, vol.

32, pp. 575-81.

Korman, S.K. and Leslie, G. (1982), 'The Relationship of Feminist Ideology and Date Expense Sharing to Perceptions of Sexual Aggression in Dating', *Journal of Sex Research*, vol. 18 (2), 114-29.

Kormos, K.C. and Brooks, C.I. (1994), 'Acquaintance Rape: Attributions of Victim Blame by College Students and Prison Inmates as a Function of Relationship Status of Victim and Assailant', *Psychological Reports*, vol. 74, pp. 545-6.

Koss, M.P. (1985), 'The Hidden Rape Victim: Personality, Attitudinal, and Situational Characteristics', *Psychology of Women Quarterly*, vol. 9, pp. 193-212.

Koss, M.P. and Dinero, T.E. (1989), 'Discriminant Analysis of Risk Factors for Sexual Victimization among a National Sample of College Women', *Journal of Consulting and Clinical Psychology*, vol. 57, pp. 242-50.

Koss, M., Dinero, T., Seibel, C. and Cox, S. (1988), 'Stranger and Acquaintance Rape: Are There Differences in the Victims' Experience', *Psychology of Women Quarterly*, vol. 12, pp. 1-23.

Koss, M., Gidycz, C. and Wisniewski, N. (1987), 'The Scope of Rape: Incidence and Prevalence of Sexual Aggression and Victimization in a National Sample of Higher Education Students', *Journal of Consulting and Clinical Psychology*, vol. 55, pp. 162-70.

Koss, M. and Harvey, M. (1987), *The Rape Victim*, The Green Press, Lexington, MA.

Koss, M.P. and Leonard, K.E. (1984), 'Sexually Aggressive Men: Empirical Findings and Theoretical Implications', in N.M. Malamuth and E. Donnerstein (eds), *Pornography and Sexual Aggression*, Academic Press, Orlando, FL.

Koss, M., Leonard, K.E., Beezley, D.A. and Oros, C. J. (1985), 'Non-stranger Sexual Aggression: A Discriminant Analysis of the Psychological Characteristics of Undetected Offenders', *Sex Roles*, vol. 12, pp. 981-92.

Koss, M.P., Woodruff, W.J. and Koss, P.G. (1990), 'Relation of Criminal Victimization to Health Perceptions among Women Medical Patients', *Journal of Consulting and Clinical Psychology*, vol. 58, pp. 147-52.

Krulewitz, J. and Payne, E. (1978), 'Attributions about Rape: Effects of Rapist Force, Observer Sex, and Sex Role Attitudes', *Journal of Applied Social Psychology*, vol. 8, pp. 291-305.

Kutchinski, B. (1988), 'Towards an Exploration of the Decrease in Registered Sex Crimes in Copenhagen', *Technical Report of the Commission on Obscenity and Pornography*, vol. 7, U.S Government Printing Office, Washington, DC.

LaFree, G.D. (1989), *Rape and Criminal Justice*, Wadsworth, Belmont, CA.

Lambert, W.W., Triandis, L.M. and Wolf, M. (1959), 'Some Correlates of Beliefs in the Malevolence and Benevolence of Supernatural Beings: A Cross Cultural Study', *Journal of Abnormal and Social Psychology*, vol. 58, pp. 162-9.

Laner, M.R. and Thompson, J. (1982), 'Abuse and Aggression in Courting Couples', *Deviant Behavior*, vol. 3, pp. 229-34.

L'Armand, K.L. and Pepitone, A. (1982), 'Judgments of Rape: A Study of Victim-Rapist Relationship and Victim Sexual History', *Personality and Social Psychology Bulletin*, vol. 8(1), pp. 134-9.

Lemert, E.M. (1951), *Social Pathology*, McGraw-Hill, New York.

Leo, J. (1987, March, 23), 'When the Date Turns into Rape: Too Often the Attacker is the Clean-cut Acquaintance Next Door', *Time*, p. 77.

Leshner, A.L. (1978), *An Introduction to Behavioral Endocrinology*, Oxford University Press, New York.

Lisak, D. and Roth, S. (1988), 'Motivational Factors in Nonincarcerated Sexually Aggressive Men', *Journal of Personality and Social Psychology*, vol. 55, pp. 795-8.

Lloyd, S.A. (1991), 'The Darkside of Courtship: Violence and Sexual Exploitation', *Family Relations*, vol. 40, pp. 14-20.

Lobel, K. (1986), *Naming the Violence: Speaking Out About Lesbian Battering*, Seal Press, Seattle.

Loh, W. (1980), 'The Impact of Common Law and Reform Rape Statutes on Prosecutions: An Empirical Study', *Washington Law Review*, pp. 552-613.

Longino, H.E. (1980), 'Pornography, Oppression, and Freedom: A Closer Look', in L. Lederer (ed), *Take Back the Night: A Closer Look*, pp. 26-41, William Morrow Company, New York.

Lorenz, K. (1971), *On Aggression*, Bantam Books, New York.

Lottes, I.L. (1988), 'Sexual Socialization and Attitudes toward Rape', in A.W. Burgess (ed), *Rape and Sexual Assault* (vol. 2, pp. 193-220), Garland, New York.

Lynn, K. (1969), 'Violence in American Literature and Folk Lore', in H.G. Graham and T.R. Gurr (eds), *Violence in America: Historical and Comparative Perspectives*, vol. I, U.S. Government Printing Office, Washington, DC.

MacEwen, K.E. (1994), 'Refining the Intergenerational Transmission Hypothesis', *Journal of Interpersonal Violence*, vol. 9(3), pp. 350-66.

MacKinnon, C. (1986), *Feminism Unmodified*, Harvard University Press, Cambridge, MA.

Mahoney, E.R., Shively, M.D. and Traw, M. (1986), 'Sexual Coercion and Assault: Male Socialization and Female Risk', *Sexual Coercion and Assault*, vol. 1, pp. 2-8.

Makepeace, J. (1981), 'Courtship Violence among College Students', *Family Relations*, vol. 30, pp. 97-102.

Makepeace, J.M. (1987), 'Social Factors and Victim-Offender Differences in Courtship Violence', *Family Relations*, vol. 36, pp. 987-91.

Makepeace, J. (1989), 'Dating, Living Together and Courtship Violence', in M. Pirog-Good and J. Stets (eds), *Violence in Dating Relationships: Emerging*

Issues (pp. 94-107), Praeger, New York.

Malamuth, N.M. (1981), 'Rape Proclivity Among Males', *Journal of Social Issues*, vol. 37(4), pp. 138-57.

Malamuth, N.M. (1984), 'Aggression Against Women', in N.A. Malamuth and E. Donnerstein (eds), *Pornography and Sexual Aggression*, Academic Press. Orlando, FL.

Malamuth, N.M. (1986), 'Predictors of Naturalistic Sexual Aggression', *Journal of Personality and Social Psychology*, vol. 50, pp. 953-62.

Malamuth, N.M. (1988), 'Predicting Laboratory Aggression Against Female and Male Targets: Implications for SexualAgression', *Journal of Personality and Social Psychology*, vol. 22, pp. 477-95.

Malamuth, N., Briere, J. and Check, J.V.P. (1986), 'Sexual Arousal in Response to Aggression: Ideology, Aggressive, and Sexual Correlates', *Journal of Personality and Social Psychology*, vol. 50, pp. 330-40.

Malamuth, N., Fesback, S. and Jaffe, Y. (1977), 'Sexual Arousal and Aggression: Recent Experiments and Theoretical Issues', *Journal of Social Issues*, vol. 33, pp. 110-33.

Margolin, L., Miller, M. and Moran P. (1989), 'When a Kiss is Not Just a Kiss: Relating Violations of Consent in Kissing to Rape Myth Acceptance', *Sex Roles*, vol. 20(5/6), pp. 231-43.

Martindale, D. (1957), 'Social Disorganization: The Conflict of Normative and Empirical Approaches', in H. Becker and A. Boskoff (eds), *Modern Sociological Theory in Continuity and Change* (pp. 340-367), Rinehart and Winston, New York.

Matoesian, G.M. (1993), *Reproducing Rape: Domination through Talk in the Courtroom*, University of Chicago Press, Chicago.

Matza, D. (1964), *Delinquency and Drift*, Wiley, New York.

Mazur, A. (1983), 'Hormones, Aggression and Dominance in Humans', in B.B. Svare (ed), *Hormones and Aggressive Behavior*, Plenum, New York.

McCahill, T.W., Meyer, L.C. and Fischman, R.M. (1979), *The Aftermath of Rape*, Lexington Books, Lexington, MA.

McCaul, K.D., Veltum, L.G., Boyechko, V. and Crawford, J.J. (1990), 'Understanding Attributions of Victim Blame for Rape: Sex, Violence, and Foreseeability', *Journal of Applied Social Psychology*, vol. 20(1), pp. 1-26.

Medea, A. and Thompson, K. (1974), *Against Rape*, Farrar, Straus and Giroux, New York.

Mellen, S.L. (1981), *The Evolution of Love*, Freeman Press, San Francisco.

Merton, R.K. (1957), *Social Theory and Social Structure*, Free Press of Glencoe, New York.

Messner, S.F. (1983), 'Regional and Racial Effects on the Urban Homicide Rate: The Subculture of Violence Revisited', *American Journal of Sociology*, vol. 88, pp. 997-1007.

Mill, J.S. (1870), *The Subjection of Women*, D. Appleton and Co., New York.

Miller, W. (1976), 'Youth Gangs in the Urban Crisis Era', in J.F. Short (ed), *Delinquency, Crime, and Society*, University of Chicago Press, Chicago.

Mills, C.S. and Granoff, B.J. (1992), 'Date and Acquaintance Rape among a Sample of College Students', *Social Work*, vol. 37, pp. 504-09.

Morgan, R. (1980), 'Theory and Practice: Pornography and Rape', in L. Lwederer (ed.), *Take Back the Night: A Closer Look*, William Morrow Company, New York.

Mosher, D.L. and Anderson, R.D. (1984), 'Macho Personality, Sexual Aggression, and Reactions to Guided Imagery of Realistic Rape', *Journal of Research in Personality*, vol. 20, pp. 77-94.

Mower, E.R. (1941), 'Methodological Problems in Social Disorganization', *American Sociological Review*, vol. 6, pp. 639-49.

Moyer, K.E. (1976), *The Psychobiology of Aggression*, Harper and Row, New York.

Muehlenhard, C.L. (1988), 'Misinterpreted Dating Behaviors and the Risk of Date Rape', *Journal of Social and Clinical Psychology*, vol. 6(1), pp. 20-37.

Muehlenhard, C.L., Friedman, D.E. and Thomas, C. M. (1985), 'Is Date Rape Justifiable? The Effects of Dating Activity, Who Initiated, Who Paid, and Men's Attitudes toward Women', *Psychology of Women Quarterly*, vol. 9(3), pp. 297-310.

Muehlenhard, C.L. and Hollabaugh, L.C. (1988), 'Do Women Sometimes Say No When They Mean Yes? The Prevalence and Correlates of Women's Token Resistance to Sex', *Journal of Personality and Social Psychology*, vol. 54, pp. 872-8.

Muehlenhard, C. and Linton, M. (1987), 'Date Rape and Sexual Aggression in Dating Situations: Incidence and Risk Factors', *Journal of Counseling Psychology*, vol. 93, pp. 186-96.

Murnen, S.K., Perot, A. and Byrne, D. (1989), 'Coping with Unwanted Sexual Activity: Normative Responses, Situational Determinants, and Individual Differences', *Journal of Sex Research*, vol. 26, pp. 85-106.

Mynatt, C.R. and Allgeier, E.R. (1990), 'Risk Factors, Self-Attributions, and Adjustment Problems among Victims of Sexual Coercion', *Journal of Applied Social Psychology*, vol. 20(2), pp. 130-53.

Nelson, E. (1982), 'Pornography and Sexual Aggression', in M. Yaffee and E. Nelson (eds), *The Influence of Pornography on Behavior*, Academic Press, London.

Okun, L. (1986), *Woman Abuse*, Suny Press, Albany, NY.

Parrot, A. (1986), *Acquaintance Rape and Sexual Assault Prevention Training Manual* (2nd ed), Cornell University Press, New York.

Parrot, A. and Bechhofer, L. (1991), *Acquaintance Rape*, John Wiley and Sons, Inc, New York.

Persell, C.H. (1984), *Understanding Society*, Harper and Row, New York.

Pollard, P. (1995), 'Rape Reporting as a Function of Victim-Offender Status: A Critique of the Lack of Effect Reported by Brackman', *Criminal Justice and Behavior*, vol. 22(1), pp. 74-80.

Poppen, P.J. and Segal, N.J. (1988), 'The Influence of Sex and Sex Role Orientation on Sexual Coercion', *Sex Roles*, vol. 19, pp. 689-701.

Post, J.B. (1978), 'Sir Thomas West and the Statute of Rapes, 1382', *Bulletin of the Institute of Historical Research*, vol. 53, pp. 24-30.

Quinsey, V.L. (1984), 'Sexual Aggression: Studies of Offenders Against Women', in D. Weisstub (ed), *Law and Mental Health: International Perspectives*, vol. 1, Pergamon Press, New York.

Quinsey, V.L., Chaplin, T.C. and Varney, G. (1981), 'A Comparison of Rapists' and Non-sex Offenders Sexual Preferences for Mutually Consenting Sex, Rape, and Physical Abuse of Women', *Behavioral Assessment*, vol. 3, pp. 127-35.

Rabkin, J.G. (1979), 'The Epidemiology of Forcible Rape', *American Journal of Orethopsychiatry*, vol. 49, pp. 634-47.

Rada, R.T. (ed) (1978), *Clinical Aspects of the Rapist*, Grune and Stratton, New York.

Rapaport, K. and Burkhart, B. R. (1984), 'Personality and Attitudinal Characteristics of Sexually Coercive College Males', *Journal of Abnormal Psychology*, vol. 93, pp. 216-21.

Richard, A.F. and Schulman, S.R. (1982), 'Sociobiology: Primate Field Studies', *Annual Review in Anthropology*, vol. 11, pp. 231-55.

Richardson, D.C. and Campbell, J.C. (1982), 'Alcohol and Rape: The Effect of Alcohol on Attribution of Blame for Rape', *Personality and Social Psychychology Bulletin*, vol. 8, pp. 468-76.

Riger, S. and Gordon, M.T. (1981), 'The Fear of Rape: A Study in Social Control', *Journal of Social Issues*, vol. 37(4), pp. 71-92.

Roscoe, B. and Benaske, N. (1985), 'Courtship Violence Experienced by Abused Wives: Similarities in Patterns of Abuse', *Family Relations*, vol. 34, pp. 419-24.

Rose, V.M. (1977), 'Rape as a Social Problem: A Byproduct of the Feminist Movement', *Social Problems*, vol. 25, pp. 247-59.

Rossiaud, J. (1978), 'Prostitution, Youth, and Society in the Towns of Southeastern France in the Fifteenth Century', in R. Forster and O. Ranum (eds), *Deviants and the Abandoned in French Society* (pp. 1-46), Johns Hopkins University Press, Washington, DC.

Rothman, E.K. (1984), *Hands and Hearts: A History of Courtship in America*, Basic Books, New York.

Rouse, L.P., Breen, R. and Howell, M. (1988), 'Abuse in Intimate Relationships: A Comparison of Married and Dating College Students', *Journal of Interpersonal Violence*, vol. 3, pp. 414-29.

Rowland, J. (1985), *The Ultimate Violation*, Doubleday, New York.

Ruggerio, G. (1980), *Violence in Early Renaissance Venice*, Rutgers University Press, Camden, NJ.

Russell, D.E.H. (1975), *The Politics of Rape: The Victim's Perspective*, Stein and Day, New York.

Russell, D.E.H. (1982), *Rape in Marriage*, Stein and Day, New York.

Russell, D.E.H. (1984), *Sexual Exploitation: Rape, Child Sexual Abuse, and Workplace Harassment*, Sage, Beverly Hills, CA.

Russell, D.E.H. (1990), *Violence in Intimate Relationships*, Prentice Hall, Englewood Cliffs, NJ.

Ryan, K.M. (1995), 'Do Courtship Violent Men Have Characteristics Associated with a "Battering Personality"?', *Journal of Family Violence*, vol. 10(1), pp. 99-111.

Sanday, P.R. (1981), 'The Socio-Cultural Context of Rape: A Cross-Cultural Study', *The Journal of Social Issues*, vol. 37, pp. 5-27.

Sandberg, G.G., Jackson, T.L. and Petretic-Jackson, P. (1987), 'College Students Attitudes Regarding Sexual Coercion and Aggression: Developing Educational and Preventive Strategies', *Journal of College Student Personnel*, vol. 28, pp. 302-11.

Scarpitti, F. and Scarpitti, E. (1977), 'Victims of Rape', *Transaction*, vol. 14, pp. 29-32.

Scher, D. (1984), 'Sex Role Contradictions: Self-perceptions and Ideal Perceptions', *Sex Roles: A Journal of Research*, vol. 10, pp. 651-6.

Schmidt, G. and Sigusch, V. (1970), 'Sex Differences in Responses to Psychosexual Stimulation by Films and Slides', *Journal of Sex Research*, vol. 6, pp. 268-83.

Schmidt, G., Sigusch, V. and Schafer, S. (1973), 'Responses to Erotic Stories: Male Female Differences', *Archives of Sexual Behavior*, vol. 2, pp. 181-99.

Schwendinger, J. and Schwendinger, H. (1985), 'Homo Economics as the Rapist in Sociobiology', in S.R. Sanday and E. Toch (eds), *Violence Against Women* (pp. 85-114), Gordian Press, New York.

Scully, D. (1990), *Understanding Sexual Violence: A Study of Convicted Rapists*, Unwin Hyman, Boston.

Scully, D. and Marolla, J. (1984), 'Convicted Rapists' Vocabulary of Motives: Excuses and Justifications', *Social Problems*, vol. 32, pp. 530-44.

Scully, D. and Marolla, J. (1985), 'Riding the Bull at Gilly's: Convicted Rapists Describe the Rewards of Rape', *Social Problems*, vol. 32, pp. 251-62.

Seligman, C., Brickman, J. and Koulack, D. (1977), 'Rape and Physical Attractiveness: Assigning Responsibility to Victims', *Journal of Personality*, vol. 45, pp. 555-63.

Shields, W.M. and Shields, L.M. (1983), 'Forcible Rape: An Evolutionary Perspective', *Ethnology and Sociobiology*, vol. 4, pp. 115-36.

Shotland, R.L. (1992), 'A Theory of the Causes of Courtship Rape', *Journal of Social Issues*, vol. 48, pp. 127-44.

Shotland, R.L. and Goodstein, L. (1983), 'Just Because She Doesn't Want to Doesn't Mean It's Rape: An Experimentally Based Causal Model of the Perception of Rape in a Dating Situation', *Social Psychology Quarterly*, vol. 46, pp. 222-32.

Shotland, R.L. and Goodstein, L. (1992), 'Sexual Precedence Reduces the Perceived Legitimacy of Sexual Refusal: An Examination of Attributions Concerning Date Rape and Consensual Sex', *Personality and Social Psychology Bulletin*, vol. 18(6), pp. 756-65.

Shotland, R. and Hunter, B.A. (1995), 'Women's 'Token Resistance' and Compliant Sexual Behaviors are Related to Uncertain Sexual Intentions and Rape', *Personality and Social Psychology Bulletin*, vol. 21(3), pp. 226-37.

Siann, G. (1985), *Accounting for Aggression and Violence*, Allen and Unwin, London.

Sigelman, C.K., Berry, C.J. and Wiles, K.A. (1984), 'Violence in College Students' Dating Relationships', *Journal of Applied Social Psychology*, vol. 14, pp. 530-48.

Sigler, R.T. and Haygood, D. (1987), 'The Criminalization of Forced Marital Intercourse', *Marriage and Family Review*, vol. l2(1-2), pp. 71-86.

Sigler, R.T. and Wenstrom, M. (1993), 'Incidence of Date Rape on a College Campus', *International Journal of Comparative and Applied Criminal Justice*, vol. 17, pp. 229-42.

Smith, J.M. (1978), *The Evolution of Sex*, Cambridge Press, New York.

Smith, R.E., Pine, C.J. and Hawley, M.E. (1988), 'Social Cognitions about Adult Male Victims of Female Sexual Assault', *Journal of Sex Research*, vol. 24, pp. 101-12.

Sorenson, S.B., Stein, J.A., Siegel, J.M. and Burnam, M.A. (1987), 'The Prevalence of Sexual Assault: The Los Angeles Epidemiologic Catchment Area Project', *American Journal of Epidemiology*, vol. 126, pp. 1154-64.

Stacy, R.D., Prisbell, M. and Tollefsrud, K. (1992), 'A Comparison of Attitudes among College Students toward Sexual Violence Committed by Strangers and by Acquaintances: A Research Report', *Journal of Sex Education and Therapy*, vol. 18, pp. 257-63.

Stein, P. (1976), *Single*, Prentice Hall, Englewood Cliffs, NJ.

Stets, J.E. and Pirog-Good, M.A. (1987), 'Violence in Dating Relationships', *Social Psychology Quarterly*, vol. 50, pp. 237-46.

Stets, J.E. and Pirog-Good, M.A. (1989), 'Sexual Aggression and Control in Dating Relationships', *Journal of Applied Social Psychology*, vol. 19, pp. 1392-412.

Stets, J.E. and Pirog-Good, M.A. (1989), 'The Marriage License as a Hitting License: A Comparison of Assaults in Dating, Cohabiting, and Married Couples', in M.A. Pirog-Good and Stets, J. E. (eds), *Violence in Dating Relationships: Emerging Issues* (pp. 33-52), Praeger, New York.

Storr, A. (1970), *Human Aggression*, Penguin, Harmondsworth, England.

Story, M.D. (1982), 'A Comparison of University Students Experience with Various Sexual Outlets in 1974 and 1980', *Adolescence*, vol. 17, pp. 737-47.

Struckman-Johnson, C. (1988), 'Forced Sex on Dates: It Happens to Men Too', *Journal of Sex Research*, vol. 24, pp. 234-40.

Stuntz, E.C. (1975), 'Women's Reactions to Rape', *Smith College Studies in Social Work*, vol. 46, pp. 35-6.

Sunday, S.R. and Tobach, E. (1985), *Violence Against Women: A Critique of the Sociobiology of Rape*, Gordian Press, New York.

Sutherland, E.H. and Cressey, D.R. (1974), *Criminology* (9th ed.), Lippincot, Philadelphia.

Sweet, E. (1985, October), 'Date Rape: The Story of an Epidemic and Those Who Deny It', *Ms./Campus Times*, pp. 56-9; pp. 84-5.

Symons, D. (1979), *The Evolution of Human Sexuality*, Oxford University Press, New York.

Taft, P. and Ross, P. (1969), 'American Labor Violence: Its Causes, Character and Outcome', in H.G. Graham and T.R. Gurr (eds), *Violence in America: Historical and Comparative Perspectives*, vol. 1, U.S. Government Printing Office, Washington, DC.

Tannenbaum, P.H. (1971), 'Emotiotional Arousal as a Mediator of Erotic Communication Effects', in *Technical Report of the Commission Obscenity and Pornography*, vol. 1, U.S. Government Printing Office, Washington, DC.

Tarvis, C. and Wade, C. (1985), *The Longest Way: Sex Differences in Perspective*, Harcourt Brace Jovanovich, San Diego, CA.

Tetreault, P.A. and Barnett, M.A. (1987), 'Reactions to Stranger and Acquaintance Rape', *Psychology of Women Quarterly*, vol.11, pp. 353-8.

Thomas, W.I. and Zaniecki, F. (1927), *The Polish Peasant in Europe and America*, Knopf and Company, New York.

Thompson, W.W.E. and Buttell, A.J. (1984), 'Sexual Deviance in America', *Emporia State Research Studies*, vol. 33, pp. 6-47.

Thornhill, R. (1980), 'Rape in Panorpa Scorpionflies and a General Rape Hypothesis', *Animal Behavior*, vol. 28, pp. 55-9.

Thornhill, R. and Thornhill, N.W. (1983), 'Human Rape: An Evolutionary Analysis', *Ethnology and Sociobiology*, vol. 4, pp. 137-73.

Tieger, T. (1981), 'Self Rated Likelihood of Raping and the Social Perception of Rape', *Journal of Clinical Psychology*, vol. 15, pp. 147-58.

Toch, H. (1977), *Police, Prisons, and the Problem of Violence*, National Institute of Mental Health, Rockville, MD.

Tong, R. (1984), *Woman Sex, and the Law*, Rowman and Allanheld, Totowa, NJ.

Trivers, R. (1972), 'Parental Investment and Sexual Selection', in B. Campbell (ed), *Sexual Selection and the Descent of Man* (pp. 136-179), Aldine Publishing Company, Chicago.

Veronen, L.J., Kilpatrick, D.G. and Resick, P.A. (1983), 'Treatment of Fear and Anxiety in Rape Victims: Implications for the Criminal Justice System', in W.H. Parsonage (ed), *Perspectives on Victimology* (pp. 148-159), Sage, Beverly Hills, CA.

Walby, S. (1990), *Theorizing Patriarchy*, Blackwell, Oxford.

Walker, P.A. and Meyer, W.J. (1981), 'Medroxyprogesterone Acetate Treatment for Paraphiliac Sex Offenders', in J.R. Hays (ed), *Violence and the Violent Individual*, Spectrum, New York.

Waller, W. (1937), 'The Rating and Dating Complex', *American Sociological Review*, vol. 2, pp. 727-34.

Waller, W. (1951), *The Family: A Dynamic Interpretation*, Dryden, New York.

Ward, S.K., Chapman, K., Cohn, E., White, S. and Williams, K. (1991), Acquaintance Rape and the College Social Scene', *Family Relations*, vol. 40, pp. 65-71.

Warner, C.G. (1980), *Rape and Sexual Assault: Management and Intervention*, Aspen, Germantown, MD.

Warshaw, R. (1988), *I Never Called It Rape*, Harper and Row, New York.

Weis, K. and Borges, S.S. (1973), 'Victimology and Rape: The Case of the Legitimate Victim', *Issues in Criminology*, vol. 8, pp. 71-115.

Weis, K. and Borges, S.S. (1977), 'Victimology and Rape: The Case of the Legitimate Victim', in D.R. Nass (ed), *The Rape Victim* (pp. 35-75), Kendall/Hunt, Dubuque, IO.

Weis, K. and Weis, S. (1975), 'Victimology and Justification of Rape', in I. Drapkin and E. Viano (eds), *Victimology: A New Focus*, vol. 5, Heath, Lexington, MA.

Wheeler, H. (1985), 'Pornography and Rape: A Feminist Perspective', in A.W. Burgess (ed), *Rape and Sexual Assault* (pp. 374-412), Garland Publishing Company, New York.

Wilder, R. (1982, July), 'Are Sexual Standards Inherited?', *Science Digest*, p. 69.

Williams, G.C. (1975), *Sex and Evolution*, Princeton University Press, Princeton, NJ.

Williams, J.E. (1984), 'Secondary Victimization: Confronting Public Attitudes about Rape', *Victimology: An International Journal*, vol. 9, pp. 66-81.

Wilson, E.O. (1975), *Sociobiology: The New Synthesis*, Belknap Press of Harvard University, Cambridge, MA.

Wilson, J. (1978), *Religion in American Society: The Effective Presence*, Prentice Hall, Englewood Cliffs, NJ.

Wilson, W. and Durenberger, R. (1982), 'Comparison of Rape and Attempted Rape Victims', *Psychological Reports*, vol. 50, pp. 198-9.

Wirth, L. (1940), 'Ideological Aspects of Social Disorganization', *American Sociological Review*, vol. 5, pp. 472-82.

Wolfgang, M. and Ferracuti, F. (1967), *The Subculture of Violence*, Tavistock, London.

Wriggins, J. (1983), 'Rape, Racism, and the Law', *Harvard Women's Law Journal*, vol. 6, pp. 103-141.

Wyatt, E.G. (1992), 'The Sociocultural Context of African American and White American Woman's Rape', *Journal of Social Issues*, vol. 48(1), pp. 77-91.

Yarmey, A.D. (1985), 'Older and Younger Adults' Attributions of Responsibility toward Rape Victims and Rapists', *Canadian Journal of Behavioral Science*, vol. 17, pp. 327-38.

Yegidis, B.L. (1986), 'Date Rape and Other Forced Sexual Encounters among College Students', *Journal of Sex Education and Therapy*, vol. 12, pp. 51-4.

Author Index

Subject Index